OF GOD WHO
COMES TO MIND

M E R I D I A N

Crossing Aesthetics

Werner Hamacher
& David E. Wellbery
Editors

Translated by
Bettina Bergo

Stanford
University
Press

Stanford
California

OF GOD WHO
COMES TO MIND

Emmanuel Levinas

Of God Who Comes to Mind
was originally published in French
in 1986 under the title
De Dieu qui vient à l'idée
© 1986, Librairie Philosophique J. Vrin

Stanford University Press
Stanford, California

© 1998 by the Board of Trustees of the
Leland Stanford Junior University

Printed in the United States of America

CIP data appear at the end of the book

Contents

PART III: THE MEANING OF BEING

Preface to the Second Edition

The text of the first edition of the present work has been reproduced here without modifications.

This work, which attempts to find the traces of the coming of God to mind [*la venue de Dieu á l'idée*], of his descent upon our lips, and his inscription in books, limits itself to the point at which, thanks to the up-welling of the human within being, there can be an interruption or suspension of the impenitent perseverance of being in its being, that of universal inter-estedness, and, consequently, of the struggle of all against all. This interruption or dis-inter-estedness is produced in human beings responding for their fellow man who, as another person, is a stranger to them. Such a responsibility is the response to the imperative of gratuitous love, which comes to me from the face of another where abandonment and the election tied to his uniqueness signify simultaneously; this is the order of being-for-the-other or of holiness [*sainteté*] as the source of every value.

This imperative to love—which is also election and love reaching him who is invested by it in his uniqueness qua responsible one—is described in *Of God Who Comes to Mind* without evoking creation, omnipotence, rewards, and promises. We have been reproached for ignoring theology; and we do not here contest the necessity of a recovery or, at least, the necessity of choosing the opportunity for a recovery of these themes. We think, however, that theological recuperation comes after the glimpse of holiness, which is primary. This is all the more true that we belong to a generation—and to a century—for which was reserved the pitiless trials of an ethics without consolation or promises; and because it is impossible—for us, the survivors—to witness against holiness, in seeking after its conditions.

We have been able to bring numerous corrections to the typesetting of the new edition thanks to the precious intervention of a reader. In effect, we owe our revisions to the extreme kindness and enlightened attention of Mr. Eugene Demont, whom we thank with humility, yet also with all our heart.

Foreword

The various texts assembled in this volume represent an investigation into the possibility—or even the fact—of understanding the word "God" as a significant word. This investigation was carried out independently of the problem of the existence or nonexistence of God; independently of the decision to be made in the wake of this alternative, and also independently of the decision concerning the sense or nonsense of this alternative itself. What is sought here is the *phenomenological concreteness* in which this signification could or does signify, even if it cuts across all phenomenality,[1] for this *cutting across* could not be stated in a purely negative fashion and as an apophantic negation. It is a matter of describing the phenomenological "circumstances" surrounding it, their positive conjuncture, and something like the concrete "staging" of what gets expressed in the abstract.

The attentive reader will probably notice that our theme leads to questions less "gratuitous" than one might imagine given its initial formulation. This is not only due to the importance that the description of the meaning attached to the name or the word "God" can take on for him who is concerned to recognize or contest—in the language of the Revelation taught or preached by positive religions—that it was indeed God who spoke, and not an evil genius or a politics hidden beneath a false name. This concern is, however, already itself philosophical.

Questions relative to God are not resolved by answers in which the interrogation ceases to resonate or is wholly pacified. The investigation could not progress, here, in a straight line. To the difficulties of the space we are exploring, there is probably always to be added the blunders and slowness of the explorer. Be that as it may, the book we present appears in the form of discrete studies which have not been brought together by a continuous writing. Thus we have borne witness to the stages of an itinerary which often lead back to the departure point. Along the way there also arise texts in which the path itself is surveyed, its perspectives glimpsed, and bearings taken. We have arranged the various essays according to the chronology of their composition. It is possible—and useful—to give the argument in a few pages at the threshold of this collection, however.

One wonders whether it is possible to speak legitimately of God without striking a blow against the absoluteness [*absoluité*] that his word seems to signify. What is it to have become conscious of God? Is it to have included him in a knowledge [*savoir*] which assimilates him, in an experience that remains—whatever its modalities—a learning and a grasping? And is not the infinity or total alterity or novelty of the absolute thus given back to immanence, back to the totality which the "I think" of "transcendental apperception" embraces, back to the system to which knowledge leads or tends across universal history? Is not the meaning of this extraordinary name of God in our vocabularies contradicted by this inevitable restitution to immanence—to the point of belying the coherence of this sovereign signifying [*signifier*] and reducing its name to a pure *flatus vocis*?

Yet what else could one seek than consciousness and experience—what else than knowledge—beneath thought, such that in welcoming the novelty of the absolute it did not, by this very welcome, strip the absolute of its novelty?[2] What is this other thought that—as neither assimilation nor integration—would neither bring the absolute in its novelty back to the "already known," nor compromise the novelty of the new by deflowering it in the correlation between thought and being which thinking itself founds? A thought would be required that was no longer constructed as a relationship binding the thinker to what is thought. Or we would need, in this thought, a relation without correlatives, a thought not held to the rigorous correspondence between what Husserl called *noesis* and *noema*, a thought not held to the visible's adequacy to the intention it should respond to in the intuition of the truth. A thought would be required in which the very metaphors of vision and aiming would no longer be legitimate.

Impossible requirements! Unless they were echoed by what Descartes

called the idea-of-the-infinite-in-us, that is, by a thought thinking beyond what it is able to contain in the finitude of its *cogito*; by an idea that
God—according to Descartes's way of expressing himself—would have
placed in us. An exceptional idea, a unique idea, and, for Descartes, the
thinking of God [*penser à Dieu*].[3] In its phenomenology, this is a thinking that does not let itself be reduced, without remainder, to a subject's
act of consciousness, or to pure thematizing intentionality. Contrary to
the ideas which always remain on the scale of the "intentional object," or
on that of their *ideatum*, and so exert a hold on it; contrary to the ideas
by which thinking progressively grasps the world, the idea of the Infinite
would contain more than it was able to do. It would contain more than
its capacity as a *cogito*. Thought would think in some manner beyond
what it thinks. In its relation to what ought to be its "intentional" correlate, thought would also be *de-ported*, falling through, not arriving at
an end [*une fin*] or at the finite [*du fini*]. Yet it is necessary to distinguish,
on the one hand, between the pure failure of the intentional aim that
reaches no end, for this would still belong to finality or to the famous
teleology of the "transcendental consciousness" destined to an end and,
on the other hand, the "deportation" or transcendence beyond every end
and every finality. The latter is a thought of the absolute in which the absolute is not reached as an end, for that would still have signified finality and finitude. An idea of the Infinite would be a thought disengaged
from consciousness, not according to the negative concept of the unconscious, but according to the thought that is perhaps most profoundly
thought; that of dis-inter-estedness which is a relationship without hold
on a being, which is not an anticipation of being—rather, a pure patience. As de-ference in passivity, it would be beyond all that which is assumed; it would be a de-ference that is irreversible like time. That is, it
is patience or length of time in its dia-chrony, where tomorrow is never
reached today. Prior to every activity of consciousness, more ancient than
consciousness, would this not be the deepest thinking of the new? Gratuitous like a devotion, a thought that would already go unrecognized in
its transcendence when one persisted in seeking, in its dia-chrony and in
procrastination, not the surplus—or the *Good*—of gratuity and devotion, but an intentionality, a thematization, and the impatience of a
grasping.

We think that one can and ought to seek, beyond this apparent negativity of the idea of the Infinite, the forgotten horizons of its abstract sig-

nification. One must bring the teleology of the act of consciousness as its turns into dis-inter-ested thought, back to the nonfortuitous conditions and circumstances of its signifying [*signifier*] in man, whose humanity is perhaps the putting in question of the good consciousness of the being that perseveres in being. We think it is fitting to reconstitute the settings indispensable to the "staging" of this turning of consciousness. This would be a phenomenology of the idea of the Infinite. It did not inter-est Descartes, for whom the mathematical clarity and distinctness of the ideas were enough, but whose teaching on the priority of the idea of the Infinite relative to the idea of the finite is a precious indication for any phenomenology of consciousness.[4]

We think that the idea-of-the-Infinite-in-me—or my relation to God—comes to me in the concreteness of my relation to the other man, in the sociality which is my responsibility for the neighbor. Here is found a responsibility that I contracted in no "experience," but of which the face of the other, through its alterity and through its strangeness, states the command that came *from who knows where*. From who knows where: it is not as if this face were an image referring back to an unknown source or an inaccessible original, like a residue and a witness borne of a dissimula-tion and the makeshift of some missed presence. It is not as if the idea of infinity were the simple negation of every ontological determination that one persisted in seeking in its theoretical essence, thereby suspecting in it the "bad infinite" beneath which the tedium of the frustrated tenden-cies of an impeded finality were dissimulated. Neither would it be the "bad infinite" in which an interminable series of failures were excused, and in which was postponed the impossibility of coming to an end which opened onto a negative theology. Rather, it is as if the face of the other man, who from the first "asks for me" and orders me, were the crux of the very scheme of this surpassing by God, of the idea of God, and of every idea in which He would still be intended, visible, and known—and in which the Infinite were denied by thematization, or in presence or rep-resentation. It is not in the finality of an intentional aiming that I think infinity. My deepest thought, which carries all thought, my thought of the infinite, older than the thought of the finite,[5] is the very diachrony of time. It is noncoincidence, dispossession itself. This is a way of "being dedicated" before any act of consciousness, and more deeply so than in consciousness, by way of the gratuity of time (in which philosophers managed to fear a vanity or privation). A way of being dedicated that is devotion. An unto-God [*A Dieu*] that is precisely not intentionality in its noëtico-noematic complexion.

This is a dia-chrony which no thematizing and inter-ested movement of consciousness—whether as memory or as hopes—can reabsorb or re-cuperate in the simultaneities it constitutes. It is like a devotion that, in its dis-interested-ness, misses precisely no goal but is diverted—by a God "who loves the stranger" rather than showing himself—toward the other man for whom I have to respond. A responsibility without concern for reciprocity: I have to respond for an other without attending to an other's responsibility in regard to me. A relation without correlation, or a love of the neighbor that is a love without eros. For-the-other-man and thereby unto God! This is how a thought thinks more than it thinks. As demand and responsibility, all the more imperious and urgent for being under-gone with more patience, such is the concrete origin or the original situ-ation where the Infinite places itself in me, where the idea of the Infinite commands the spirit, and the word God comes to the tip of one's tongue. Here is inspiration and, thus, the prophetic event of the relation to the new.

Yet this is also—with the placing in me of the idea of the Infinite—a prophetic event beyond its psychological particularity: it is the beating of the primordial time in which, for itself or of itself, the idea of the Infi-nite—deformalized—signifies. God-coming-to-the-idea, as the life of God.

PART I

A Rupture of Immanence

§ Ideology and Idealism

Ideology and Morality

Ideology usurps the appearances of science, but the statement of its concept ruins the credit of morality. The suspicion of ideology deals morality the hardest blow it could ever receive. This suspicion probably marks the end of an entire human ethics and, in any case, overturns the theory of duty and of values.

Understood as a set of rules for conduct founded upon the universality of maxims or upon a hierarchically ordered system of values, morality carried within itself a rationale. It had its evidence and was apprehended in an intentional act analogous to knowing. Like the categorical imperative, axiology belonged to the *logos*. The relativity of morality in relation to history, its variations and variants as a function of social and economic structures, did not fundamentally compromise this rationale. Both the historical situation and social particularism allowed themselves correctly to be interpreted as determining the "subjective" conditions of access to the *logos* and the time necessary for this access. These were the variable conditions of a clear-sightedness that did not fall omniscient from the sky and that knew periods of obscurity. The relativism that the experience of these conditions seemed to invite was attenuated to the degree to which historical evolution let itself be understood as the manifestation of reason to itself; as a progressive rationalization of the Subject up to the absolute point of a reason becoming free act, or a practical, effective reason. Utilized in the Marxist critique of bourgeois humanism, the notion of ideology received much of its persuasive force in Nietzsche and in Freud.

3

That the appearance of rationality might be more insinuating and more resistant than a paralogism, and that its powers of mystification might be dissimulated to the point where the art of logic was insufficient for its demystification, and that the mystification might mystify the mystifiers—proceeding from an intention unconscious of itself: here lay the novelty of this notion of ideology.

It is possible, however, to think that the strange notion of *suspect reason* did not arise in a philosophical discourse that would simply have let itself slide into suspicions instead of producing proofs.[1] The meaning of this reason imposes itself in the "desert that grows," in the rising moral misery of the industrial era. A meaning that *signifies* in the moaning or in a cry denouncing a scandal to which Reason—capable of thinking, as an *economy*, a world wherein one sells the "poor for a pair of sandals"—would remain insensitive without this cry.[2] This is a prophetic cry, barely discourse; it is a voice that cries in the desert, a revolt of Marx and Marxists beyond Marxian science. It is a meaning which rends like a cry that is not reabsorbed in the system that absorbs it, and wherein it does not cease resounding in a voice other than that which carries coherent discourse. It is not always true that not-to-philosophize is still to philosophize! The interrupting force of ethics does not attest to a simple relaxing of reason, but to placing in question the *act of philosophizing*, which cannot fall back into philosophy. But what a singular reversal! By way of its historical relativity, by way of its normative allures, which one deems regressive, ethics is the first victim of the struggle it instigated against ideology. Ethics loses its status of reason for a precarious condition within the Ruse of reason. It passes for an unconscious effort, certainly, but also is susceptible to becoming conscious and, consequently, courageous or cowardly in view of deceiving both others and its own followers or preachers. Its rationality, one of pure semblance, is the ruse of a war of one class opposed to the other, or a refuge of frustrated beings, a bundle of illusions commanded by interests and needs for compensation.

Ideology and "Disinterestedness"

That ideology—like reason in Kant's transcendental dialectic—might be a necessary source of illusions is probably a still more recent view. If we believe Althusser, ideology always expresses the manner in which consciousness's dependency in regard to the objective or material conditions that determine it—and which scientific reason grasps in their objectivity—is experienced by this consciousness. We must at once ask ourselves if this does not teach us, at the same time, a certain eccentricity of consciousness relative to the order controlled by science—and to which science doubtlessly belongs—a dislocation of the subject, a gaping, a "game" between the subject and being.

If illusion is the modality of this game, it does not make this game, or this gap, or this exile, or this ontological "statelessness" of consciousness illusory. Could this gap be the simple effect of the incompleteness of science which, in its coming to completion, would erode to a filament the subject whose ultimate vocation should only be in service to the truth and which, once science were completed, would lose its reason for being? But it is then this indefinite deferment of scientific completion that would signify the gap between the subject and being. As this gap is found in the possibility that the subject would have of forgetting science, which, having put ideology back into its place and having certainly caused the latter to lose the pretension of being a true knowledge and of directing efficacious acts, should have brought ideology back to the rank of a psychological factor to be modified by praxis like any other factor of the real. Science will not, however, have kept this ideology, henceforth inoffensive, from continuing to assure the permanence of a subjective life that lives from its demystified illusions. This is life where under the nose of science one commits great follies, where one eats and distracts oneself, where one has ambitions and esthetic tastes, where one weeps or becomes indignant, forgetting the certainty of death and all of the physics, psychology, sociology that, behind life's back, command this life. The gap between the subject and reality, attested by ideology, would thus hold either to an always deferred completion of science or to this ever-possible forgetting of it.

But does this gap come from the subject? Does it come from a *being* concerned about its being and persevering in being, from an interiority clothed in an essence of a personage, from a singularity taking pleasure in its ex-ception, concerned with its happiness—or with its salvation—with its private intentions in the midst of the universality of the true? Is it the subject himself who will have dug out a hollow for ideology, between himself and being? Does this hollow not derive from a prior rupture with the illusions and the ruses that filled it; does it not derive from an interruption of essence, from a non-place, from a "utopia," from a pure interval of the *ēpochē*[3] opened by disinterestedness? There, science would not yet have consoling dreams to be interrupted, nor megalomania to be brought back to reason; but there alone science would have found the distance necessary to its impartiality and its objectivity. Ideology would thus have been the symptom or the sign of a "non-place" where the objectivity of science eludes all impartiality. How to decide between the terms of this alternative? Perhaps another moment of the modern mind will suggest the meaning of the option to choose. And also a more complete analysis of disinterestedness.

The Uninterrupted Science

Modern epistemology is little concerned with this unconditional condition—about this necessity to tear oneself from being in order to place oneself, as a subject, upon an absolute or utopian ground, on a terrain that makes disinterestedness possible. Epistemology even mistrusts it: any distancing from reality favors ideology, in the eyes of epistemology. The conditions of rationality are henceforth all on the side of knowledge itself, and on that of the technical activity that results from it. A sort of neoscientism and neopositivism dominates Western thought. It extends to disciplines having man as their object, it extends to ideologies themselves, whose mechanisms one dismantles and whose structures one sets forth. The mathematical formalization practiced by structuralism constitutes the objectivism of the new method, which is so much its consequence. Never in the new science of man shall value serve as a principle of intelligibility. For it is precisely in value that the great Lie would take refuge: impulse or instinct, a mechanical phenomenon objectively detectable in man, gives us by its spontaneity the illusion of the subject and, by its term, the appearance of an end. The end poses as value and the impulse, consequently, garbed in practical reason, is guided by this value promoted to the rank of a universal principle. All a drama to be reduced! We must remember Spinoza, that great demolisher of ideologies, still unaware of their name—or recall his knowledge of the first genus. It is the desirable that is valued, it is not value that gives rise to desires.

In the ambiguity of the desire that still lets itself be understood, either as provoked by the value of its end or as founding value by the movement that animates it, only the second term of the alternative endures. The death of God began there. It has resulted, in our day, in the subordination of axiology to desires understood as impulses, organized according to certain formulas in those machines of desire that would be men. The new theory of knowledge no longer ascribes any transcendental role to human subjectivity. The scientific activity of the subject is interpreted as a detour by which the diverse structures to which reality is reduced show themselves and are arranged in a system. What one called, in times past, the effort of intelligence in invention would thus be only an objective event of the intelligible itself and, in some manner, a purely logical sequence. Contrary to Kantian teachings, true reason would be without interest. Structuralism is the primacy of theoretical reason.

Contemporary thought thus moves in a world of being without human traces, where subjectivity has lost its place in the midst of a spiritual landscape comparable to the one before the astronauts who first set foot on the moon, whence the earth itself appeared as a dehumanized star. Entrancing spectacles, never before seen! From the "déjà vu" to the voyages yet to come! Discoveries from which one carries off pounds of stones composed of the same chemical elements as our terrestrial minerals. Perhaps they respond to the problems that up until now seemed insoluble to the specialists; perhaps they widen the horizon of specific problems. They will not tear apart the ideal line that is certainly no longer the encounter of the sky and the earth, but which marks the limit of the Same. Within the infinity of the cosmos offered up to his movements, the cosmonaut, or the space pedestrian—man—finds himself confined without being able to set foot outside.

Has science produced the *beyond being* in discovering the totality of being? Has it given itself the place or non-place necessary to its own birth, to maintaining its objective spirit? The question remains. The superhuman adventure of the astronauts—to refer to this adventure as if to a parable—shall certainly go at some point beyond all the knowledge that permitted it. There will then be the old biblical verses recited by Armstrong and Collins. But perhaps this *ideological* recitation will have expressed only the foolishness of *petits bourgeois* Americans, an expression inferior to their courage. And it will have expressed the infinite resources of rhetoric—that is, of rhetoric in the Platonic sense, which flatters its audience, according to the *Gorgias*, and which "is to justice as cookery is to medicine" (465 c); but also of a rhetoric foreshadowed in all the fullness of its ideological essence as a "spurious counterfeit of a branch of the art of government" (463 d). And already rhetoric as a power of illusion of language, according to the *Phaedrus*, independent of all flattery and of all interest: "not only relative to judiciary debates nor to all those of the pop- ular Assembly . . . but . . . relative to all uses of the word . . . we shall be capable of making anything equal to anything else" (261 d–e). A rhetoric that is not attached to the discourse that seeks to win a trial or a place, but a rhetoric gnawing away the very substance of the word precisely to the degree to which the latter finds itself apt to "function in the absence of all truth." Is this not already the eventuality of significations reducible to the play of signs detached from what is signified? But from then on, rhetoric becomes an ideology more desolate than any ideology, and one which no science could salvage without running the risk of sinking down into the issueless game that it would like to interrupt. An ideology crouching in the depths of the *logos* itself. Plato believes he can escape it by way of good rhetoric. But already he hears in discourse the simian im- itation of discourse.

Yet there is also in the parable of interstellar navigation the foolishness attributed to Gagarin, declaring that he had not found God in the sky. Unless we take this seriously and hear in it a very important avowal: the new condition of existence in the weightlessness of a space "without sites" is still experienced, by the first man to be launched into space, as a *here*, as the *same* without a veritable alterity. The marvels of technology do not open the *beyond* where Science, their mother, was born! No outside at all in all these movements! What an immanence! What a bad infinite! That which Hegel expresses with a remarkable precision, "Something becomes an Other, but the Other is itself a Some thing, thus it becomes similarly an Other and so forth to infinity. This infinity is the bad or negative in- finity inasmuch as it is nothing other than the negation of the finite which, moreover, is consequently reborn as well, as it is not suppressed."[4]

The bad infinity proceeds from a thinking, incompletely thought, of an idea of the understanding. But the thinking that is beyond under- standing is necessary to understanding itself. Is not a rupture of Essence shown objectively in the modern spirit?

The Other Man

What therefore are this movement and this life, manifested "objec- tively" in modern times—neither illusory ideology, nor yet Science—by which within being there occurs something like a *dislocation*, in the form of the subjectivity or the humanity of the subject? Does not the visible face of this *ontological interruption*—of this *ēpochē*—coincide with the movement "for a better society"? The modern world is no less stirred up by this—all the way to its religious depths—than by the denunciation of ideologies; although, like the miser crying "stop thief," in this movement the world is prompt to suspect itself of ideology. Is it not to return to morality to demand justice for the *other man*? To the very morality of morals, indisputably! Yet the invincible concern for the other man in his destitution and his homelessness—in his nakedness—in his condition or noncondition of a proletarian, this concern escapes the suspect finality of ideologies; the *search* for the other man who is still far away is already the *relationship* with this other man, a relationship in all its rectitude—a trope specific to the approach of the neighbor, which is already proximity. Here we see something coming that is other than the complacency in ideas agreeing with the particularism of a group and its interests. *In the form* of the relationship with the other man who, in the nakedness of his face, belongs—like a proletarian—to no fatherland, there occurs a transcendence, a departure from being and thus *impartiality* itself through which shall be possible, notably, science in its objectivity and humanity in the form of the I.

Like the requirements of scientific rigor, like anti-ideology, the revolt against a society without justice expresses the spirit of our age.[5] A revolt against a society without justice, though in its injustice it be balanced, governed by laws, subject to a power and constituting an order, a State, a city, a nation, a professional corporation; a revolt for a society that is other, yet a revolt that recommences as soon as the other society is established; a revolt against the injustice that is founded as soon as order is founded—a new tonality, a tonality of youth, within the old Western progressivism. As though it were a question of a justice that shows itself to be senile and decrepit from the moment institutions are there to protect it; as though, in spite of all recourse to the doctrines and sciences, political, social, and economic, in spite of all references to the reason and the techniques of Revolution, man were sought in the Revolution inasmuch as it is a disorder or permanent revolution, a rupturing of frameworks, an obliteration of qualities that, like death, frees man from everything and from the whole. As though the other man were sought, or approached, within an alterity where no administration could ever reach him; as though, through justice, there should open in the other man a dimension that bureaucracy, even if it had a revolutionary origin, blocks up by its very universality, by the entry of the singularity of the other into a concept that universality comprises, and as though *in the form* of a relationship with the other stripped of all essence—with an *other*, who is thus irreducible to the individual of a genus, or to the individual of the human race—there opened up the *beyond* of essence or, in some idealism, *dis-interestedness* in the strong sense of the term,[6] or in the sense of a suspension of essence. The economic destitution of the proletarian—and already his exploited condition—would be this absolute destitution of the other as other, de-formation to the point of formlessness, beyond the simple change of form. Is this an idealism of suspect ideology? Yet it is a movement so little ideological—so little similar to resting in an established situation, to self-satisfaction—that it is the putting into question of the self, posing itself directly as de-posed, as for the other. It is a putting into question that signifies not a fall into nothingness but a responsibility-for-the-other, a responsibility that is not *assumed* as a power, yet a responsibility to which I am straightaway exposed, like a hostage; a responsibility that signifies, all things considered, to the very bottom of my "position" within myself, my substitution for the other.[7] To transcend being *in the form* of disinterestedness! Here is a transcendence that comes to pass *in the form* of an approach of the neighbor[8] without a recovery of breath, to the point of being substituted for him.

A relationship of idealism behind ideology. Western thought learns this not merely from the movements of the young of our century. Plato articulates a *beyond* relative to institutional justice, outside of the visible and the invisible, outside of appearing, as that of the dead judging the dead (*Gorgias* 253 e), as though the justice of the living could not pass through humans' clothing. That is, as though it could not pierce the attributes that, in the other, are offered to knowledge, attributes that show him but also cover him over, as though the justice of the living judging the living could not deprive the judged of the qualities of their natures, which they always have in common with those that also cover the judges; and as though this justice, consequently, could not bring together people who were not persons of quality and, in the proximity of the other [*autrui*], go out toward the absolutely other [*autre*]. In the myth of the *Gorgias* (523 c–d), with extreme precision, Zeus reproaches the "last judgment," which he intends to reform in a spirit worthy of a god, for remaining a tribunal in which "fully dressed" men are judged by men, themselves also fully dressed and "having placed before their souls a screen which is made of eyes, ears, and bodies in its entirety." A screen wholly made up of eyes and ears! The essential point: once thematized, an other [*autrui*] is without uniqueness. He is returned to the social community, to the community of dressed beings wherein the priorities of rank impede justice. The faculties of intuition, in which the entire body participates, are precisely what blocks the view, screens off the plasticity of the perceived, and absorbs the alterity of the other [*l'autre*] precisely by which he is not an object within our reach, but the neighbor.

That for Plato a relationship could be possible between the one and the other, "dead to the world" the one and the other,[9] and consequently lacking a common order; that a relationship could be possible without a common ground, that is, a relationship within difference; that the difference might signify a nonindifference, that this nonindifference could be developed by Plato as ultimate justice—thus it is that, with all the approximations of myth, there is pronounced, within the *essence* of being, an eccentricity, a disinterestedness. It comes to pass in the form of the relationship with an other [*autrui*], in the form of the humanity of man. Beyond essence, dis-inter-estedness; yet this, as the just judgment, and not a nothingness. Ethics does not come to be superimposed upon essence as a second layer in which an ideological gaze incapable of looking the real in the face would take refuge. The commandment of the absolute, as Enrico Castelli expressed it in a different context,[10] is not "within the system of a possible ideology"; in regard to the rationality of knowledge, it "constitutes a disorder." Signification, as the one-for-the-other, as ethics, and as the rupture of essence, is the end of the illusions of its appearing. Plato speaks of a judgment concerning, ultimately, merit. Beneath its apparent qualities, should merit be some real attribute, some inner attribute [*arrière-attribut*] of which judgment could not rid itself, leading the other back under the concept again and missing its departure? Could it be something going from me to the other as if we were, the one and the other, dead? Is the last judgment not the manner by which a being puts itself in the place of another, contrary to all perseverance in being, to all *conatus essendi*, to all knowledge that welcomes only concepts from the other? Does the last judgment not signify the substitution for the other?[11] And what can the impetus to put oneself in the place of the other mean, if not literally the approach of the neighbor?

The Other "in the Form" of the Other Man

One may be surprised by the radicalism of an affirmation wherein the rupture of the essence of being, irreducible to ideology, signifies *in the form* of responsibility for the other man who is approached in the nakedness of his face, in his noncondition as a proletarian, and always "losing his place." One may be surprised by the radicalism of an affirmation wherein the "beyond being" signifies *in the form* of my dead man's disinterestedness, which expects nothing from a dead man. It is not difficult to see that the *for* of the "for-the-other" of my responsibility for another, is not the *for* of finality; that the *for the other* of him who is exposed to another without defense or covering, in an incessant dis-quietude of not being open, and in the disquietude of knotting oneself up within oneself, is an opening of self, a disquietude going to the point of enucleation [*dénucléation*]. We shall not again take up this theme frequently developed elsewhere.[12] But where should the absolute "otherwise" of the "beyond being" articulated by Plato and Plotinus take place against the unrendable identity of the Same—whose ontological obstinacy is incarnate or persists stubbornly in an I—if not in the substitution for another?

Nothing, in effect, is absolutely other in the being served by knowledge wherein variety turns into monotony. Is this not the thought of Proverbs (14:13): "Even in laughter the heart is sorrowful, and the end of that mirth is heaviness"? The contemporary world, scientific, technical, and sensualist, sees itself without exit—that is, without God—not because everything there is permitted and, by way of technology, possible, but because everything there is equal. The unknown is immediately made familiar and the new customary. Nothing is new under the sun. The crisis inscribed in Ecclesiastes is not found in sin but in boredom. Everything is absorbed, sucked down and walled up in the Same. The enchantment of sites, hyperbole of metaphysical concepts, the artifice of art, exaltation of ceremonies, the magic of solemnities—everywhere is suspected and denounced a theatrical apparatus, a purely rhetorical transcendence, the game. Vanity of vanities: the echo of our own voices, taken for a response to the few prayers that still remain to us; everywhere we have fallen back upon our own feet, as after the ecstasies of a drug. Except the other whom, in all this boredom, we cannot let go.

The alterity of the absolutely other is not an original quiddity of some sort. As a quiddity, this alterity has a ground in common with the quiddities from which it stands out. The notions of the *ancient* and the *new*, understood as qualities, are insufficient to the notion of the absolutely other. The absolute *difference* cannot itself sketch out the ground common to those who differ. The other, absolutely other, is the Other [*l'autre, absolument autre, c'est Autrui*]. The Other is not a particular case, a species of alterity, but the original exception to the order. It is not because the Other is a novelty that it "gives rise" [*donne lieu*][13] to a relationship of transcendence—it is because responsibility for the Other is transcendence that there can be something new under the sun.

My responsibility for the other man; the paradoxical and contradictory responsibility for a foreign freedom—going, according to an expression of the Talmudic tractate (*Sota* 37 B), to the point of responsibility for his responsibility—does not arise from a respect destined to have the universality of a principle, nor from a moral evidence. My responsibility is the exceptional relationship in which the Same can be concerned by the Other without the Other being assimilated to the Same. A relationship in which one can recognize the inspiration for attributing, in this rigorous sense, spirit to man. It does not matter! Cutting across the rhetoric of all our enthusiasms, in the responsibility for the other, there occurs a meaning from which no eloquence could distract—nor even any poetry! A rupture of the Same without being taken up again by the Same into his customs, without aging—it is novelty, transcendence. The rupture expresses itself altogether in ethical terms. To the crisis of meaning that is attested by the "dissemination" of verbal signs which the signified no longer succeeds in dominating, since it would only be its illusion and ideological ruse, there is opposed the meaning prior to "things said," repelling words, and incontestable in the nakedness of the face, the proletarian destitution of the other, and in the offense undergone by him. This is probably what was taught by the sages of the Talmud who already knew a time in which language had eroded the significations it was supposed to carry, when they spoke of a world in which prayers cannot pierce the sky, for all the heavenly doors are closed except that through which the tears of the injured pass.[14]

That the other [*l'autre*] *qua* other not be an intelligible form tied to other forms in the process of an intentional "disclosure," but a face, proletarian nakedness, destitution; that the other [*l'autre*] be another [*autrui*]; that the departure from oneself be the approach of the neighbor; that transcendence be proximity, that proximity be responsibility for the other, substitution for the other, expiation for the other, condition—or uncondition—of a hostage; that responsibility as response be the preliminary Saying; that transcendence be communication, implying, beyond a simple exchange of signs, the "gift," the "open house"—here we have a few ethical terms through which transcendence signifies in the form of humanity, or ecstasy as dis-interestedness. Here is an idealism prior to Science and Ideology.

§ From Consciousness to Wakefulness

Starting from Husserl

> . . . I sleep, but my heart waketh . . .
> —Song of Solomon 5:2

The Insecurity of Reason

Husserlian phenomenology intervenes at the level of the human, where reason signifies the manifestation of beings to a true knowledge, one concerned about their *presence* in the original, about their *presence* in their identity as beings, or their presence as being. It should signify an insecurity of rationality that beings might appear without remaining in their being; that there might be, by way of signs or through words, beings appearing without their being; that, in images, beings offer only their resemblance in the place of their identity; that the images cover them over or detach from them like parings; that there might be resemblances between them and, consequently, semblances. It should signify an insecurity of rationality that, of all the modes of appearing [*apparoir*], appearance would be the ever-possible flip-side of beings. All this, since philosophy took its first steps, should signify an insecurity of rationality. Reason, as a modality of knowledge, should have to be on its guard before certain games that bewitch it. It should be held to vigilance in order to confound illusions. One must not sleep, one must philosophize.[1]

The novelty of criticism is that these bewitching games might be played out in reason itself, and without running up against its rational movement—unbeknownst to it, as it were; that there might consequently be a necessity, against lucidity itself, for an exercise of reason that is *other* than its spontaneous and unforeseen exercise. That there might be a necessity for vigilance against evidence and its daydreams. In other words, that a philosophy *distinct from "good sense"* and scientific research might be necessary is the novelty of criticism. Kantianism, in which we agree to see the "beginning of the end" of philosophy, will have been the decisive moment of this call to a philosophy different from science. Here is a moment characterized by the denunciation of the transcendental *illusion*—that is, of the radical malice within good faith, or within a reason innocent of all sophism and which, paradoxically, Husserl called naïveté. It is as if rationality (that is, according to the Western understanding of it as the absorption of knowledge by being) were still an intoxication; as if, all erect in its vigilance as lucidity, the reason that identifies being slept on its feet or walked like a somnambulist, and were still dreaming, as if, in its sobriety, it still slept off the effect of some mysterious wine.

And this vigilance and dogmatism continue to be interpreted as forms of knowledge [*savoirs*], more extended, clearer, and more adequate. The fact that reason might be naive and still insufficiently awakened, that it might have to guard against its own assurance, is shown, in effect, in Kant's work. It is shown in the theoretical adventure wherein reason, as always in the West, is invested with the mission of truth and does its utmost to discover being; there where, consequently, in reason or by reason, being exhibits itself as being. It is the presence of being *qua* being, or the lucidity of re-presentation, that still gives us in Kant the standard for sobriety, disinebriation, and vigilance. This vigilance is interpreted in its turn as activity; that is, as a remaining-the-same or as a returning-to-its-identity under every affection (as an immanence) and thus as an invulnerability, a nonfissionability, an individuality under the blows of affection. This is an invulnerability in undergoing [*subir*] that shall be called the unity of the "I think." It is a solidity that will signify "I want," but will immediately be understood as a grasping, as transcendental apperception—the passivity of the wound received turning back into assumption, synthesis, and thus into a synoptic simultaneity of presence. The limit of rationality—or vigilance—will be understood as a limit of activity. And in Kant the vigilance of the rational will have surpassed this limit in morality which shall be full vigilance, full rationality, and full—that is, free—activity. It is nevertheless remarkable that the notion of the rational, initially reserved for the order of knowledge [*connaissance*]—and tied, consequently, to the problem of being as being—abruptly will have taken in Kant a meaning within an order other than that of knowledge. This is true even though, of this adventure—essential to humanity in the Western tradition—reason keeps its pretense to activity (in spite of the passivity to which reason, as categorical imperative, does not fail to attest). That is, it is so even though reason keeps its initial or ultimate belonging to the category of the Same. Reason is identity that posits itself as I [*comme Moi*]. It is an identity that identifies itself—that returns to itself—through the force of its form. It is that which is produced precisely as self-consciousness: an act of identification or identification in act. A force that returns to itself according to an itinerary traced only through the world and the history of humanity. The rationality of reason would thus leave nothing in the form of consciousness outside itself. The energy of the return to the self which is identification—this *vis formae*, force or power of the form—is the activity of every act, and if it is a sobering up, then it is a sobering up in the Same, a coming-back-to-oneself.

Adequation and Life

Preoccupied with reason as the presence of being in the original, and invoking intuition as the principle of principles and the rationality of reason, Husserlian phenomenology has nevertheless been the most rigorous critique of evidence. And it has been this all the way to the evidence of logico-mathematical sequences (which phenomenology nonetheless preserved against any psychologization, to the point of passing for their supreme guarantee, notably since the *Prolegomena*).[2] Without ever disputing knowledge's privilege of possessing the origin of meaning, phenomenology does not cease to search behind the lucidity of the subject and the evidence that satisfies this lucidity, something like a supplement [*surcroît*] of rationality. This supplement would not return to the unconditional principle of a deduction nor to some sort of intensification of light, nor again to the enlargement of the objective horizon of appearing, which would have "to suppress" the partial character of the given by restoring that part of being manifested to the gaze of knowledge, to the totality of the universe that it promises.

Sometimes, in the Husserlian *corpus*, the recourse to the subjective takes the appearance of such a concern for the totality. This is so to the degree that, *qua* psychological, the subjective belongs to the totality of the world and of being. Thus, in his *Phenomenological Psychology*,[3] the subjective modes of appearing of the world and of nature, the *Erscheinungsweisen* or the aspects of the real are still a part of being, varying as they do according to the orientations and the movements of the body—

and still more profoundly, according to the hyletic layer of lived experience in its role as abridgments or "silhouettes" (*Abschattungen*), and constituting "the subjective aspects" of the object (and even the hyletic layer
stripped of this role and considered as itself experienced). Also part of being is, no doubt, that which is prior to these subjective orientations, the
social conditions of the investigation and identification of the true (of
which Husserl does not speak). All this is still being and still forms a part
of the world.[4] To ignore this subjective part of being is not only to be
thrown back toward abstractions, it is to falsify a knowledge that was
content with a truncated reality. And yet this psychic side does not constitute a "region" of being. It does not integrate itself into the world or
associate itself dialectically with nature in order to "form a system" with
it, since its phenomenological description is a privileged path toward the
Reduction, that is, toward the "absolute" of consciousness whose meaning is indebted to nothing that might be the existence of the world. The
"sphere of the world swims in the subjective," according to a picturesque
formula from the *Phenomenological Psychology*.[5] The element in which the
world swims does not have the status of this world, it does not even have
the status of the whole, since it is by way of this element alone that the
very equilibrium of every status—or the identification of the Same—is
assured.

Consequently, a supplement of rationality relative to the rationality of
evidence is obtained in phenomenology by a change of level or by a deepening, which is carried out in the following very precise manner: in a subject absorbed, in all lucidity, by his object, it is a question of awaking a
life that evidence absorbed and made us forget, or rendered anonymous.
More generally still, it is a question of descending from the entity illuminated in evidence toward the subject, which is extinguished rather than
announced therein.

The necessity of going toward the subject and reflecting upon consciousness and intentional life, wherein world and objects are "noemati-
cally" present, is certainly motivated in diverse manners, at diverse moments within the presentation of the Husserlian *corpus*, although the
movement motivated is always the same.

In the first edition of *Logical Investigations*, phenomenology, as a descriptive psychology, must allow us to avoid certain equivocations that
slide into the data,[6] owing to the confusion between subjective and objective.[7] This requires a theory of knowledge that makes possible "the sure

and final determinations, if not of all objective distinctions and evidence, at least of the majority of them."[8] Yet slippages of meaning can also occur because of language and symbolism, against which objective evidence is defenseless:

> Though it would be ideal analysis and not the phenomenological analysis of concrete experiences that would form a part of the domain originally proper to pure logic, the latter remains no less indispensable for the advancement of the former. . . . Logic is first and foremost given to us in an imperfect form: the concept appears to us as a more or less fluctuating verbal signification; the law appears as an assertion no less fluctuating because it constructs itself with concepts. It is true that we do not lack logical evidence for all that. We apprehend the pure law with evidence and we know that it is founded upon pure forms of thought. But this evidence is tied to the significations of words that were alive in the accomplishment of the act of judging which articulated the law. By virtue of an equivocation that passes unnoticed, other concepts can slide into these words after the fact, and, for the significations of professions that have been modified, one may appeal wrongly to the evidence experienced previously. Or, inversely, this false interpretation born of an equivocation can also misrepresent the meaning of the propositions of pure logic (for example, the meaning of empirico-psychological propositions), and induce us to abandon evidence experienced previously and the unique signification of pure logic. For logical ideas and for the pure laws constituted with them this manner of being given therefore cannot suffice. Thence is born the great task of *bringing to clarity and distinction*, according to the requirements of the *theory of knowledge, logical ideas*, concepts, and laws. It is here that phenomenological analysis, etc., intervenes.[9]

Husserl remarks in the same way a little further on, "But the most complete evidence can become confused, it can be falsely interpreted, that which it discloses in all certitude can be rejected."[10] On these slippages of meaning, which owe nothing to the incompetence of the logicians, "formal logic and transcendental logic" unceasingly insist, thirty years later.

The logic that the mathematician-logician can successfully carry out, without attending to psychic acts in which his theory is experienced, therefore requires "a descriptive psychology" reflecting upon this lived experience. Obscurities might come to trouble the gaze of the mathematician or his language, or they might slip into the results of his calculation while these rested as acquired knowledge in some writing, but outside of thought. Reflection would have to verify the intuitive purity of this logic, *unaltered by the gaze turned toward the objective.* For everything comes to pass as though the lucidity of the *Anschauung* (intuition) turned toward the object was not sufficiently lucid, and as though it remained in a mind insufficiently awakened. It is only through reflection upon the experience of consciousness that objective terms are maintained in an evidence which, by itself and without transparency for itself, awakens to itself only in reflection.

When we leave it to itself, the motivation of phenomenology through the instability of the evidence in which objects of the world or logico-mathematical relations appear is connected with motifs that invite us to the theory of knowledge whose problem is formulated, in diverse ways, in the first pages of the *Logical Investigations.* "How shall we understand that the *in itself* of objectivity reaches *representation*, and thus could again become in some sense subjective?"[11] This formulation of the theory of knowledge refers us, to be sure, to the study of the general structure of cognition [*connaître*] and, consequently, to the analysis of consciousness and to the meaning of the objectivity of objects (from the perspective of the *Logical Investigations,* it was a question of distinguishing this analysis and this meaning from the *acts* of consciousness, and of preventing any confusion between them). But between these two motivations—the instability of evidence left to itself and the reference to the general problematic of the theory of knowledge—the tie is established practically, in the de facto exercise of phenomenology.

In *Ideen I,* the passage to phenomenology is called a *transcendental Reduction.* It is accomplished there on the Cartesian path: starting from the nonadequation of evidence relative to the world and to the things therein, through the suspension of belief in the existence of this world and these objects which assert themselves despite the uncertainty, and moving to the search for certainty or adequate evidence from reflection upon the *cogitatio* to which this belief itself belongs—in order to measure in it the degree of its uncertainty and certainty. Or *in order to throw light upon the meaning or the modality of naive evidence!* There lies an alternative that, in the *Ideen I,* is an ambiguity. Is it a question of preserving, in the form of an ideal of certainty, the ideal of intuition espousing fully the claim of thought, in order to measure all certainty according to this standard? Phenomenology would then have as its goal a return to the reduced consciousness, and a questioning and requestioning of the alleged sufficiency of the world given in the naive evidence of the man-in-the-world or of being, given as world. Phenomenology would have this goal, having discovered that in the intuition directed upon the world, or upon a consciousness integrated into the world as psychological consciousness, thought is never filled by the presence of that at which it aims, but opens onto a process of infinite filling up. The apodicticity of internal intuition—in which the internal intuition may be judged and circumscribed—would be the finality of the transcendental reversal. Yet one may also say that it is a question of liberating meaningful thought from the norms of adequation. This would liberate thought from its obedience to being, understood as an event within the identification of the identical, as an event of identification that is only possible as a gathering into a theme, as representation and as presence. Where this liberation was essential, the reduction would be not a discovery of uncertainties compromising certainty, but an awakening of the spirit beyond certainties or uncertainties, modalities of the knowledge of being. The Reduction would be an awakening in which a rationality of thought is profiled—as the significance of meaning—contrasting with the norms that command the identity of the Same. This is, perhaps (beyond the horizons that Husserl's texts open implicitly and where his spoken thought stands firmly) a rationality of spirit that is not translated either into systems of knowledge or into certainties, and which the irreducible term of "awakening" designates. Even in the *Ideen I*, the first term of the alternative we just formulated prevails incontestably. Beyond the critique raised against the *certainty* of various evidence, the reduction certainly makes possible the description of evidence into which uncertainties enter as traits characterizing new modalities of evidence (and, consequently, new modes of being). In any case, in *Ideen I*, the passage to a more profound rationality is still the passage from a knowledge less perfect to one more perfect. It is a passage from an order in which the recovery of what one intended by what one actually saw is impossible, to the order of adequate identification, which would be that of apodicticity.

Notice, however, that in the *Cartesian Meditations* this apodictic rationality is interpreted otherwise. It no longer results from the "adequation" between intuition and the "signitive" act,[12] which intuition fulfills. The intuition of the internal meaning is, in its turn, incapable of filling the "signitive intention." Beyond a core of "living presence" of the I to itself, there "extends only an indeterminate horizon of a vague generality, a horizon of that which, in reality, is not the immediate object of experience, but only the object of thoughts which necessarily accompany it. To this horizon belongs the I's past, which is almost always totally obscure . . . ."[13] However, the limit of the apodictic and the nonapodictic does not reduce to that which separates the "core" from its horizons. This is a limit that nothing indicates or asserts in the texts (§§6–9) that Husserl's *Cartesian Meditations* devotes to apodicticity. In this sense, in the "living presence of the I to itself," the adequation between what is "intended" [*visé*] and what is "seen" [*vu*] is not the essential thing. "Apodicticity may, in some cases, belong to inadequate evidence. It possesses an absolute indubitability of a special and well-determined order, that which the scholar attributes to all principles . . . ."[14] The positive determination of apodicticity, which does not go "together with adequation," is lacking in these perplexed pages in which, on various occasions, are acknowledged the difficulties attached to the notion of apodicticity "provisionally neglected" therein.[15]

Must we not admit that the specific and exceptional indubitability of the apodictic refers to the *unique* situation of the *Cogito-Sum* (without letting itself be abstracted from it)? This situation would define apodicticity; it is not some arbitrary criterion, external to these circumstances, which would render the situation apodictic. "To deny the apodicticity of the *I am* is not possible unless one limits oneself to these arguments (namely, to the arguments in favor of the doubt reborn in the evidence of the *I am*) in an entirely external manner."[16] And yet the necessity of submitting the apodicticity of the transcendental experience[17] to criticism (itself also apodictic), in a reflection upon reflection, is not contested. We are even told that this criticism would not lead to an infinite regression.[18] Now, we cannot expect that some adequate intuition will arrest this regression. Only the evidence of an idea "in the Kantian sense of the term" could make this infinity of criticism thinkable. The apodicticity of the transcendental Reduction shall thus be a reflection upon reflection, only assembling into an "idea in the Kantian sense of the term" that which is a process without completion of the criticism of criticism. The apodicticity of the *Cogito-Sum* rests upon the infinity of "iteration."[19] Apodictic indubitability does not come from any new characteristic of evidence that would assure it a better opening onto being or a new approach thereto. It is due only to the deepening of the evidence, to a change of level where, from the evidence that throws light on the subject, the subject awakes as from a "dogmatic slumber." In the "living presence of the I to itself,"[20] does not the adjective "living" designate this wakefulness which is only possible as an incessant awakening? In "living presence" and "living evidence," the adjective comes to add itself *emphatically* to the qualifications suitable to evidence *qua* essence of the truth. It does so in order to cause the *Cogito-Sum* to be heard as a modality of the *living* [*du vivre*] itself, which identifies itself in its immanence but awakens from this immanence in the manner of an I-that-holds-itself-at-a-distance, torn out of the state of soul of which it was a part. Does the adjective "living" [*vivant*] not express the apodicticity of the subjective, which is not only a degree of certainty, but the mode of life, the *living* [*vivre*] of life? Does this adjective not reveal how important the word *Erlebnis* [experience] is? From the beginning of the Husserlian discourse, this word designates the subjectivity of the subjective. Lived experience and life would thus be described not by the ecstasy of intentionality, nor by the *out-of-oneself* of being-in-the-world. It would not even be described—as in the *Phenomenological Psychology*,[21] where life is lived before the *hyle* [matter] of the sensible takes on the function of *Abschattung*, and where it seems to exhaust itself in self-identifying—by the assembly, in the passive synthesis of time, into "presence to oneself," in the perfect knowledge of self-consciousness, and in perfect immanence. Presence to oneself as a living presence to oneself, in its very innocence, casts its center of gravity outside itself: the presence of oneself to oneself always *awakens* from its identity as a state, and presents itself to an I which is "transcendent in immanence."

Vigilance as I

At the level of the Ego—where subjectivity is at its most alive—there intervene, in Husserl, the terms "sleep" and "sleeplessness" [*veille*]. The Ego is situated outside of immanence while belonging to it—as "transcendence in immanence"—which must signify the following: a *difference* in relation to the "remaining-the-same" or to the "finding-oneself-the-same-anew," which is the duration (or the temporalization, as one says today) of immanent time or the flow of lived experience. But this is a difference other than that which separates the intentional object from this flow. What might this exteriority signify, which tears at the innermost of the intimate? What is the meaning of this "soul within the soul," this alterity, there where everything is nevertheless coincident with self or rediscoveries of self,[22] this unreality at the heart of lived experience? What might this exteriority—which would not be an intentional ecstasy—signify? A retro-cendence: that which is identified in immanence and recovered there, detaches itself from itself or comes to its senses, like the instant at which sleep gives way and where, in awakening, the lived experience before us discolors as a dream that is past and may only be remembered. Transcendence in immanence, the strange structure (or the *depth*) of the psyche as a soul within the soul; it is the awakening that always recommences in sleeplessness itself; the *Same* infinitely carried back in its most intimate identity to the *Other*. It would be absurd to isolate this Other [*Autre*] from that infinite relation and freeze it as ultimate—that is, as the Same in its turn—in some impenitent attachment to the rationalism of the Same.[23] In awakening, between the Same and the Other there is shown a relationship irreducible to adversity and conciliation, alienation and assimilation. Here the Other [*Autre*], instead of alienating the uniqueness of the Same that he troubles and holds, only calls the Same from the depths of himself toward what is deeper than himself; there where nothing and no one can replace him. Would this already be toward responsibility for the other [*autrui*]? The Other calling the Same at and to the depths of himself! This is a heteronomy of freedom that the Greeks have not taught us.[24] Transcendence in immanence—this is precisely the nonbelonging of the I to the tissues of its states of consciousness, which thus in their immanence do not stiffen by themselves.

Awakening is the I sleeping and not sleeping, *for whom* takes place all that comes to pass in immanence itself:[25] an awakened heart, a nonbeing, a nonstate in the depth of moods slumbering in their identity, an insomnia or a throbbing in the ultimate recess of the subjective atom.

This vigilance of the I coming from the depths of the subjectivity that transcends its immanence, this *de profundis* of the spirit, this bursting at the heart of the substance, this insomnia is described in Husserl, certainly, as intentionality. The I-in-wakefulness, *keeping watch on the object* [*veille à l'objet*], remains an objectivizing activity even beneath its axiological or practical life. It is on the alterity of the object or the shock of the real that the sobering up of awakening here depends. The affect undergone, the stimulation received, these shall come from the object, from that which "stands out" (*sich abhebt*) in immanence. The awakening responds again to an alterity to be assimilated by the I. It is indeed this assimilation that is expressed by the optical metaphor of the *ray*, which, from the awakened I, directs itself to the object that had awakened it, which directs itself upon itself as knowledge, or as the mind assimilating that which strikes it. To be sure.

Nevertheless, in the *Ideen I* the division of intentional consciousness into "actualities" and "potentialities" already supposed the fact of intentionality in such a way that the latter was not equivalent, at the outset, to the radiance of the I, while the I would there characterize only the active intentionality attesting to itself in attention. In *Experience and Judgment* and *Phenomenological Psychology*, on the other hand,[26] it is intentionality as such that coincides with the vigilance of the I affected and already waking. This I is *never numbed to the point of absence*. Even in the passivity of consciousness, where one cannot yet speak of knowledge proper, the I keeps watch. Even if this virtual intentionality must blossom into knowledge and into evidence that bring forgetfulness to the underlying life of the I or that put this life to sleep, the *possibility of awakening* already makes the heart of the I beat, from the disturbed and living interior, "transcendent in immanence." "To examine it close up, sleep has meaning only relative to wakefulness and carries, in itself, the potentiality for waking up."[27]

Must the analysis not be pushed, consequently, beyond the letter of Husserl's text? In the identity of the state of consciousness present to itself, in this silent tautology of the prereflective, there *keeps watch* a difference between the same, and the same that is never in phase, a difference that identity does not manage to encompass. This is precisely *the insomnia* that one cannot state otherwise than by these words, which have a *categorial* signification. A scission of identity, *insomnia* or *keeping watch*— otherwise than being—depend upon "logical" categories no less august than those that sustain and found being—such as dialectical negativity, for example, to which insomnia cannot be brought back. An irreducible category of the difference *at the heart* of the Same, which pierces the structure of being, in animating or inspiring it. Husserl compares the I to the unity of Kant's transcendental apperception,[28] and this certainly will have its justification. But the identity of this identical I is torn by the difference of insomnia, creating a void which is always recreated, not by a detachment from everything acquired but by a resistance, as it were, to any condensation of this same void, which comes over me like somnolence (or like the being of the being). Insomnia, like an enucleation of the very atomicity of the one (over which the unity of transcendental apperception still prevails, synthesizing the given), or like a dis-appointment of its very punctuality.[29]

Here is an insomnia or a rending that is not the finitude of a being, incapable of rejoining itself and of "remaining at rest" in the form of a mood, but rather transcendence rending or inspiring the immanence which at first sight envelops it, as if there could be an idea of the Infinite; that is, as if God could abide within me.[30] This is a wakefulness without intentionality but awakened ceaselessly from its very state of wakefulness, sobered from its own identity, for what is deeper than oneself. Subjectivity as a susception[31] of the Infinite, this is submission to a God both interior and transcendent. *In oneself,* liberation *of* self. A freedom of awakening, freer than the freedom of the beginning which is fixed in a principle.[32] This freedom resembles that which flashes in the proximity of the neighbor, in responsibility for the other man, where, nevertheless, as the uniqueness of the noninterchangeable, in the condition or noncondition of a hostage, I am unique and elected. Is this an analogy with the proximity of the other [*autrui*], or the preliminary necessary to awakening? Without intentionality, otherwise than being: is not *keeping vigil* already to substitute oneself for the Other [*Autrui*]? In any case, it is starting from the Other that Husserl will describe the transcendental subjectivity, tearing the I from its isolation in itself. But the unity of transcendental apperception and the lucidity of knowledge, recognized together as a subject, are not without phenomenological justification. They [unity and lucidity] are necessary to awakening. The I is in itself, and in itself it is *here,* and here it is in the world. It must be torn out of this rootedness. Husserl's transcendental Reduction has, as its vocation, to awaken the I from numbness, to reanimate its life and its horizons lost in anonymity. The intersubjective Reduction, starting from the other [*l'autre*], will tear the I out of its coincidence with self and with the center of the world, even if Husserl never ceases, for all that, to think about the relationship between me and the other in terms of knowledge.

The Reduction as Awakening

The account of apodicticity, indubitability *sui generis,* comes to an end in §9 of the *Cartesian Meditations* with the avowal of the difficulties attached to the problems that it raises. Presence to oneself invokes a meaning no longer described by adequation, just as it is not destroyed by the nonadequation between the intended [*visé*] and the seen.[33] The path leading to the Reduction from a phenomenological psychology of perception is, if we believe the *Krisis*, better than the path followed in *Ideen I* and the *Cartesian Meditations*,[34] based on Descartes. Subjective life will reveal its transcendental dignity by its anteriority relative to the real which is identified in it, but which absorbs and reduces subjective life to anonymity. As though in cognition itself, inasmuch as it bears upon an identical and identifiable object, the opening were also a closing! As though the thought that identifies a world or inhabits it were immediately blocked up or *embourgeoisée* by this same world![35] As though, consequently, the adventure of cognition were not all of the spirituality of thought, as if it were rather the falling asleep of a wakefulness! An opening blocked up by that which shows itself therein, not in order to bring about a dialectic of the part and the whole. As though the part necessary to the knowledge of the whole indeed absorbed the gaze—like reason fallen to the rank of understanding—causing us to forget the indigence of the part taken for a whole, and thus dissimulating the whole instead of revealing it. But as though the enlargement—under a greater light— of the objective horizon (where the object shows itself and where it borders other objects which it dissimulates) were not yet the lifting of the naïveté of the gaze turned toward its theme. It is the life underlying the gaze that Husserlian phenomenology awakens. It is not a question of adding a theme internal to the external theme, but rather of reanimating—or of reactivating—this life in order to reach, under the name of indubitable being, the living presence. *It is a question, in presence, of rediscovering life.* As though consciousness, in its identification of the Same, fell asleep in "being awakened" to things; as though the object contemplated were that which paralyzes and petrifies life in cognition.

   Above all, the Reduction will be the approach that—beneath the rest *in itself* wherein the Real, referred to itself, is fulfilled—will show or awaken the life against which thematized being already balked in its sufficiency. Here is a life suitably enough called absolute existence, but whose absoluteness shall be ab-solution or sobering, awakening, or held-in-wakefulness in the exposition of what is "reduced" to new reductions; here is a life undoing the dogmatism subsisting or returning under ideal identities; a life reactivating dormant intentions, reopening forgotten horizons, disturbing the Same in the midst of its identity where the *watching over* becomes a *state* of soul; a life disturbing the state of watch-fulness which, from its rest, finds itself already indebted to the Same wherein it lolls, still or already.

For the I that is wakefulness itself, but also for the I that discovers itself the same—the intersubjective reduction! The latter is not directed only against the solipsism of the "primordial sphere" and the relativism of the truth resulting from it, with the view to assuring the objectivity of knowl-edge as an accord among multiple subjectivities. The constitution or the explication of the meaning of an I [*Moi*] other than I [*moi*],[36] starting from the *analogy between animate bodies*—a passive synthesis being ac-complished in the primordial I—tears the I from its hypostasis, from the *here*, which its somnambulist's tread is insufficient to separate from the center of the world. The spatial interchangeability of the *here* and the *there* does not only constitute the homogeneity of space. By the inter-changeable here and there, the I [*Moi*], albeit so evidently *primordial* and hegemonic in its *hic et nunc* and its identification, becomes *secondary*, sees itself other, is exposed to another, and already has accounts to give. Does not the counter-nature or the "marvel" of reflection upon oneself, prac-ticed in the egological Reduction, owe its likelihood to this intersubjec-tive tearing from the primordial, to the reduction of the I to its previous and forgotten secondariness? The secondariness where, under the gaze of another, the primordial sphere loses its priority, its privileges, and its suf-ficiency, is an awakening where the egological—and egotism and ego-ism—flee like dreams. In Husserl this secondariness is tempered or even balanced by the reciprocity of intersubjective relations, and this proceeds from a tenacious tradition for which mind is equivalent to knowledge and freedom, to beginning—and in which the subject, though enucle-ated, persists as the unity of the transcendental apperception.

Does the preliminary exposition to the Other [*l'Autre*] of the primor-dial sphere, in its identity and "natural pride," signify enslavement? Is the gaze of the Other straightaway objectivation and reification? Is it not the case that, in the exposition of the primordial level to the other [*l'autre*], the Same, straightaway devoted to Another [*Autrui*], is elected and, in its responsibility, irreplaceable and unique? Vigilance—a wakefulness arising in the awakening, the awakening waking up the state into which vigil itself falls and is fixed—is vocation, and, concretely, responsibility for Another.

Against the simple abstraction that, in starting from the individual consciousness, rises to "Consciousness in general" by the ecstatic or angelic omission of its terrestrial weight, by intoxication or by the idealism of a magical sublimation, the Husserlian theory of the intersubjective reduction describes the astonishing possibility of the sobering up, where the I is liberated from itself and awakens from dogmatic slumber.[37] The reduction as explosion of the Other in the Same, toward absolute insomnia, is a category under which the subject loses the atomlike consistency of the transcendental apperception.

In Husserl, this Reduction is expressed, to the end, as a passage from one knowledge [*connaissance*] to a better knowledge [*connaissance*]. The apodicticity of the Reduction remains characterized as indubitable knowledge, as the living presence of the Cogito. *Life* may certainly not enter into philosophical discourse other than as *presence* to a reflection. Yet Husserl will not separate the *living* from life and presence, the condition of philosophical discourse. Always, for him, the very spirituality of the spirit remains knowing [*savoir*]. And for philosophy this necessity of remaining, *qua* knowledge, a knowledge of *presence* and of being, cannot but signify—and this no more for Husserl than for the entirety of Western philosophy—the ultimate figure of the meaningful [*le sensé*]. Or, which amounts to the same, this necessity cannot but signify that the meaningful has its meaning in the ultimate, in the fundamental, in the Same. The spirit remains founded upon the presence of being, it is the event of this presence. This meaning that, when it shows itself, cannot but show itself in consciousness, shall not separate itself from the adventure of consciousness which is ontological. Never shall philosophy, starting from the presence of being, be awakened from it or speak of the awakening in terms other than those of knowledge [*savoir*]. Never shall it reduce the knowledge of ontology to one of the modalities of wakefulness where already modalities much *deeper* arise; never shall philosophy think the vigil—and the awakening from which the vigil lives—as Reason without understanding it within cognition [*connaissance*], without reducing its very significance to the *manifestation* of meaning. To awaken from presence and being will not signify for philosophy an adventure of the spirit, except as a profusion of free images, poetry or dreams, drunkenness or slumber.

Vigil

Is not the *living* of life an exceeding?[38] Is it not a rupture of the container by the uncontainable which precisely, thus, animates or inspires?

Should not awakening be inspiration? Irreducible terms. The *living* of life—an incessant bursting of identification. As if, like a dazzling or burning, life were, beyond the *seeing*, already the pain of the eye exceeded by light; beyond contact, already the ignition of the skin touching—but not touching—the ungraspable. The Same, disturbed by the Other who exalts him. To live is not an ecstasy, it is an enthusiasm. Enthusiasm is not drunkenness, it is a sobering up. A sobering up always yet to be further sobered, a wakefulness watchful for a new awakening, the Same always awaking from itself—Reason. Non-rest or non-perdurance in the Same, a non-state: should we call the *otherwise*, which thus withdraws itself [*se dédit*] from being, a "creature"? Perhaps. But on condition that it not be understood as a lesser being, nor as some sort of modification or derivation of being. For the priority or the ultimacy of the Same—as also consciousness, knowledge, thematization, and being—put themselves into question. The frame of ontology is here broken, with the subject passing from the Same—excluding or assimilating the other—to the awaking of the Same by the other, sobering up from its identity and its being.

I have described elsewhere the enucleation of the *subject* as *substance*, where we started from responsibility for the Other as substitution for him, by the order of the Infinite, and where the Infinite—neither theme nor interlocutor—awakens me to vigilance, to watchfulness over the neighbor.[39]

This is an awakening irreducible to knowledge [*savoir*] and Reason, which does not confine itself to lucidity. But knowledge constitutes a privileged modality of awakening. It justifies itself to the degree that *responsibility for another*, and the condition—or noncondition—of a hostage which this responsibility signifies, cannot, before the third party, do without comparison. Thus it is compelled to the comparison of incomparables, to objectivization, and to consciousness and to philosophical knowledge itself.[40]

The question that these pages have posed consisted in asking ourselves whether intelligence and significance are invariably figures of the Same, of knowledge and being, or whether, on the contrary, signification only espouses these figures at a certain level of vigilance, while in identity's rest, intelligibility already drops off to sleep, it already "goes bourgeois" in the presence that is satisfied with its place.

"Going bourgeois" or sufficiency: a strange "alteration" of the Same by itself, whereas it ought to have been preserved from this by its identity and its power to assimilate the other. Here is an alienation, a "fattening up," which disowns alterity by resisting violently, in its integrity, that which transcends and still affects it.[41]

We are asking whether reason, always brought back to the search for rest, appeasement, conciliation—always implicating the ultimacy or priority of the Same—does not already thereby absent itself from living reason. It is not that reason should be equivalent to the *search* for an equality with oneself—for an adequation with oneself—which would be *better* than the adequation already attained. Against this out-of-date and unjustifiable romanticism, like the one that prefers war to peace, the classicism of plenitude is beautiful in its lucidity. But we are asking whether lucidity—as perfection of knowing—is the most awakened wakefulness [*la veille la plus éveillée*]; even if it were necessary to acknowledge that vigilance, itself, demands to be recognized with lucidity. We are asking whether the *watching* [*veillée*] is a nostalgia for the equal, and not a patience of the Infinite. We are asking whether, consequently, as vigilance and watching, reason is not the unresorbable derangement of the Same by the Other—an awakening that shakes the state of wakefulness—or a derangement of the Same by the Other in the difference that, precisely as non-indifference, does not lend itself to the adversities and reconciliations in which the community—however formal it be—triggers the dialectical movement. Here the difference remains without any community and non-indifference—the unique relation of awakening—is not reduced to nothing. It is a restlessness, a deepening or shaking of every foundation, and thus of presence or simultaneity (by which origin and ultimacy are fixed in time) into dia-chrony, into an exposition to the other in the form of a wound or of vulnerability. It is not the passivity of inertia or of the effect, but rather sensibility: a pain of what dazzles and burns. There is more light in the eye than its state can receive, more contact than the skin can touch: the Same held in wakefulness by an other. It is a relation between the Same and the Other that, for the philosophy of the Same, can only be provisional.

Yet is this not the description of transcendence? A relation between the Same and the Other that could not be interpreted as a state, even if this were lucidity; a relation that owes itself to vigilance which, as dis-quiet, does not rest in its theme, in representation, in presence, or in Being. The vigilance—as the waking up in awakening—signifies the de-fection of the identity. This is not identity's extinction but its substitution for the neighbor. Substitution is an order or disorder in which reason is no longer either knowledge or action, but in which, unseated in its state by the Other—unseated from the Same and from being—reason is in ethical relationship with an other, it is proximity of the neighbor.

These questions concern the ultimate, and even the possibility or the impossibility of the ultimate. Must we think that the identification of the Same, in which being responds for its presence, is reason in its spiritual vigilance, but that, in check at each of its ages, it requires all of human history to find its assurance anew and, consequently, to fulfill itself dialectically through the ruptures and happy reunions of identity, up to the final triumph of *identification* in the Absolute Idea, as the identity of this rational movement and of being? Must we not dread, on the contrary, in the identity of the Same and in its return to itself wherein reason as identification lays claim to its triumph—that is, in the identity of the Same to which thought aspires by itself as to some rest—must we not fear there an hebetude, a petrifaction or a fattening up or a laziness? The dilemma can also be stated in this way: does the other, who eludes identification, pass himself off abusively—or for a while only—as the adversary of the Same, in a diabolical game played to confuse what is but a cognition impatient to lead to something and refusing the methodology of history? Is this a game that the spirit will thwart in its patience as the concept [*du concept*], assured as it is to finish in its own time with the other? Or should we understand the other altogether differently—according to an alterity of which a few traits were traced up to now—as an incessant putting in question, without ultimacy, of the priority and the quiet of the Same, like the burning without consumption of a inextinguishable flame? This is an undergoing [*susception*] more passive than any passivity, leaving behind it not even a cinder. Yet it is an undergoing out of which meaning emerges: the more in the less or the one for the other—an undergoing of the impulse, a waking up in the heart of the awakening itself, a sobering up always deeper, an insomnia more vigilant than the lucidity of the evidence in which rests the Same—and this, already and again—a dream in its present. Beyond the dialectic that remains, in spite of its restlessness, a consciousness of the Same in its completion—or still more simply, which remains the very idea of completion or the ultimate.

§ On Death in the Thought of Ernst Bloch

The Importance of This Theme for the Truth of Bloch's Thought

The Marxism of Ernst Bloch is deliberately humanistic. It is a view that would justify itself as much by the mature texts of Marx as by those of his youth. Never would the doctrine of Marx—which wants to be a science concerned with objectivity—suppress "real humanism." "As real, precisely, and non-formal, this doctrine is put back on its feet."[1]

As a new philosophy and not a simple "secularization" (that is, a technical application or realist "abasement") of truths already acquired by the tradition of spiritualism and of "spirituality," Marxism would draw its force as much from the moral reaction aroused, even among those privileged by the unjust regime, by the misery of the neighbor, as by the objective analysis of reality.[2] These are two sources of the revolutionary consciousness—which would be the true self-consciousness—confluent or springing from the same subterranean origin. "Misery, inasmuch as it comprehends its causes, becomes the lever of the revolution"; "the humanity which conceives itself through action" is identified with the "red march of the intelligentsia." However, these propositions would not be more Marxist than the Husserlian-style idea of an authentic access to the misery of man "enslaved, humiliated, and despised" starting from revolt or, inversely, of an access, starting from misery, to the "force of the revolt directed against the cause of misery."[3]

However, in the philosophy of Ernst Bloch, which at first glance is only an interpretation of Marxism, this idea is powerfully amplified by

an attention turned toward all the works of the human spirit. In these
works innumerable harmonics are awakened: the universal culture sets
about vibrating by sympathy. A singular resonance! Taking as his own
the formula "to overturn all the relations in which man remains humiliated, enslaved, declassed, and despised," Ernst Bloch nevertheless recovers the valuable modes of human civilization: philosophy, art, and religion. They represent for him the expression of human hope, the anticipation of the future in which humanity, today absent, will exist. This is
an anticipation for which Marxism would be the adequate and rigorous
formulation that alone makes possible the interpretation, in spirit and in
truth, of the works of the past, still abstract and poor [*plus pauvres*].
Marxism abandons the heavens to speak the language of the earth. To be
sure. But "a good intellectual content (*ein guter Gehalt*) is not weakened
when one sets it aright and it is still more evident that this content is not
secularized when, put back on its feet, it is realized."[4] That is, Bloch
adds, unless we understand secularization in the Marxist sense as the suppression of all the elevation in which man does not appear. This goes, in
effect, for world culture as Bloch sees it, as it does also for the Old Testament seen by the Christians: this Testament would only prefigure the
authentic meaning of revelation, although the Church preserves it among
the Holy Scriptures.

Bloch's philosophy thus wants deliberately to ignore the "cultural revolution." It already places itself, on this point, in a postrevolutionary era.
In culture, understood as hope [*espérance*], humanity is already rediscovered, at least because it seeks itself despite the struggle of the classes. Humanity is thus found not in a sort of compromise, not in order to atten-
uate this struggle, but in order to intensify it, precisely because this struggle would be the sole path toward the real universality hoped for by
human culture. The revaluation of these hopes and their affirmation constitute the magisterial work of Bloch devoted to the interpretation of
world civilization. A refined hermeneutic that in no way resembles the
coarseness of the common reduction "of the superstructures" to the economic infrastructure. Bloch's eminent personal culture—scientific, historical, literary, musical—is at the level of the "documents" he interprets
and which he very obviously takes pleasure in interpreting, as if he were
scoring, for an orchestra assembling all the geniuses of the earth, the
counterpoint of the Marxist concepts. In his philosophy, which is in this
sense consistent with Greek wisdom, the *human* is thus treated, starting

from *being* and, at the same time, in its irreducibility to the things of the world. The spectacle of the misery and frustration of the neighbor, of his debasement under a regime of economic exploitation, and the rigorously ethical discourse that it engenders, rejoins, according to Bloch and in Bloch, the logical discourse on being, or ontological discourse. This spectacle determines the awakening of ontological discourse.[5] The fulfillment of man is the fulfillment of being in its truth. But never, perhaps, has a body of ideas presented a surface upon which ethics and ontology, in the opposition in which these are understood in an unfinished world, are in superimposition to each other without our being able to say which is the writing that carries the other. Is this still entirely consistent with the reason of Athens?[6]

For this confluence of philosophical and ethical discourses to be convincing, however, for the order of what has come, by convention, to be called nature, in its cold splendor or in its scientific and astronomic legality, to take on a meaning for man recognized in his dis-aster,[7] a response must be given to the problem of death. Without this the position of Bloch would remain at the state of some Marxist homily. It is necessary that man, finally taking his place in a world become his order, his native land, his home [*chez soi*] (this is the term *Heimat* that Bloch utilizes to designate the realization of the utopian), it is necessary that man find there not only the social justice always promised out of the universal logos of nature by idealism. Idealism must not only console man for the violences he undergoes in reality, by assuring him of the freedom of his transcendental consciousness in which the being of the real is constituted and in which, at least in its necessities, being is understood.[8] The accord between being and man requires, beyond these consolations, the alleviation of the Ego's inevitable anguish before death. This would not be possible unless justice and the fulfillment of Being could receive a new meaning and show a very intimate kinship, and unless the subjectivity of the subject in his relation to Being might admit an unsuspected modality in which death loses its sting.[9]

The Pure Future

Ernst Bloch understands Marxism as a philosophical moment. He sees it, notably, in the extension of the *Phenomenology of Spirit* wherein labor receives, for the first time, a categorial dignity. The Marxist ambition to transform the world would not signify some indeterminable priority of action, which would come to be substituted for the search for truth, and bend the world to a value that did not come from such a search. The truth of being, precisely as truth—and without the intervention of some sort of voluntarism interrupting Reason—is conditioned by *labor*, the fundamental relationship between subject and object. *The act would form a part of the manifestation of being.* This is certainly not possible except by way of a new notion of the intelligibility of being—a Marxian contribution to the history of philosophy prior in significance to its contributions to politics and economics—understood as covering particular regions of the Real. The intelligibility of being, which is also its "gesture of being,"[10] would coincide with its *completion of the incomplete*: on the one hand with its materiality—as a *potential* having to pass into the *act* as Aristotle taught; on the other hand with its humanity, with that by which, precisely, the potential passes into the act and is determined. That by which potential is determined is not initially an "operation" of mind—a pure judgment, a pure synthesis of the understanding from the idealism born of Kant. The act is labor. Nothing is accessible, nothing *shows* itself without being determined by the intervention of humans' corporeal labor. This is a labor that is not some sort of blind thrust, that is, a mechanical causality accompanied if need be by intentions in the manner of epiphenomena, nor a causality corresponding, or not corresponding, after the fact, with some finality proper to man, making itself truth or error according to the success or the failure of this pragmatic correspondence. This is a labor that is not a concern for *oneself* in the manipulation of "usable things" (*Zuhandenes*), bordering on the alienation of self in techniques. It is labor as a transcendental condition of truth. It is labor producing being with matter in the double sense of the term "to produce": *to make* and *to present* being in its truth. This is praxis: labor as a transcendental condition of the sense datum, a specific appearing [*apparoir*] of matter. But already the appearing of the sensation supposes labor, which no image precedes. A notion in no way hybrid, praxis is forged in a perspective that remains philosophical. One would be wrong to see therein a simplification or an incomprehension of the problem of knowledge. It is as laborer that man is subjectivity.

The truth of being is thus the actualization of potential, or History. A determination of the indeterminate, it goes toward that which is as yet nowhere. It is not separated from hope. Hope is here in its place of birth.

But to conceive truth in this way is to denounce as purely ideological—under the jurisdiction of an incomplete knowledge—the notion of a being that would be real for all eternity, or would unfold in a time imitating in its mobility an immobile eternity of fulfillment. To posit praxis as conditioning truth is to take time seriously. It is to understand by "future" that which really has not come to pass and which does not preexist itself in any way—neither as implicated in the folds of the explicit, nor as deep within the mystery of intimacy; neither as God gathering up time in his transcendence, nor as *Deus sive Natura.* A God without transcendence to be sure, but containing the future in the eternity of Nature. The future of praxis has not yet taken place in any sense. It is a future of utopia in the opening of pure experience. Without praxis, the activity that perfects being—"being," that is, here, humanity—could neither begin nor continue in its long patience in science and effort.

We must certainly note here the analogy between Ernst Bloch's utopianism and the great intuitions of contemporary philosophy, which is sensitive to the future as the essential in temporality. The irreducible novelty of each instant of the Bergsonian duration, putting in question anew the definitiveness of the past on which it freely confers a new meaning, already attests a break with the time of the *Timaeus.* Since his *Two Sources of Morality and Religion,*[11] duration is married to the relationship with the neighbor in a creative generosity, and according to a sociality other than that of sociologists and historians. But precisely in this way it is on the path of internalization, of pure spirituality where, by way of holiness, the future makes itself present, and takes place without showing itself in the time of the World, and without being conscious of its utopianism.[12] History is conjured away; the misery of the world is either rapidly passed over or avoided in the subterranean passages of the soul hollowed out beneath the foundations of the ghettos reserved for the poor, deeply enough so as not to run up against them and not to provoke any collapse. This is not an insufficiency of the heart, but a conceptual deficiency of a philosophy. For Ernst Bloch, the humanization of the Real could not bypass the world.

One knows, on the other hand, that in Heidegger's celebrated analyses of time, the "ecstasy" of the future is privileged over those of the present and the past. But it is to the finitude of human existence, "destined to being," which in its existence is "unto-death" [*pour-la-mort*], that human time owes its originality as a "temporalization starting from the future."

"Being-for-death,"[13] as a potential-to-be most proper to man because absolutely untransferable (each one dies for himself without a possible replacement), as the anguish wherein the imminence of nothingness occurs, is the original future. It is the most authentic modality of the humanity of man. This schema of the pure future stands opposed to that which emerges from Bloch's thought. The nothingness of the utopia is not the nothingness of death, and hope is not anguish. This is glaringly obvious. But it is not death that, in Bloch, opens the authentic future, and it is relative to the future of utopia that death itself must be understood. The future of utopia is the hope of realizing that which is not yet. It is the hope of a human subject still alien to himself, a pure facticity—pure *Dass-sein*; of a separated subject invisible to itself, still at a distance from the place where, in uncompleted being, it could truly *be there* (*Dasein*),[14] but also the hope of a subject acting for the future, whose subjectivity does not therefore return, in the last resort, to the tension over itself—to the concern for self of ipseity[15]—but rather to the dedication to a world to come, a world to fulfill, to utopia.

Death, Where Is Your Victory?

One should not see in these ideas the ease of a feigned optimism, opposing the proletarian hope to the pessimism attested by the desperate philosophy of capitalist decomposition. In the messianic movement of history that he sketches, Bloch does not wish to ignore the core of human singularity. On the contrary, he reproaches the philosophers of the "flow of consciousness," James and Bergson, for ignoring in their descriptions the substances or nodes that interrupt the continuity of time, and in which history is again taken up. Against the moderns he invokes the Plato of the *Parmenides*, who glimpsed these points as instants that are neither in movement nor at rest. The facticity of the human subject—the *Dass-sein*—is a zone of obscurity in being, to the point that, for each one, the *here* begins only at a certain distance from the space that it occupies. Ernst Bloch certainly does not take lightly the "*conatus essendi*" (the perseverance in being), nor the struggle for life, nor the anguish about the end—all part of that night in which man struggles. The seriousness he attaches to this only allows us to measure the gap between the unfulfilled and the fulfilled, and the plenitude of the anthropological signification thus attributed to a process nevertheless thought of in terms of ontology.

In the obscurity of pure facticity, in the desert of being and its indetermination into which the subject is thrown, hope is introduced. This is a hope for a home, for a *Da-sein*. Man in his dereliction is not yet in the world! From the depths of his obscurity the subject works for this hoped-for future. Bloch refuses to take as the essence of man his *de facto* situation. Under the traits of the man "without a dwelling place," Bloch divines him who, "being closer to his humanity," can feel, as if it were a garment, that which at first sight seems to stick to him like his skin.[16]

The ultimate meaning of subjectivity would thus be entirely ecstatic. Not by way of intentionality becoming conscious of being, but by the praxis that *produces* it, and by which the subject is in its entirety *work* [*oeuvre*]. The egoism of the I is, if we may express ourselves this way, placed inside out, turned back like a garment. But the being *for* which the I *is* rejoins, at its utopian fulfillment, the Good which is no longer beyond being: in the good is abolished the opposition of man to the world. There man, "close to his humanity," is *satisfied* without confining himself, through happiness, within a separate destiny, without retiring under the shell of a skin. He leaves to death only this shell to bite on [*coquille à croquer*]!

A victory over death that is certainly unimaginable, it is nevertheless hoped for in utopian fashion. In Ernst Bloch, this victory is distinguished from the analogical—but purely rhetorical, logical, and dialectical—constructions of the philosophical tradition. It is thus distinguished by the evocation of "premonitions" or "presentiments" experienced "before the hour," and in which the co-naturality of man and being glimmers as an extreme possibility, like the privileged instants of the contemplation of the One of which Plotinus speaks. This evocation is often taken up, and constitutes the most remarkable trait of what one could call the "mysticism of immanence," ventured in the *Principle of Hope*.

The subject, in the obscurity of the brute facts, works for a world to come, for a better world. His work is historical. It is not at the level of the utopia. In the immediate future, it only succeeds partially. This work is thus also failure. The melancholia of this failure is the manner in which man adapts himself to his historical development [*devenir*]; this is his manner of standing in incomplete being. This melancholia therefore does not derive from anguish, as all affectivity should derive, if we believe Heidegger. Quite to the contrary: it is the anguish of death that would be a modality of melancholia. The fear of dying is fear of leaving a work undone! Ernst Bloch shows that the utopian work of completion might co-incide with the essence of man, and that the "concern to work" might not be, as Heidegger often thought, agitation and distraction, and a way of deserting, illusorily, a finite destiny. He shows this by evoking the privileged moments in which the obscurity of the subject is traversed by a ray, coming as if from the utopian future. There, a place is left for "the consciousness of the glory of the utopia in man."[17] Bloch calls these instants, in which the light of utopia penetrates for an instant into the obscurity of the subject, *astonishment*. It is an astonishment that is a question.

An unformable question, for being in its completion is without references; the words *to be* would already be too much.[18] Yet this is an unformable question by which is nourished every subsequent human question. This is so even if every subsequent question—and even philosophy, and especially the scientific question—weakens and smothers the astonishment that carries them, by the formulation of questions and responses. An astonishment like this does not depend upon the "quiddity" of that which astonishes, but on the *how* of the relation to things. It can be provoked by

> the manner in which a leaf is stirred by the wind. But that which is thus understood can also be filled with a content more familiar and more significant (*mit bekannteren, höheren Inhalt*). This can be a child's smile, a young girl's gaze, the beauty of a melody rising from a trifle, the contemptuous clap of a rare word which does not refer to anything in a very firm fashion. But this more signifying *content* is not necessary to give rise to and fulfill the intention-symbol [*l'intention-symbole*] going towards the *Tua res agitur* [Your cause is at stake] which thus appears.[19] It is the most profound astonishment, without any derivation, an element of the authentic under the figure of a question echoing within itself.[20]

But we must refer to the entirety of the text we are using here, where the description of "astonishment" is made relative to a simple "it is raining," drawn from Knut Hamsun's *Pan*.[21] Among the "most signifying" situations where this astonishment is produced, and where death cannot touch man because humanity has there already quit the individual, Bloch evokes the battlefield of Austerlitz in Tolstoy's *War and Peace*, where Prince Bolkonski contemplates the pure height of the sky, and *Anna Karenina* with Karenin and Vronski at the bedside of the gravely ill Anna.

A victory over death divined in astonishment, that is, there where philosophy begins! Bloch conforms to the Western tradition: the agreement of man and being is announced with philosophy. Despite all the exaltation that rouses the utopian fulfillment, nothing would come—either from on high or from without—to disturb or disquiet the immanence of the history, nevertheless messianic and eschatological, which is expressed in this thought. The astonishment is at once a question and a response. It is a question by way of its disproportion with the obscurity of the subject; it is a response through its plenitude. "Everything can be *to such a degree our own 'being'* that we might no longer have any need for a question, but rather that the latter be posed fully in astonishment and might finally become happiness: a being that would be a happiness."[22]

An abolition, within the "being arrived at its end" or transformed by praxis, of the opposition man/being! We must think this abolition with vigor. Is there not, there in Ernst Bloch's approach, a most remarkable intellectual move, beyond any dialectical artifice and independent of his personal credo? We are inclined to accord him an importance that is considerable and all his own. The transformation of the world that is, properly speaking, its formation or its in-formation; the introduction of forms into matter by praxis, in the Aristotelian sense of actualization, this "objective" process is *so intimately or so authentically, so properly (eigentlich) tied to this praxis*, that this objectivity is exalted into a *possessive*, into the possessive of *tua res agitur*. Must we not think that the original place of the possessive is here, rather than in the appropriation of things, in property? Consequently, there is a remarkable movement starting from this *tua res agitur*: more originally—and more properly—than starting from inalienable death, the identity of the I is identified and takes the consistency of the consciousness which is, if not that of Horace's "*non omnis moriar*" [let me not die in entirety], at least that of the "*non omnis confundar*" [let me not be utterly destroyed].

To the end, human fulfillment coincides with being moving to its complete determination. Being's coming to itself is certainly impossible without the end of man's misery: of my misery, and especially the misery of another. Misery is alienation, which is not only a sign or metaphor of incompleteness, but its original mode:

> Humanity obtains a place in a democracy rendered really possible, just as democracy represents the first place of human habitation. . . . Marxism well practiced, carefully liberated, and rid of its bad neighbors is, from the outset,

humanity in act,[23] a human face in its fulfillment. Marxism searches for the path, the only one objectively suitable to this; it commits itself to, and follows this path in such a way that its future is at once inevitable and offers a home.[24]

This path is also that of the intelligibility of being, of its coming to itself, and of its having become supreme objectivity. Decidedly, Marx is, for the humanity in search of itself, "the truth, the way and the life." The constitution of "a place of human habitation" and the "gesture" of being *qua* being would be the same event, the same *Er-eignis* (in the Heideggerian sense):[25] the same event of self-appropriation or of dis-alienation, of the appearing of the possessive of the "*Tua res agitur.*"

But this salvation of man and of being is thought in terms of an ontology in two dimensions, because it excludes all reference to height, as if there were some fear that one might confuse height and sky. In the present essay, which has no critical intentions and in which we are above all asserting the force of certain of Bloch's concepts, we must not be astonished that height remains, to the end, conceived on the model of the supernatural. And for this legitimate reason height remains suspect, whereas in the presentation Bloch makes of certain exceptional experiences of the utopian outcome, being is put in some way in the *superlative*, in order to throw light on the obscurity of the subjective. Is a passage not therefore suggested from the notion of being to the certainly admissible notion of the creature?[26] And would not the evident elevation of the superlative notion of being have to lead to the elaboration of a dimension of height less contestable than that of the pre-Copernican universe?

§ From the Carefree Deficiency to the New Meaning

For Mikel Dufrenne

At this stratum where the symbiosis of man and world
is originally effected, one could always discover the
expressions, stammering and ambiguous, of this exigency
according to which man is a task for man.
—Mikel Dufrenne, *Pour l'Homme*

I

The cases of human deficiency—of man's inferiority to his task as a man, where man finds himself impotent to respond to that which one expects of him—belong to daily experience. Physical, economic, and political causes have a hold over man as if he were but one natural reality among others. The elevation of human identity to the rank of transcendental subjectivity does not annul the effect which the penetration of metal can have, as a knife point or revolver's bullet, into the heart of the I, which is but viscera. "All the vigor of the human spirit is compelled to succumb to the smallest atom of matter," states the *Logic of Port Royal*. Does not the deficiency of man stem from this death, understood as the irrecusable door to nothingness, and understood as coming to strike a being whose meaning is reduced to ess*a*nce,[1] to the task or the mission of being, that is, to the exercise of the activity expressed by the verb of verbs, by the verb *to be* which one lightly calls auxiliary? A verb of verbs, in effect, it states an activity that effects no change, either of quality or of place, but precisely the very identification of the identical, and thus as the non-restlessness of identity, as the act of its rest, an apparent contradiction in terms, which the Greeks did not hesitate to think as *pure act* and which is probably only thinkable where one can be astonished about the firm earth beneath one's feet and the celestial vault with fixed stars over one's head. The deficiency of man begins, consequently, in the traumatism of the end, breaking the energy of *esse*, in the "finitude of human ess*a*nce." The imminence of nothingness, the threat of instances of violence that can bring its date closer, the diversion that turns the attention away from it, but also the faith that denies this imminence—all these permit human "matter" to be modeled at will.

This essential energy of humanity, or this courage to be—as a source of courage *tout court*—shows itself concretely in the maintenance of its identity against all that would come to alter its sufficiency or its *for itself.* It shows itself in humanity's refusal to undergo any cause exercised upon it without its consent. In all things one awaits from man a free and rational decision. Consent should be given, the decision should already be made, from the moment of the first awareness [*prise de conscience*]. Nothing happens to man that might not be to some degree assumed, nothing could touch him without the mediation of reflection.

This is an activity that, nevertheless, cannot ignore what risks alienating it. It is in this sense active only in the form of free willing, and not as *omnipotence.* The finitude of man is also the distinction in him between the will and the understanding. But the dream of infinite power remains no less his *idée fixe.* As a given, the non-ignorance or the knowledge of the *other* permits the surmounting of finitude: the knowledge of understanding, raising itself to Reason, stretches power [*puissance*] to the infinite and, with the philosophy of Hegel, claims to leave nothing else outside. Absolute thought would be the coincidence of the will and the understanding in Reason. The very fact that this excellence demands time—"as we have all been children before being men" (which, for Descartes, without compromising the human freedom of middle age, would explain the sometimes picturesque congestion of our world)—founds, in Hegel, the will within power. The process of history signifies a process of integration of the totality of the given into the infinity of the Idea. Man consequently rejoins the divinity, which since the Greeks is described by this coincidence of will and knowledge, united in the thinking of thought [*la pensée de la pensée*] by this intelligible necessity. It is asserted as identical and unalterable, established upon the unshakable terrain which is the earth in the astronomical system; an empirical fact, but one underlying everything; a founding fact in the act of its rest, and the founder of the very concept of foundation. This is presence "under the sun" and presence in the broad daylight of knowledge; that is, in the two senses of the expression *under the sun*, which the word "onto-logy" unites.

The disappointment to which human deficiency gives rise thus finds attenuation in the evocation of the incompleteness of the historical process that promises the universal integration of Being within the Idea; this is an incompleteness in which the pure act would still be only free will. But this deficiency can be explained also by the abdication of the freedom, which, *qua* freedom, exposes itself, without contradicting itself, to an unhappy choice. Sin would explain mortality itself and would thus be the ultimate ground for unfreedom, although confirming the essential freedom of man. Consequently, deficient humanity—criminal, immoral, diseased, arrested or retarded in its development—should have to be separated—whether incarcerated, interned, colonized, or educated—from the true humanity—good, healthy, and mature. The deficiency would not compromise man, always considered as active and free ess*a*nce. But is it certain that, in pure activity, in the self-consciousness that man reaches in Humanity—as a global and homogeneous State—death, as nothingness, loses its sting and ceases to be the point at which deficiency commences?

II

That the possibility of the human fiasco be attached to the "being's act" and to the finitude of this act doomed to death as nothingness—a finitude without which the act would have no meaning as act, although the age of metaphysics, forgetful of ess*a*nce in its truth, might have erected it into an eternal act in its onto-theology—is doubtless one of the rigorous teachings of Heideggerian thought. This thought—despite the perspectives that it opens brilliantly, toward new thoughts through its phenomenological audacities—takes its place, by this attachment to the act even unto death, no less than does the Hegelian dialectic, among the outcomes of the philosophical tradition of our continent.

Human ipseity exhausts its meaning *in being there* [*à être là*], in being-the-there, unfolding itself as being-in-the-world. But being-there is a *manner* that comes back to having-to-be; an ess*a*nce that before any theoretical formulation of the question is already a questioning about the ess*a*nce of being. This is a questioning that is not an attribute of some kind, or an adjective of the human substance, but the manner, the modality, the *how*, the adverbial quality of being which *has to be*. Man, according to many of the passages of *Sein und Zeit*, passes for having but one methodological privilege: because his being unfolds in the manner of a questioning about the ess*a*nce of being, he should be the path that would lead to the response. But the questioning about ess*a*nce in man inverts its objective genitive into a subjective genitive (*viz.*, the famous Heideggerian *Kehre* [turn]; it is this version and not a simple moment in the evolution of the philosopher). The ess*a*nce of being is to be-in-question, and it is insofar as being is equivalent to being-in-question, insofar as *esse* carries on in this *in-the-course-of-placing-itself-in-question*, that man questions himself on the ess*a*nce of being. It is therefore not a questioning of an anthropological event, engaging the human region of the Real. It is *qua* adventure of *esse* taken absolutely (as *Sein überhaupt* [Being in general]) that the being in question plays in the *being-there* [*Da-sein*] of man *having-to-be* [*ayant-à-être*] and, as such, questioning.

Yet in Heidegger this reduction of humanity to the task of being goes to the point of a quite remarkable deduction of ipseity itself out of the ess*a*nce of being. The ess*a*nce of being or *being-in-question* is in question in the *being-there* as *having-to-be*, which is the being of man. *Man is*: this is equivalent to man *has* to be. The "property" indicated in the *having* [*avoir*] of the having-to-be [*de l'avoir-à-être*] measures all that which is ir-recusable—irrecusable *to the point of dying*—in the strict obligation to be, included in the *to* of the *to be*... It is in this sense that Heidegger can say at the beginning of section 9 of *Sein und Zeit* that *being-there* is charac-terized by *Jemeinigkeit*,[2] or "mineness"; it is because being there is essen-tially *Jemeinigkeit*, that the man who *has-to-be* [*a-à-être*] is I. And not the inverse! Ipseity is like the emphasis of the *to* [*à*]... Ess*a*nce—as the "ges-ture" or the carrying on of being—thus proceeds, and as early as *Sein und Zeit*, in its being-in-question as the appropriation by the *being-there*, which *has* to be, as *Er-eignis*. And man exhausts the meaning of his hu-manity and his ipseity in articulating the *Er-eignis* of being.

Yet Heidegger develops this manner of being in question as *Er-eignis*, starting from *being-there*, as an adventure toward death: temporality and finitude. This finitude, as such, already contains the possibility of a defi-ciency: that is, of a falling back into everyday life, beclouding the "a priori certitude" of the end, unburdening existence, reassuring it about death, distracting it, permitting it to take pleasure in the very being that never-theless is doomed to the end. We find, here again, human deficiency as the reverse of its task of being, which is the task or the destiny of man.

What is nonetheless striking in this analysis—already inclined to glimpse the meaning of the human starting from a passivity and from a passive state [*d'un passif*] more passive than any suffering and any pa-tience, which are simply correlative of acts—is its fidelity to the idea of assumption [*assomption*], of com*pre*hension, of grasp. It is the resurgence of courage behind the passivity. The *being-toward-death* or being unto death is still a being-able-to-be, and death, according to a significant terminology, is the *possibility* of impossibility and not at all an extreme instant, torn from all assumption; not at all an impossibility of being-able, beyond all seizure or all dispossession, and beyond all welcome, pure abduction. The affective dispositions (*Stimmungen*) which, for Heidegger, signify so many ways for the *being-there*, for humanity, to correspond with the ess*a*nce that is to be—that is, to seize the power to be—all refer, for him, to the anguish where being unto death affronts courageously and desperately—freely!—the nothingness where humanity *is* thus faithfully its ontological destiny, between to be and not to be. Anguish and man in it are all ontologies. But the end of the ess*a*nce is no longer in question. It is taken. Being toward death, as being exhausted [*être à bout*], as being at the end, is certitude, *Gewissheit*, at its highest degree of *Gewissen* [conscience] and as origin of moral consciousness. The imminence of death—the very future of temporality—menaces with nothingness. Nothingness alone menaces in death.

III

We wonder whether the human, considered from the starting point of ontology as freedom, as will to power and as assuming in its totality and its finitude the ess*a*nce of being—if the human, considered from the starting point of anguish (as a gaze plunged into the abyss of nothingness), which is experienced in all emotion and all dis-quiet—if the human, considered from the starting point of the ontology to which is subordinated, and on which is founded, and from which would derive, and wherein would reside, European philosophy's law and its moral and political obedience and all that the Bible seemed to bring it—we wonder whether this humanity is still equal to that which in human deficiency strikes the modern intelligence. Modern intelligence is that which saw, in Auschwitz, the outcome [*aboutissement*] of law and obedience—flowing from the heroic act—in the totalitarianisms, fascist and nonfascist, of the twentieth century. Modern intelligence has its reasons, even if eternal Reason had, one day, to renounce them. This intelligence draws them from very recent memories—and in what is still current actuality—in which human deficiency has lost its appearance as an exception in the submission to propaganda, to terror, and to all the technologies of conditioning wherein the omnipotence of men shows itself a correlative of the certainty that one may make anything of man. Men are thus dehumanized by the delegation of powers in which they sought the exaltation of power. These are the victims, but equally dehumanized are those who commanded and who, upon analysis, found themselves to be instruments of a mechanism, a dialectic, a system, or of money. Can one say that they do not put in question the axioms of Marxist analysis itself which, simultaneously, recognized the facts of alienation and conditioning as a function of economic structures and which, despite the social convulsions before which the simple free will acknowledged its impotence, rejoined humanist optimism, announcing a triumphant humanity at the point of being born, thanks to a lucidity integrating and utilizing these convulsions as necessary to human efficacy? And the phenomenon of Stalinism and the resurgence of nationalist conflicts between states on the socialist path gave to the possibilities of human degradation a meaning different from that which they could have received from an innocent barbarism, from original or nonoriginal faults, and from diversion. The success of psychoanalytical theses in this period after the—at least provisional—debacle of fascism (a success that itself is indebted to the memory of totalitarianism) has habituated us to the idea of unmediated traumas, that is, of a hold upon freedom unbeknownst to us; to a smuggled penetration into a disarmed humanity, to procedures in which reason was washed with brains and no longer resembled either the unity of transcendental apperception, or a practical Reason.

But in our time human deficiency takes on a new meaning *by way of the consciousness we have of this deficiency.* It is experienced in an ambiguity: that between despair and frivolity. The exaltation of the human in its courage and heroism—in its identity as pure activity—is inverted into a consciousness of bankruptcy, but also of play. This is a play of influences and impulses. It is a play played without players, or stakes; a game without a subject and not a rational rigor, whether Stoicist, Spinozist, or Hegelian. It is this reversal of the crisis of meaning into the irresponsibility of the game which is, perhaps, despite its ambiguity, the most perversely subtle modality of the human fiasco. A gracious disorder of simple glints of being, experienced as less constraining in its arbitrariness, as succumbing to the drug—than the social and even logical law, which is always repressive. Being receives itself, finding itself to its liking.[3] The rigorous law exposes itself as hypocritical, for it remains stubbornly in its rigor, all the while showing its wear [*usures*] and nonsense. Death, without losing its signification as an end, adds to the lightness of being the gratuity of the vain. "Vanity of vanities":[4] the expression of Ecclesiastes is marvelously precise. A vanity with an exponent: Death would only be striking its semblances of acts, for there would be no more acts, there would be no more subject, nor activities. There would only be caprices of epiphenomena, and these already other than themselves. Into the abyss of death vanish vain simulacra of signifieds. Here is a crisis of language in which are dissolved all the syntheses, every work of the constituent subjectivity. It is the end of the world, whose nuclear arsenals reveal its popular and anguishing aspect. It is perhaps to that point that the human fiasco leads.

IV

Neither preaching nor consolation is philosophical speech. But the fiasco of the human appears to us to arise in the extension of a certain exaltation of the Same, of the Identical, of Activity, and of Being—if only as their being put into question anew. Does this not suggest, by that very placing again into question, another significance; another meaning, and another way of signifying? One may wonder whether the discord between Meaning and Being—the permanent risk, for Meaning, that it be expelled from being and wander about there as if out of its element, exiled and persecuted—does not hearken back to a rationality that does without confirmation by Being, one to *which the fiasco of the rationality of the Same is a necessary and bearable test*? A novel rationality or one more ancient than the rationality of the solid earth "under the sun," that is, of positivity. This rationality, consequently, does not amount to the ontological adventure with which, from Aristotle to Heidegger, it coincides, and into which were dragged, along with traditional theology, which remained a thinking of identity and of being, the God and the man of the Bible or their homonyms. This was an adventure that was mortal to the first of these, according to Nietzsche, and to the second one as well, according to contemporary antihumanism. It was mortal in any case to the homonyms: to man-in-the-world and to the God establishing himself in the back-worlds, under the same sun as the world. For a long time, one passed off the meaning that does not triumph, that does not install itself in the absolute repose of the earth under the vault of heaven, as purely objective, or as romantic, or as the unhappiness of the unhappy consciousness. One did not wonder whether un-rest, dis-quiet, the question, and, consequently, Search and Desire, low-ranked among the positive values, were a simple decrease of repose, of response and possession, that is to say, insufficient thoughts of the identical, indigent modes of knowledge—or whether, in these relations unequal to themselves, there is not thought, rather, difference, irreducible alterity, the "un-containable," the Infinite or God. One did not wonder, by chance, whether knowledge, response, results were not themselves precisely a psyche insufficient for the thoughts here necessary, and poorer than the question which is always also a request addressed to another, were it only a prayer without response. One did not ask oneself if demand, search, and desire—far from carrying in them only the hollowness of need—are not the bursting of the "more" in the "less," which Descartes called the idea of the infinite. Is it not of these thoughts that Blanchot speaks when he says, "we have a premonition that the *dis-aster* is thought."[5] These thoughts are other than those which, in intentional consciousness, "will [*veulent*]," to their measure, the correlative, the repose, and the identity of the *astronomic* positive.

One limits the human to equality to self and to being. One limits the human to activity in self-consciousness, to the identical, to the positive, which makes possible the firm ground; one does this without considering the "passive synthesis" of time, that is, the aging that comes about, although no one brings it about, and which signifies, without anyone saying it, *adieu* to the world, to the firm ground, to presence and to ess*a*nce: dis-inter-estedness by way of passing.[6] But does not dis-inter-estedness, as this leavetaking and this *adieu*, signify an unto God [*à-Dieu*]? The passive synthesis of time, of patience, is a waiting without an awaited term, and one that the determinate waitings deceive, filled as they are by that which corresponds to a grasp and a *comprehension*. Time as an awaiting—as patience, more passive than any passivity correlative of acts—awaits the ungraspable.[7]

Is what is ungraspable in this awaiting still contained in the hypostasis of the *being*, in which the language that names it encloses it?[8] Or is the *between-the-two* of this mode perhaps the manner in which the human is affected or inspired, where it *places itself in question*, and from whence it questions? A patience of awaiting, time is a question, a search, a demand, and a prayer. These may be thoughts more thoughtful [*pensantes*] than the positive ones that one would nevertheless like to substitute for them; as though patience and time were some negative theology separated from its god by indifference. On the contrary, therein lies a degree of passivity in which searching and questioning still seem buried, that is, held in the secret of their fortuity [*aléa*] of patient awaiting. The word of the prophet (Isaiah 65:1), which we cite by way of illustration, expresses this admirably. "I am sought of them that asked not for me, I am found of them that sought me not." Thoughts more thoughtful! Patience and length of time that must not even be understood as the makeshift of a parsimonious revelation of the Infinite to human finitude. These thoughts undergo, or suffer, the refusal or the challenge that strikes—or astonishes—finitude. By this striking or astonishing, the Infinite precisely transcends beyond being, but it also thereby inspires finitude, traumatically, and is thought.[9] The *in-* of the Infinite is not a simple negation, but rather time and humanity. Man is not a "fallen angel who remembers the heavens"; he belongs to the very meaning of the Infinite. This is a meaning inseparable from patience and awaiting; inseparable also from time, against which, as though these were "subjective contingencies," the insidious question returns—the only supposedly serious one—about the existence of God. This question is only the return of ontology and of its pretense to hold the ultimate measure of meaning. It is perhaps against ontology that the word of the prophet we just cited also bears witness. The term that is parallel to "*to be found* [*être trouvé*]" still remains the verb expressing the passive form of *to seek* [*rechercher*]. Transcendence *finds* by ever remaining a search (this is its life) and even patience, passive to the point of forgetting its own demand—or prayer—in the pure length and the pure languor and the silence of time. A traumatic inspiration—a traumatism without tangency, a traumatism felt in advance: fear! It is necessary to contest the Heideggerian phenomenology of affectivity, which would be rooted in the anguish of finitude. The non-eudaimonic, non-hedonistic affectivity of fear does not wait to be aroused for a threat implicating my being, as if the dread of God could only trouble me by the sanction that threatens me.[10]

Yet no doubt the ultimate sense of this patience and this fear—that of the question and the search that bury themselves therein—shows itself in the analysis that we have attempted elsewhere.[11] This is the reversion of this waiting for God into the proximity of another, into my responsibility as a hostage; a reversion of this fear, as foreign to fright before the Sacred as it is to the anguish before Nothingness, into fear for the neighbor.[12]

PART II

The Idea of God

§ God and Philosophy

The Priority of Philosophical Discourse, and Ontology

1. "Not to philosophize is still to philosophize." The philosophical discourse of the West asserts the amplitude of an all-inclusiveness [*englobement*] or an ultimate comprehension. It compels every other discourse to justify itself before philosophy.

Rational theology accepts this vassalage. If, for the benefit of religion, it pulls out some domain over which the supervision [*contrôle*] of philosophy is not exercised, then this domain shall have been, on good grounds, recognized as philosophically unverifiable.

2. This dignity of an ultimate and royal discourse comes to Western philosophy by virtue of the rigorous coincidence between the thought in which philosophy stands and the reality in which this thought thinks. For thought, this coincidence signifies the following: not to have to think beyond that which belongs to the "gesture or movement of being [*geste d'être*]"; or at least not to have to think beyond that which modifies a previous adherence to the "gesture of being," such as ideal or formal notions. For the being of the real, this coincidence signifies: to illumine thought and what is thought by showing itself. To show itself, to be illumined, is precisely to have a meaning; it is precisely to have intelligibility *par excellence*, underlying any modification of meaning. Consequently, it is necessary to understand the rationality of the "gesture of being" not as an eventual characteristic that would be attributed to it [the gesture of being] when some reason comes to know it. Intelligibility is precisely that a

thought might know the rationality of the gesture of being. It is necessary to understand rationality as the incessant upsurge of thought driven by the energy of the gesture of being or by its manifestation, and we must understand reason starting from this rationality. Meaningful thought, thought of being: these would be pleonasms and equivalent pleonasms, justified, however, by the vicissitudes and privations to which this identification of the thought of the meaningful and of being is exposed *de jure*.

3. Philosophical discourse must therefore be able to embrace God—of whom the Bible speaks—if, that is, this God has a meaning. But once thought, this God is immediately situated within the "gesture of being." He is situated therein as a *being* [*étant*] *par excellence*. If the intellection of the biblical God—theology—does not reach the level of philosophic thought, it is not because theology thinks God as a *being* without making clear to begin with the "being [*être*] of this being," but because in thematizing God, theology has brought him into the course of being, while the God of the Bible signifies in an unlikely manner the beyond of being, or transcendence. That is, the God of the Bible signifies without analogy to an idea subject to *criteria*, without analogy to an idea exposed to the summons to show itself true or false. And it is not by accident that the history of Western philosophy has been a destruction of transcendence. Rational theology, fundamentally ontological, endeavors to accommodate transcendence within the domain of being by expressing it with adverbs of height applied to the verb "to be." God is said to exist eminently or *par excellence*. But does the height, or the height above all height, which is thus expressed, still depend on ontology? And does not the modality that this adverb asserts, borrowed from the dimension of the sky stretched above our heads, govern the verbal sense of the verb "to be," to the point of excluding it—as ungraspable—from the *esse* that shows itself, that is to say, that shows itself as meaningful in a theme?

4. One can, to be sure, also claim that the God of the Bible has no meaning; that is, he is not thinkable properly speaking. This would be the other term of the alternative. "The concept of God is not a problematic concept, it is not a concept at all," writes Jeanne Delhomme in a recent book, prolonging a major line of the philosophical rationalism that refuses to receive the transcendence of the God of Abraham, or of Isaac and Jacob, among those concepts without which there would be no

thought.[1] That which the Bible raises above all comprehension has here not yet reached the threshold of intelligibility!

The problem that is posed, consequently, and which shall be our own, consists in asking ourselves whether meaning [*le sens*] is equivalent to the *esse* of being; that is, whether the meaning which, in philosophy, is meaning is not already a restriction of meaning; whether it is not already a derivation or a drift from meaning; whether the meaning equivalent to essence—to the gesture of being, to being *qua* being—is not already approached in the presence which is the time of the Same. This supposition can only be justified by the possibility of going back, starting from this allegedly conditioned meaning, to a meaning that would no longer express itself in terms of being, nor in terms of beings. We must ask ourselves whether, beyond the intelligibility and the rationalism of identity, of consciousness, of the present and of being—beyond the intelligibility of immanence—the significance, the rationality, and the rationalism of transcendence are not themselves understood. Our question is whether, beyond being, a meaning might not show itself whose priority, translated into ontological language, will be called *prior* to being. It is not certain that, going beyond the terms of being and beings, one necessarily falls back into the discourse of opinion or of faith. In fact, while remaining outside of reason, or while wanting to be there, faith and opinion speak the language of being. Nothing is less opposed to ontology than the opinion of faith. To ask oneself, as we are attempting to do here, whether God cannot be uttered in a reasonable discourse that would be neither ontology nor faith, is implicitly to doubt the formal opposition, established by Yehuda Halevy and taken up by Pascal, between, on the one hand, the God of Abraham, Isaac, and Jacob, invoked without philosophy in faith, and on the other the god of the philosophers. It is to doubt that this opposition constitutes an alternative.

The Priority of Ontology and Immanence

5. We have said that for Western philosophy meaning or intelligibility coincides with the manifestation of being, as if the very affair of being led, in the form of intelligibility, toward clarity, and thence became intentional thematization in an experience. This is a thematization from which derive, or to which are susceptible, all the potentialities of experience, as they press toward it or await thematization. In the thematic ex-

position the question of being or of truth is exhausted. But if being *is* manifestation—if the exertion or action of being comes back to this exhibition—then the manifestation of being is only the manifestation of "this exertion." That is, it is a manifestation of manifestation, a truth of truth. Philosophy thus finds in manifestation its matter and its form. Philosophy would thus remain in its attachment to being—to the existent or to the being of the existent—an intrigue of knowledge and truth, an adventure of experience between the clear and the obscure. It is certain that this is the sense in which philosophy carries the spirituality of the West, wherein spirit remained coextensive with knowledge. But knowledge [*savoir*]—or thought, or experience—should not be understood as some sort of reflection of exteriority in an inner forum. The notion of reflection, an optical metaphor borrowed from thematized beings or events, is not the characteristic of knowledge. Knowledge only comprehends itself in its own essence, starting from consciousness, whose specificity eludes us when we define it with the aid of the concept of knowledge, which itself supposes consciousness.

It is as a modality or a modification of *insomnia* that consciousness is consciousness of... , an assembling in being or in presence that—up to a certain depth of vigilance, where vigilance must clothe itself in justice—has import for insomnia.[2] Far from being defined as a simple negation of the natural phenomenon of sleep, insomnia—as wakefulness or vigilance—comes out of the logic of the categories, prior to all anthropological attention and dullness. Always on the verge of awakening, sleep communicates with wakefulness; while attempting to escape from it, sleep remains attuned to it in *obedience to the wakefulness* that threatens and calls to it, the wakefulness that *demands*. The category of insomnia cannot be reduced to the tautological affirmation of the Same, or to the dialectical negation, or to the "ecstasy" of thematizing intentionality. Keeping awake [*veiller*] is not equivalent to *attending to* [*veiller à*]... , where there is already a searching for the identical, rest, and sleep. It is in consciousness alone that the keeping awake [*le veiller*], already paralyzed, is inflected toward a content that is identified and assembled into a presence, into the "gesture of being," and is absorbed in it. Insomnia as a category—or as a meta-category (but it is by way of it that the *meta* takes on a meaning)—does not come to be inscribed in a table of categories starting from a determining activity exerted upon the other as a *given*, by the unity of the Same (and all activity is only identification and crystallization of the

Same against the Other, although affected by the Other) in order to assure to the Other, consolidated in a being, the gravity of being. Insomnia—the wakefulness of awakening—is disturbed at the heart of its formal or categorial *equality* by the *Other* who cores out [*dénoyaute*] all that
which in insomnia forms a core as the substance of the Same, as identity,
as repose, as presence, as sleep.[3] It is cored out by the Other who tears
this rest, who tears it from the inner side [*de l'en-deçà*] of the *state* where
equality tends to settle. There precisely lies the irreducible, categorial
character of insomnia: the Other in the Same who does not alienate the
Same, but precisely wakes him. This awakening is like a demand that no
obedience equals, and no obedience puts to sleep: a "more" in the "less."
Or, to utilize an antiquated language, there lies the spirituality of the soul
which is ceaselessly awakened from its state of soul [*état d'âme*], in which
the staying awake itself already closes up on itself or goes to sleep, resting within its state's boundaries. This is the passivity of Inspiration, or
the subjectivity of a subject sobered up from its being. Here we find the
formalism of insomnia, more formal than that of any form that defines,
delimits, encloses; formally more formal than that of the form that encloses in presence and in *esse*, filling itself with content. This is insomnia
or wakefulness, but it is a wakefulness without intentionality, dis-inter-
ested. An indetermination—but one that is not an appeal to form, one
that is not materiality. A form not *fixing* its own pattern as a form, not
condensing its own emptiness into content. A non-content—Infinity.

6. Consciousness has already broken with this dis-interestedness.[4]
Consciousness is identity of the Same, presence of being, presence of
presence. It is necessary to think of consciousness starting from this emphasis of presence.[5] Presence can only be as a return of consciousness to
itself, outside of sleep. In this sense, consciousness goes back to insomnia even if this return to itself, as consciousness of self, is only the forgetting of the Other who wakes the Same from within; even if the freedom
of the Same is still only a waking dream. Presence is only possible as an
incessant recovery of presence, as an incessant re-presentation. The "without-ceasing" of presence is a repetition; it is its recovery, its apperception
of representation. Yet the re-covery does not describe re-presentation. Re-
presentation is the very possibility of the return, as the possibility of the
always, or of the presence of the present. The unity of apperception, the
"I think"—which is to be discovered in re-presentation, and to which a

role has thus devolved—is not a manner of making presence purely subjective. The synthesis accomplished by the unity of the *I think*, behind experience, constitutes the act of presence, or presence as an act, or presence in action. This encompassing movement is accomplished by the unity that has become a core [*noyautée*] in the "I think" and which, as synopsia,[6] is the structure necessary to the actuality of the present. The operative concept of transcendental idealism which is the "activity of mind" does not rest upon some empirics [*empirie*] of the deployment of intellectual energy. It is rather the extreme purity—extreme to the point of tension—of the presence of presence, which is Aristotle's being in act, a presence of presence; an extreme tension to the point of the bursting of *presence* into an "experience had by a subject" in which presence precisely returns upon itself and fills itself up and is fulfilled. The psychic life [*psychisme*] of consciousness is this emphasis of being, this presence of presence; an overbidding of presence with no way out, with no subterfuge, with no possible forgetting in the folds of some sort of implication that could not be unfolded. The "without-ceasing" is a making explicit, without any chance of being dimmed [*estompement*]. It refers to an awakening in the form of lucidity, but also to a keeping watch over being. It is an attention to... , and not an exposition to the other, which is already a modification of Insomnia's formalism without intentionality. The fact remains that through consciousness nothing in being can dissimulate itself. Consciousness is a light that illumines the world from one end to the other; all that sinks into the past is re-membered [*se sou-vient*] or is rediscovered by history.[7] Reminiscence is the extreme consciousness that is also universal presence and ontology: all that which is able to fill the field of consciousness was, in its time, received, perceived, and had an origin. Through consciousness the past is but a modification of the present. Nothing can, or could, come to pass without presenting itself. Nothing can, or could, smuggle itself into consciousness without being declared, without showing itself, and without letting itself be inspected as to its truth. Transcendental subjectivity is the figure of this presence: no signification precedes that which I give.

Consequently the process of the present unfolds through consciousness like a "held note" in its *forever*, in its identity as the same, in the simultaneity of its moments. The process of the subjective does not come from the outside. It is the presence of the present that involves consciousness; and this in such a way that philosophy, in search of the transcendental operations of the apperception of the *I think*, is not some unhealthy and accidental curiosity. Philosophy is representation, the reactualization of representation; that is, the emphasis of presence, the remaining-the-same of being in its simultaneity of presence, in its forever and in its immanence. Philosophy is not only knowledge of immanence, it is immanence itself.[8]

7. Immanence and consciousness, as gathering the manifestation of manifestation, are not shaken by the phenomenological interpretation of affective states. Neither are they shaken by the voluntary life of the psyche, which places at the heart of consciousness the emotion or anguish that would overturn consciousness's impassiveness or, starting from fear or from trembling before the sacred, would understand immanence and consciousness as original lived experiences. It is not by accident that, in Husserl, the axiological and the practical levels hide a representative ground.

These levels remain experience—experience of values, or experience of the willed as willed. The representative ground that Husserl brings to light in them consists, moreover, less in some serenity of theoretical intention than in the identification of the identical in the form of ideality. It consists in assembling, or in representation in the form of a presence and in the form of a lucidity that lets nothing escape. In a word, the ground consists in immanence.

8. But let us note this well: the interpretation of affectivity, as a modification of representation or as founded upon a representation, succeeds to the degree to which affectivity is taken at the level of a tendency—or at that of concupiscence, as Pascal would say—at the level of an aspiration that can be satisfied in pleasure or which, if unsatisfied, remains a pure lack that causes suffering. Beneath such an affectivity is again found the ontological activity of consciousness—investment and comprehension, through and through, that is, presence and representation (of which the specifically theoretical thematization is but one modality). This does not exclude the possibility that, on a path other than that of the tendency going toward its end, there breaks forth an affectivity that cuts through the shape and designs of consciousness and steps out of immanence; an affectivity that is transcendence. We shall attempt, precisely, to express the "elsewhere" of this affectivity.

9. A religious thought that appeals to religious experiences allegedly independent of philosophy insofar as it is founded upon experience, already

refers to the "I think" and is entirely connected to philosophy. The "narrative" of the religious experience does not shake philosophy and, consequently, could not break the presence and the immanence of which philosophy is the emphatic accomplishment. It is possible that the word "God" may have come to philosophy from a religious discourse. But philosophy—even if it refuses it—understands this discourse as that of propositions bearing on a theme; that is, as having a meaning that refers to a disclosure, to a manifestation of presence. The messengers of the religious experience do not conceive another signification of meaning [*signification de sens*]. The religious "revelation" is henceforth assimilated to philosophical disclosure—an assimilation that even dialectical theology maintains. That a discourse might speak otherwise than to say what has been seen or heard outside, or felt internally, remains unsuspected. From the outset, then, the religious being interprets what he lived through as experience. In spite of himself, he already interprets God, of whom he claims to have an experience, in terms of being, presence, and immanence.

From here comes our previous question: can discourse signify otherwise than by signifying a theme? Does God signify as a theme of the religious discourse that names God, or as a discourse that precisely, at least at first sight, does not name him, but says him in another way than by denomination or evocation?

The Idea of the Infinite

10. The thematization of God in religious experience has already conjured away or missed the excess of the intrigue that breaks the unity of the "I think."[9]

In his meditation on the idea of God, Descartes has sketched, with unequaled rigor, the extraordinary course of a thought proceeding to the point of the breakup of the *I think*. While thinking of God as a being, Descartes thinks of him nevertheless as an eminent being, or he thinks of him as a being who *is* eminently. Before this *rapprochement* between the idea of God and the idea of being, we must certainly ask ourselves whether the adjective *eminent* and the adverb *eminently* do not refer to the height of the sky over our heads and thus overflow ontology. Be that as it may, Descartes maintains a substantialist language here, interpreting the immeasurableness of God as a superlative way of existing. But for us his unsurpassable contribution does not lie here. It is not the proofs of

God's existence that matter to us here, but rather the breakup of consciousness, which is not a repression into the unconscious but a sobering or a waking up [*réveil*] that shakes the "dogmatic slumber" that sleeps at the bottom of all consciousness resting upon the object. As a *cogitatum* of a *cogitatio* that contains *at first sight* the *cogitatio*, is the idea of God (understood as signifying the uncontained *par excellence*) the very absolution of the absolute here? This idea of God surpasses every capacity, its "objective reality" as a *cogitatum* causes the "formal reality" of the *cogitatio* to break apart. Perhaps this overturns—in advance—the universal validity and the original character of intentionality. We shall say this: the idea of God causes the breakup of the thinking that—as investment, synopsia, and synthesis—merely encloses in a presence, re-presents, brings back to presence, or lets be.

Malebranche was able to measure the full implications of this event: there is no idea of God, or God is his own idea. We are out of the order in which one passes from the idea to the being. The idea of God is God in me, but it is already God breaking up the consciousness that aims at ideas, already differing from all content. This is a difference that is not, to be sure, an emergence, as if encompassing the idea of God had ever been possible; neither is it some escape from the empire of consciousness, as if a *comprehension* could ever have been effected here. And yet it is an idea of God, or God in us, as though the not-letting-itself-be-encompassed were also an exceptional relation with me, as though the difference between the Infinite and that which had to encompass and comprehend it were a non-indifference of the Infinite to this impossible encompassing, a non-indifference of the Infinite for thought: the placing of the Infinite in thought, but wholly other than the thought, which is structured as a comprehension of the *cogitatum* by a *cogitatio*. This is a placing-in that is like a passivity unlike any other [*mise comme passivité non pareille*], because it cannot be assumed (it is perhaps in this passivity—from beyond all passivity—that we must recognize awakening [*réveil*]). Or, contrariwise, as if the negation of the finite included in Infinity signified not some negation coming from the formalism of negative judgment, but precisely the *idea of the Infinite*, that is, the Infinite in me. Or, more exactly, as though the psyche of subjectivity were equivalent to the negation of the finite by the Infinite; as though—without wanting to play on words—the *in* of the Infinite signified at once the *non-* and the *within*.[10]

11. In the form of the idea of the Infinite, the actuality of the *cogito* is thus interrupted by the unencompassable; it is not thought but undergone, carrying in a second moment of consciousness that which in a first moment claimed to carry it. After the certitude of the *cogito*, present to itself in the second Meditation, after the "halt" that the last lines of this Meditation signal, the third Meditation announces that "I have, in some manner, in me firstly the notion of the infinite rather than the finite, that is of God rather than myself." The idea of the Infinite, *the Infinite in me*, can only be a passivity of consciousness. Is this still consciousness? At stake is a passivity that one could not assimilate to receptivity. The latter is a fresh grasping in welcoming, an assuming under the blow received. The breakup of the actuality of thought in the "idea of God" is a passivity more passive than any passivity, like the passivity of a trauma through which the idea of God would have been placed in us. An "idea placed within us": does this figure of style suit the subjectivity of the *cogito*? Does it suit consciousness and its manner of holding a content, which always consists in leaving behind the marks of its grasp? Does consciousness not get its origin from its presence of consciousness [*présent de conscience*]? Does it not get its contents from itself? Can an idea be placed in a thought and renounce its Socratic seal of nobility, its immanent birth in reminiscence, that is, its origin in the very presence of the thought that thinks it, or in the recuperation of this thought by memory? Now, in the idea of the Infinite is described a passivity more passive than any passivity appropriate to a consciousness: it is the surprise or susception of the unassumable, more open than any opening—an awakening [*éveil*]—but suggesting the passivity of the created one.[11] The placing in us of an unencompassable idea overturns this presence to self which is consciousness; it thus forces through the barrier and the checkpoint, it confounds the obligation to accept or adopt all that enters from without. It is thus an idea signifying with a significance prior to presence, to all presence, prior to every origin in consciousness, and so an-archic, accessible only in its trace.[12] It is an idea signifying with a significance that is straightaway older than its exhibition, one that does not exhaust itself in exhibition, one that does not derive its meaning from its manifestation. It is thus an idea that breaks with the coincidence of being and appearing in which meaning or rationality reside for Western philosophy; it is an idea that breaks up synopsia. It is more ancient than recollectable thought, which representation retains in its presence. What can this significance more

ancient than exhibition mean? Or, more precisely, what can the antiquity of a signification mean? In exhibition, can it enter into a time other than the historic present, which already annuls the past and its dia-chrony by re-presenting it? What can this antiquity mean if not the trauma of awakening [*éveil*]? As though the idea of the Infinite—the Infinite in us—awakened a consciousness that is not sufficiently awake. As though the idea of the Infinite in us were exigency and signification, in the sense in which an order is signified in exigency.

Divine Comedy

12. As we have already said, it is not in the negation of the finite by the Infinite, understood in its abstraction and in its logical formalism, that we must interpret the idea of the Infinite, or the Infinite in thought. It is, on the contrary, the idea of the Infinite, or the Infinite in thought, that is the proper and irreducible figure of the negation of the finite. The *in-* of the infinite is not a *non-* or *not* of some kind: its negation is the subjectivity of the subject, which is behind intentionality. The difference between the Infinite and the finite is a non-indifference of the Infinite with regard to the finite, and is the secret of subjectivity. The figure of the Infinite-placed-in-me, which if we believe Descartes is contemporary with my creation,[13] would signify that the not-able-to-comprehend-the-Infinite-by-thought is, in some way, a positive relation with this thought. But it is a relation with this thought as passive, as a *cogitatio* almost dumbfounded, and no longer commanding—or not yet commanding—the *cogitatum.* Here we find a dumbfounded *cogitatio* not yet hastening toward the adequation between the term of the spontaneous teleology of consciousness and this term given in being. This adequation is the destiny of the essential teleology of consciousness going to its intentional term and conjuring up the presence of re-presentation. Better still, the not-able-to-comprehend-the-Infinite-by-thought would signify precisely this condition—or noncondition—of thought, as though to say the incomprehension of the Infinite by the finite did not amount merely to saying that the Infinite is not finite. And as if the affirmation of the difference between the Infinite and the finite had to remain a verbal abstraction, without consideration of the fact of the incomprehension of the Infinite precisely by thought—which, by way of this incomprehension, is posited as thought, as a posited subjectivity, that is, is posited *qua* self-

positing, itself. The Infinite has nothing to add to itself anew in order to affect subjectivity. Its very in-finity, its difference with respect to the fi-nite, is already its nonindifference with respect to the finite. This amounts to the *cogitatio not comprehending* the *cogitatum* which affects it ab-solutely. The Infinite affects thought by simultaneously devastating it and calling it; through a "putting it in its place," the Infinite puts thought in place. It wakes thought up. This is a waking up that is not a reception or welcome of the Infinite, a waking up that is neither recollection [*re-cueillement*] nor assuming, both of which are necessary and sufficient for *experience*. The idea of the Infinite puts them in question. The idea of the Infinite is not even assumed, like the love that is awakened by the tip of the striking arrow, but in which the subject, stunned by the trauma, im-mediately finds himself again in the immanence of his state of soul. The Infinite signifies precisely the hither side of its manifestation—its mean-ing is not reduced to manifestation, to the representation of presence, or to teleology; its meaning is not measured by the possibility or the impos-sibility of the truth of being, even if the signification from the hither side had to show itself, in one way or another, if only by its trace, in the enig-mas of the saying.[14]

13. What then is the intrigue of meaning, other than that of re-pre-sentation and empirical experience [*empirie*], which is formed in the idea of the Infinite—in the monstrosity of the Infinite *placed* in me—an idea which in its passivity beyond all receptivity is no longer an idea? What is the meaning of the traumatism of the awakening, in which the Infinite could neither be posited as a correlate of the subject, nor enter into a structure with him, nor make itself his contemporary in a co-presence, but in which the Infinite transcends the subject? How is transcendence thinkable as a relationship, if it must exclude the ultimate—and the most formal—co-presence, which the relationship guarantees to its terms?

The *in-* of the infinite designates the depth of the affection by which subjectivity is affected through this "placing" of the Infinite within it, without prehension or comprehension. A depth of undergoing [*subir*] that no capacity comprehends, and where no foundation supports it any longer, this is a depth in which every process of investment fails, and where the bolts that close the rear doors of interiority burst. Here is a placing without recollection, devastating its site like a devouring fire, bringing down [*catastrophant*] the site in the etymological sense of the term "catastrophe."[15] A dazzling where the eye holds more than it can hold; an ignition of the skin that touches and does not touch that which, beyond the graspable, burns. A passivity, or passion, in which Desire is recognized, in which the "*more* in the *less*" awakens with its most ardent, most noble, and most ancient flame, a thought destined to think more than it thinks.[16] But this is a Desire of another order than those characteristic of affectivity and hedonic or eudaimonic activity wherein the Desirable is invested, attained, and identified as an object of need, and wherein the immanence of representation and of the external world is rediscovered. The negativity of the *In-* of the Infinite—otherwise than being, divine comedy—hollows out a desire that could not be filled, one nourished from its own increase, exalted as Desire—one that withdraws from its satisfaction as it draws near to the Desirable. This is a Desire for what is beyond satisfaction, and which does not identify, as need does, a term or an end. A desire without end, from beyond Being: dis-inter*estedness*,[17] transcendence—desire for the Good.

But if the Infinite in me signifies Desire of the Infinite, are we sure of the transcendence that there *passes*? Does not desire restore the contemporaneousness of the desiring and the Desirable? This could again be expressed otherwise: does not the desiring one derive from the Desirable a complacency [*complaisance*] in desiring, as if it had already grasped the Desirable by its intention? Is not the disinter*estedness* of the Desire for the Infinite an inter*estedness*? A Desire for the good beyond being, a transcendence—we have said this without concerning ourselves with the manner by which interestedness is excluded from the Desire for the Infinite, and without showing how the transcendent Infinite merits the name "Good" while its very transcendence can, it seems, only signify indifference.

14. Love is only possible through the idea of the Infinite, through the Infinite placed in me, by the "more" that ravages and wakes up the "less," turning away from teleology, and destroying the time and the happiness [*l'heure et le bonheur*] of the end. Plato compels Aristophanes to make an admission that, in the mouth of the master of Comedy, resounds in a singular fashion. "These are people who pass their whole lives together; yet they could not explain what they desire of one another."[18] Hephaestus will say that they wish to become "one instead of two,"[19] thus restoring an end to love and bringing it back to the nostalgia for what was in the past. But why do the lovers not know how to say what they demand of

each other, the one from the other, beyond pleasure? Diotima will place the intention of Love beyond this unity, but will discover it indigent, needy, and liable to vulgarity. The celestial and the vulgar Venus are sisters. Love finds pleasure in the very anticipation of the Lovable one; that is, it enjoys the Lovable through the representation that fills the anticipation. Pornography is perhaps this, arising in all eroticism, as eroticism buds in all love. Losing the immeasurableness of Desire in this enjoyment, love becomes concupiscence in Pascal's sense of the term, an assumption and an investment by the *I*. The *I think* reconstitutes in love both presence and being, inter*estedness* and immanence.[20]

Is the transcendence of the Desirable possible, beyond the inter*estedness* and the eroticism in which the Beloved is found? Affected by the Infinite, Desire cannot go to an end to which it might be equal; in Desire, the approach creates distance [*éloigne*] and enjoyment is only the increase of hunger. In this reversal of terms, transcendence or the disinter*estedness* of Desire comes to "pass." How? And in the transcendence of the Infinite, what is it that dictates to us the word Good? In order that disinter*estedness* be possible in the Desire for the Infinite—in order that the Desire beyond being, or transcendence, might not be an absorption into immanence, which would thus make its return—the Desirable, or God, must remain separated in the Desire; as desirable—near yet different—Holy. This can only be if the Desirable commands me [*m'ordonne*] to what is the nondesirable, to the undesirable *par excellence*; to another. The referring to another is awakening [*éveil*], awakening to proximity, which is responsibility for the neighbor to the point of substitution for him. We have shown elsewhere[21] the substitution for another at the heart of this responsibility, which is thus an enucleation of the transcendental subject, thus also the transcendence of goodness, the nobility of pure *enduring*, an ipseity of pure election. Love without Eros. Transcendence is ethical, and the subjectivity which in the final analysis is not the "I think" (which it is at first sight), or the unity of the "transcendental apperception," is, as responsibility for the other, subjection to the other. The I is a passivity more passive than any passivity, because it is from the outset in the accusative, oneself—which had never been in the nominative—under the accusation of another, although without sin. The hostage for another, the I obeys a commandment before having heard it; it is faithful to an engagement that it never made, and to a past that was never present. This is a wakefulness—or opening of the self—absolutely exposed, and sobered up from the ecstasy of intentionality. We have designated this manner for the Infinite, or for God, to refer, from the heart of its very desirability, to the undesirable proximity of the others, by the term "illeity"; this is an extra-ordinary turning around of the desirability of the Desirable, of the supreme desirability calling to itself the rectilinear rectitude of Desire. A turning around by which the Desirable escapes the Desire. The goodness of the Good—of the Good that neither sleeps nor slumbers—inclines the movement it calls forth to turn it away from the Good and orient it toward the other, and only thus toward the Good. An ir-rectitude going higher than rectitude. Intangible, the Desirable separates itself from the relationship with the Desire that it calls forth and, by this separation or holiness, remains a third person: He at the root of the You [*Tu*]. He is Good in this very precise, eminent sense: He does not fill me with goods, but compels me to goodness, which is better than to receive goods.[22]

To be good is a deficit, a wasting away and a foolishness in being; to be good is excellence and elevation beyond being. Ethics is not a moment of being, it is otherwise and better than being; the very possibility of the beyond.[23] In this ethical turnabout, in this reference [*renvoi*] from the Desirable to the Undesirable, in this strange mission commanding the approach to the other, God is pulled out of objectivity, out of presence and out of being. He is neither object nor interlocutor. His absolute remoteness, his transcendence, turns into my responsibility—the non-erotic *par excellence*—for the other. And it is from the analysis just carried out that God is not simply the "first other," or the "other *par excellence*," or the "absolutely other," but other than the other, other otherwise, and other with an alterity prior to the alterity of the other, prior to the ethical obligation to the other and different from every neighbor, transcendent to the point of absence, to the point of his possible confusion with the agitation of the *there is* [*il y a*].[24] This is the confusion wherein substitution for the neighbor gains in disinter*estedness*, that is, in nobility; wherein the transcendence of the Infinite thereby likewise arises in glory. It is a transcendence that is true by way of a dia-chronous truth and, being without synthesis, it is higher than the truths lacking enigmas.[25] In order that the formula, "transcendence to the point of absence," not signify the simple explicitation of an ex-ceptional word, it was necessary to restore this word to the meaning of every ethical intrigue, to the divine comedy without which this word could not have arisen. A comedy taking place in the ambiguity between temple and theater, but wherein the laughter sticks in your throat at the approach of the neighbor, that is, of his face or his forsakenness.

Phenomenology and Transcendence

15. The exposition of the ethical meaning of transcendence, and of the Infinite beyond being, can be carried out starting from the proximity of the neighbor and from my responsibility for the other.

Until proximity and responsibility were described, we seemed to be constructing the abstraction of a passive subjectivity. The receptivity of finite knowledge is the assembling of a dispersion of the given into a simultaneity of presence, in immanence. The passivity "more passive than any passivity" consisted in suffering an unassumable trauma—or, more precisely, in having already suffered it in an unrepresentable past that was never present. The unassumable [*inassumable*] trauma is to be stricken by the *in-* of the infinite,[26] devastating presence and awakening subjectivity to the proximity of the other. The uncontained, breaking the container or the forms of consciousness, thus *transcends* the essence or "the act" of knowable being, which follows its course of being in presence. It transcends the inter*estedness* and simultaneity of a representable or historically reconstitutable temporality; it transcends immanence.

This trauma—as unassumable—is inflicted upon presence by the Infinite. It is this affectation of presence by the Infinite—this affectivity—that takes shape as a subjection to the neighbor. This is a thinking thinking more than it thinks—Desire—a reference to the neighbor—a responsibility for the other.

This abstraction is nevertheless familiar to us beneath the empirical event of obligation to the other and as the impossible indifference—impossible without avoidance—to the misfortunes and faults of the neighbor, as an irrecusable responsibility for him. A responsibility whose limits are impossible to fix, whose extreme urgency cannot be measured. To reflection, this responsibility is astonishing in every way, extending all the way to the obligation to answer for the freedom of the other, all the way to being a responsibility for his responsibility, whereas the freedom that would require an eventual engagement, or even the assumption of an imposed necessity, cannot find for itself a present that encompasses the possibilities of the other. The freedom of the other could not form a common structure with my freedom, nor enter into a synthesis with mine.

The responsibility for the neighbor is precisely that which goes beyond legality and obliges beyond the contract. It comes to me prior to my freedom, from a nonpresent, from an immemorial. Between me and the other there gapes a difference which no unity of transcendental apperception could recover. My responsibility for the other is precisely the non-indifference of this difference: the proximity of the other. An extraordinary relation in the absolute sense of the term, it does not reestablish the order of representation in which all of the past returns. The proximity of the neighbor remains a dia-chronic break, or a resistance of time to the synthesis of simultaneity.

Biological human fraternity, considered with the sober coldness of Cain, is not a sufficient reason that I be responsible for a separated being. The sober, Cain-like coldness consists in reflecting on responsibility from the standpoint of freedom or according to a contract. Yet responsibility for the other comes from what is prior to my freedom. It does not come from the time made up of presences, nor from presences sunken into the past and representable, the time of beginnings or assumptions. Responsibility does not let me constitute myself into an *I think*, as substantial as a stone or, like a heart of stone, into an in- and for-oneself. It goes to the point of substitution for the other, up to the condition—or the noncondition—of a hostage.[27] This is a responsibility that does not leave me time: it leaves me without a present for recollection or a return into the self. And it makes me late: before the neighbor I "compear" rather than appear.[28] I respond from the first to a summons. Already the stony core of my substance is hollowed out. But the responsibility to which I am exposed in such a passivity does not seize hold of me as if I were an interchangeable thing, for no one here may substitute himself for me. In appealing to me as to someone accused who can not challenge the accusation, responsibility binds me as irreplaceable and unique. It binds me as elected. To the very degree to which it appeals to my responsibility, it forbids me any replacement. As unreplaceable for this responsibility, I cannot slip away from the face of the neighbor without avoidance, or without fault, or without complexes; here I am pledged to the other without any possibility of abdication.[29] I cannot slip away from the face of the other in its nakedness without recourse. I cannot escape it in its forsaken nakedness, which glimmers through the fissures that crack the mask of the personage or his wrinkled skin, in his "with no recourse," which we must hear as cries already cried out toward God, without voice or thematization. There the resonance of silence—the *Geläut der Stille*—certainly resounds.[30] An imbroglio to be taken seriously: this is a relation to... that which is without representation, without intentionality, and not repressed. It is the latent birth, in the other, of religion; prior to the emotions and to the voice, prior to "religious experience" that speaks of revelation in terms of the disclosure of being, when it is a question of an unusual access, at the heart of my responsibility, to an unusual derangement of being. Even if one immediately tells oneself, "it was nothing." "It was nothing"—it was not being, but otherwise than being. My responsibility in spite of myself—which is the manner by which the other is incumbent upon me, or how he disturbs me, that is, the way in which he is close to me—is a hearing or an understanding of this cry. It is awakening. The proximity of the neighbor is my responsibility for him: to approach is to be the guardian of one's brother; to be the guardian of one's brother is to be his hostage. This is immediacy. Responsibility does not come from fraternity, it is fraternity that gives responsibility for the other its name, prior to my freedom.

16. To posit subjectivity in this responsibility is to glimpse in it a passivity, never passive enough, of a consummation for the other whose very light glimmers and illuminates out of this ardor, without the cinders of this consummation being able to make themselves into the kernel of a being that is in-itself and for-itself, and without the I opposing to the other any form that might protect it or bring to it a measure. It is the consummation of a holocaust. "I am ashes and dust," says Abraham, interceding for Sodom.[31] "What are we?" says Moses, still more humbly.[32]

What is signified by this summons in which the subject is cored out as if enucleated, and receives no form capable of assuming it? What do these atomic metaphors signify, if not an I [*moi*] torn from the concept of the Ego [*Moi*] and from the content of obligations for which the concept rigorously furnishes the measure and the rule? What do these metaphors signify if not an I that is left, precisely in this way, to a responsibility beyond measure, because it increases in the measure—or in what is beyond measure—that a response is made? It increases gloriously. An I that one does not designate but which says, "here I am." "Each of us is guilty before everyone, for everyone and for everything, and I more than the others," says Dostoevsky in *The Brothers Karamazov*. This is an I who says "I," and not one who singularizes or individuates the concept or the genus: it is I

[*Moi*], but an I [*moi*] unique in its kind who speaks to you in the first person. That is, unless one could maintain that it is in the individuation of the genus or in the concept of the Ego [*Moi*] that I awaken and expose myself to the others; which is to say, that I begin to speak. Here is an exposition that does not resemble the self-consciousness or the recurrence of the subject to himself, confirming the ego [*moi*] by itself. This is rather the recurrence of awakening, which one can describe as the shiver of incarnation, through which *giving* takes on meaning, as the original dative of the *for the other*, in which the subject becomes heart and sensitiveness and hands that give. Yet it is thus a position already de-posed from its kingdom of identity and substance, already in debt, "for the other" to the point of substitution for the other and altering the immanence of the subject in his innermost identity. This is the subject, irreplaceable for the responsibility there assigned to him, and who therein discovers a new identity. But insofar as it tears me from the concept of the Ego [*Moi*], the fission of the subject is a growth of obligation in proportion to my obedience to it; it is the augmentation of culpability with the augmentation of holiness, an increase of distance in proportion to my approach. There is no rest here for the self in the shelter of its form, in the shelter of its concept of ego! There is no "condition," were it only one of servitude. This is an incessant solicitude for solicitude, an excess of passivity in the responsibility for the responsibility of the other. In this way proximity is never close enough; as a responsible I, I never finish emptying myself of myself. An infinite increase in one's exhaustion, wherein the subject does not simply become aware of this expenditure, but is its site and its event, and, if we may say this, its goodness. *The glory of a long desire!* The subject as hostage has been neither the experience nor the proof of the Infinite, but the witnessing of the Infinite, a modality of this glory, a witnessing that no disclosure has preceded.

17. This growing surplus of the Infinite, which we have dared to call *glory*, is not an abstract quintessence. It has a meaning in the response, given without any possible evasion, to the summons that comes to me from the face of the neighbor: it is the hyperbolic exigency that immediately overflows the response. This is a surprise for the respondent himself, by which—ousted from his interiority as an ego and a "being with two inner sides"—he is awakened, that is, exposed to the other without restraint and without reserve. The passivity of such an exposure to the

other is not exhausted in various ways of being open to undergo the gaze or the objectifying judgment of the other. The openness of the I exposed to the other is the bursting open or the turning inside-out of interiority. Sincerity is the name of this extraversion.[33] Yet what can this inversion or this extraversion mean if not a responsibility for the others such that I keep nothing for myself? What can it mean if not a responsibility such that everything in me is debt and donation, and that my being-there is the ultimate *being-there*, in which the creditors overtake the debtor? Or a responsibility such that my position as a subject, in its *as for me*, is already my substitution for the others, or expiation for the others. This is a responsibility for the other—for his misery and his freedom—which does not go back to any engagement, to any project, or to any previous disclosure, in which the subject would be posited for itself before being-in-debt. This signifies an excess of passivity in proportion (or in disproportion) to which devotion for the other does not close itself up in itself like a mood, but in which, henceforth, devotion too is dedicated to the other.

This excess is *saying*. Sincerity is not an attribute that, eventually, receives the saying. It is only by saying that sincerity, as exposition without reserve, is possible. Saying makes a sign to the other, but in this sign, it signifies the very donation of the sign. Saying opens me to the other, before saying something said, before the said that is spoken in this sincerity forms a screen between me and the other. It is a saying without words, but not with empty hands. If silence speaks, it is not by some ecstasy of intentionality, but through the hyperbolic passivity of giving, which is prior to all willing and all thematization. This is a Saying bearing witness to the other of the Infinite, which tears me open as it awakens me in the Saying.

Thus understood, language loses its function as luxury; the strange function of doubling thought and being. As witnessing, Saying precedes every Said. Before uttering a Said, the Saying is already a bearing witness of responsibility (and even the Saying of a Said is a bearing witness, insofar as the approach of the other is responsibility for him). Saying is thus a way of signifying prior to any experience. It is pure witnessing: the truth of the martyr that depends upon no disclosure, even if this were a "religious" experience; this is an obedience preceding the hearing of the order. A pure witnessing that bears witness not to a previous experience but to the Infinite, it is inaccessible to the unity of apperception, it is nonappearing, and it is disproportionate to the present. It could not encompass the Infinite; it could not comprehend it. The Infinite concerns me and encircles me, speaking to me through my own mouth. And there is no pure witnessing except of the Infinite. This is not a psychological wonder, but the modality according to which the Infinite *comes to pass*, signifying through him to whom it signifies, understood insofar as, before any engagement, I respond for the other.

As if placed under a leaden sun, suppressing every shadowy nook in me, every residue of mystery, every dissimulated thought, every "as for me," and every hardening or relaxing of the structure by which escape would be possible, I am the witnessing, or the trace, or the glory of the Infinite, breaking the bad silence that shelters the secret of Gyges. This is the extraversion of the interiority of the subject: he would make himself visible before making himself a seer! The infinite is not "in front of" me; it is I who express it, but I do so precisely in giving a sign of the giving of signs, of the "for-the-other" in which I am dis-interested: here I am [*me voici*]. A marvelous accusative: here I am under your gaze, obliged to you, your servant.[34] In the name of God. Without thematization! The sentence in which God comes to be involved in words is not "I believe in God." The religious discourse prior to all religious discourse is not dialogue. It is the "here I am," said to the neighbor to whom I am given over, and in which I announce peace, that is, my responsibility for the other. "In making language flower upon their lips . . . Peace, peace to him who is far off, and to him who is near, says the Eternal . . . "[35]

Prophetic Signification

18. The transcendental condition of some kind of ethical experience was not at issue in the description just developed. Ethics as substitution for the other, as donation without reserve, breaks up the unity of transcendental apperception, which is the condition of all being and experience. As dis-inter*estedness* in the radical sense of the term, ethics signifies the improbable field wherein the Infinite is in relation with the finite without contradicting itself through this relation, where, on the contrary, it *comes to pass* only as Infinity and as awakening. The Infinite transcends itself in the finite, it *passes* the finite in that it orders the neighbor to me [*il m'ordonne le prochain*] without exposing itself to me. This is an order that slips into me like a thief, despite the taut weave of consciousness; a trauma that surprises me absolutely, always already *passed* in a past that was never present and remains ir-representable.

One might give the name "*inspiration*" to this intrigue of infinity in which I make myself the author of what I hear. Inspiration constitutes, on the hither side of the unity of apperception,[36] the very psyche of the soul. It is inspiration or prophetism in which I am the interpreter of what I utter. "The Lord God has spoken, who can but prophesy," says Amos,[37] comparing the prophetic reaction to the passivity of the fear that seizes him who hears the roaring of wild animals. Prophetism as pure witnessing, pure because prior to all disclosure; this is a subjection to an order prior to the understanding of the order. It is an anachronism that, according to the recoverable time of reminiscence, is not less paradoxical than a prediction of the future. It is in prophetism that the Infinite passes—and awakens—and, as transcendence refusing objectification and dialogue, signifies in an ethical way. The Infinite *signifies* in the sense in which one says, *to signify an order*; it orders [*il ordonne*].

19. In sketching the contours of prophetic witnessing behind philosophy where transcendence is always to be reduced, we have not entered into the moving sands of religious experience. That subjectivity be the temple or the theater of transcendence, and that the intelligibility of transcendence take on an ethical sense, certainly does not contradict the idea of the Good beyond being. This is an idea that guarantees the philosophical dignity of an enterprise in which the significance of meaning separates from the manifestation or the presence of being. But one can only wonder whether Western philosophy has been faithful to this Platonism. Western philosophy discovered intelligibility in terms set in conjunction with each other, the ones posited relative to the others, or the one signifying the other, and it is thus that for philosophy, being, thematized in its presence, is illuminated. The clarity of the visible—signified.[38] The trope proper to the significance of signification is written: "the-one-for-the-other." However, significance becomes visibility, immanence, and ontology to the degree to which the terms are united into a whole, in which their very history is systematized, in order to be clarified.

In the pages presented here, transcendence as the ethical one-for-the-other has been formulated in terms of significance and intelligibility.[39] The trope of intelligibility takes shape [*se dessine*] in the ethical one-for-the-other; it is a significance prior to that which is taken on by the terms in conjunction within a system. Does this significance, more ancient than all patterns, *take form*, however?[40] We have shown elsewhere the latent birth of the system and of philosophy, starting from this august intelligibility, and we will not return to it here.[41]

The intelligibility of transcendence is not ontological. The transcendence of God can neither be said nor thought in terms of being, the element of philosophy behind which philosophy sees only night. But the rupture between philosophical intelligibility and what is beyond being, or the contradiction there would be in com-prehending the infinite, does not exclude God from the significance that, although not ontological, does not amount to simple thoughts bearing on a being in decline, nor to views without necessity, nor to words that play.

In our time—is this its very modernity?—a presumption of ideology weighs upon philosophy.[42] This presumption cannot appeal to philosophy; in it the critical spirit would not rest content with suspicions, but owes it to itself to provide proofs. Yet the presumption, irrecusable, draws its force from elsewhere. It begins in a cry of ethical revolt, a bearing witness to responsibility. The presumption begins in prophecy. In the spiritual history of the West, the moment at which philosophy becomes suspect is not insignificant. To recognize with philosophy—or to recognize philosophically—that the Real is reasonable and that alone the Reasonable is real, and not be able to stifle or to cover the cry of those who, in the morning after this recognition, intend to transform the world, is already to walk in a domain of meaning which the inclusion cannot comprehend.[43] It is to walk among reasons that "reason" does not know, and which have not begun in Philosophy. A meaning seems thus to bear witness to a beyond that would not be the *no man's land*[44] of non-sense in which opinions pile up. *Not to philosophize would not be still to philosophize*, nor to succumb to opinions. This is a meaning borne witness to in interjections and in cries, before disclosing itself in propositions; a meaning signifying like a command, like an order that one signifies. Its manifestation in a theme already flows from its signifying as ordering; ethical signification signifies not *for* a consciousness that thematizes, but *to* a subjectivity that is all obedience, obeying with an obedience preceding understanding. A passivity more passive than that of the receptivity of knowing, more passive than the receptivity assuming that which affects it; this is, consequently, a signification in which the ethical moment is not founded upon any preliminary structure of theoretical thought, or of language, or of some particular tongue. Here, language exerts upon signification nothing more than the hold of a form investing matter, which recalls the distinction between form and signification, where signification shows itself in this distinction and through its references to a linguistic system. This is so even though this *said* must be *unsaid*—and it must be unsaid in order to lose its linguistic modification [*altération*]; even though signification must be reduced and must lose the "stains" that its exposition to the light or its sojourn in the shadows gave it; even though a rhythm of alternation is substituted for the unity of discourse, from the said into the unsaid and from the unsaid into the unsaid anew. This is a bursting open of the omnipotence of the *logos*, of the *logos* of system and simultaneity; a bursting open of the *logos* into a signifier and a signified that is not *only* a signifier. It goes against the attempt to amalgamate the signifier and the signified, and to hunt down transcendence in its first or last refuge by delivering to language, *qua* system of signs, all of thought, in the shadow of a philosophy for which meaning is equivalent to the manifestation of being and to the manifestation of the *esse* of being.

Transcendence as signification, and signification as the signification of an order given to subjectivity before any statement: a pure one-for-the-other. Poor ethical subjectivity, deprived of freedom! Unless this would be but the trauma of a fission of oneself come to pass in a venture risked with God or through God. But in fact even this ambiguity is necessary to transcendence. Transcendence owes it to itself to interrupt its own demonstration and monstration, its phenomenality. It requires the blinking and the dia-chrony of the enigma, which is not merely a precarious certitude but breaks up the unity of transcendental apperception, wherein immanence always triumphs over transcendence.

§ Questions and Answers

· *The conversation reproduced in the following pages—with a few modifications that leave intact its improvised essence—took place at the University of Leyden, on the occasion of the university's 400th anniversary celebration in March 1975. Invited to participate, Emmanuel Levinas also responded, for over two hours, to questions the Dutch philosophers posed about his work. This meeting took place on May 20, 1975. Some of these questions, numbered and written out, were given to him in advance, at the beginning of the session.*

Professor Andriaanse of Leyden agreed to organize and supervise a recording of this dialogue. The transcript was given its final form thanks to his collaboration.

Improvisation constitutes, perhaps by its exacting urgency and its inevitable digressions, which are its freedom, a mode of expression all its own. Without absolving himself from any responsibility, Emmanuel Levinas submits these traces of an oral examination.

T. C. FREDERIKSE I would like to know whether, in your philosophy, you do not judge history too negatively, apparently in reaction against the Hegelian philosophy of history in which the other has an effective role only by way of his place in the totality. Is it not possible to judge history more positively, as an open event wherein the neighbor comes to me from out of our common past and proposes to me, or invites me to enter with him into a new future? Grammatically, is it not true that the vocative only has its justification [*d'être*] when one privileges the verb in the imperfect and the future tenses? While reading *Totality and Infinity* I had

79

the impression that the face of the other emerges, as it were, from nothingness, which gives a ghostly character to your philosophy.

E. LEVINAS You say that in *Totality and Infinity* the other [*l'autre*] appears in a ghostly manner. The other must be received independently of
his qualities, if he is to be received as other. If it weren't for this, which is a
certain immediacy—it is even immediacy *par excellence*; the relationship
to the other [*autrui*] is the only one to have no value except when it is immediate—then the rest of my analyses would lose all their force. The relationship would be one of these thematizable relations that are established
between objects. It seemed to me that forgetting all of these "incitements"
to thematization was the only manner for the other to count as other.

You say, there are no events in a pure vocative. I do not think that the
face of the other [*d'autrui*] only gives rise to the vocative in the form of
impersonal relations. That is Buber. I have always attempted to look for
the event—formal to be sure, if everything I just said about the exclusion
of qualities of character and social condition, and predicates in general, remains valid—that is produced in the relation to another. Three notions to
keep in mind: first, proximity. I have tried to define it otherwise than by a
reduced space separating the terms that one calls close. I have tried to pass
from spatial proximity to the idea of the responsibility for another, which
is an "intrigue" much more complex than the simple fact of saying "you"
[*tu*], or of pronouncing a name. And I have tried, in looking behind or
into responsibility, to formulate the notion—very strange in philosophy—
of *substitution*, as the ultimate meaning of responsibility. *Appearing*, here,
would not be the ultimate event, although in phenomenological philosophy the ultimate event must appear. Here, under the ethical mode, a "category" different from knowledge is thought about. The principal task behind all these efforts consists in thinking the Other-in-the-Same [*l'Autre-
dans-le-Même*] without thinking the Other [*l'Autre*] as an other Same
[*Même*]. The *in* does not signify an assimilation: the Other disturbs or
awakens the Same; the Other troubles the Same, or inspires the Same, or
the Same desires the Other, or awaits him (does time's duration not come
from this patient awaiting?). There exists a transition of meaning from
each of these verbs to all the others. The Same is not, consequently, at rest;
the identity of the Same is not that to which all his meaning can be reduced.
The Same contains more than he can contain. This is Desire, and searching, and patience, and the length of time. It is a question of a very singular

temporality, foreign to Greek philosophy. In Plato's *Timaeus*, the circle of the Same comes to surround the circle of the Other. Ultimately, everything grows quiet in the Same, as in Hegel, there is an identity of the identical and the nonidentical. And one thinks that the disquieting [*inquiétude*] of the Same by the Other is an insufficiency. In my essays, the dis-quieting of the Same by the Other is the Desire that shall be a searching, a questioning, an awaiting: patience and length of time, and the very mode of surplus, of superabundance. Searching, this time, not as the expression of a lack, but as a manner of carrying the "more in the less." These are the veritable terms toward which all my research, which on first sight might appear as purely ethical, theological, or edifying, is incessantly returned.

M. SPINDLER Do you feel you have responded to the question of M. Frederikse concerning the philosophy of history?

E.L. Yes and no. History was not at the starting point of my reflection. Nevertheless, I think that an event of unlimited responsibility for another is something other than a vocative, a summons of no consequence; it certainly has a historic meaning, it bears witness to our age and marks it. If, in order to be historical, an analysis must refer in a very precise way to specific situations, account for them, and announce how all this will turn out, be completed in the absolute or be spoiled definitively, then I have no philosophy of history. I do think that the *unlimited* responsibility for another, as an enucleation of oneself,[1] could have a translation into history's concreteness. Time, in its patience and its length, in its awaiting, is not an "intentionality," nor a finality (a finality of the Infinite—how laughable!), it belongs to the Infinite and signifies dia-chrony in the responsibility for another. I was taken one day, in Louvain, after a lecture on these ideas, to a student house that is there called "pedagogy." I found myself surrounded by South American students, almost all priests, but above all preoccupied by the situation in South America. They spoke to me of what was happening there as of a supreme trial of humanity. They questioned me, not without irony: where would I have encountered concretely the Same, preoccupied by the Other to the point of undergoing a fissioning of itself? I replied: at least here. Here, in this group of students, of intellectuals who might very well have been occupied with their internal perfection and who nevertheless had no other subjects of conversation than the crisis of the Latin American masses. Were they not hostages? This utopia of conscience found itself historically fulfilled in the room in which I found myself. That history should be concerned by these utopias of conscience, I believe seriously.

H. HEERING Would it not be useful to draw a connection here with the second written question? "We find the word 'justice' used for the relationship with the other and also for the relationship with the third party. However, these are very distinct relationships, according to your thought. Do they not require a terminological distinction?"

E.L. It is not easy to speak of the way in which things were written fifteen years ago. It is a question of the appearance of the third party [*le tiers*], why there is the third party. I ask myself sometimes whether it cannot be justified in this way: to make possible a dis-interested responsibility for another excludes reciprocity. But should another [*autrui*] be without devotion to the other [*l'autre*]? A third party is necessary there. Be that as it may, in the relationship with another I am always in relation with the third party. But he is also my neighbor. From this moment on, proximity becomes problematic: one must compare, weigh, think; one must do justice, which is the source of theory. The entire recovery of Institutions— and of theory itself, of philosophy and of phenomenology, which explicate what appears—is done, according to me, starting from the third party. The word "justice" is in effect much more in its place, there, where equity is necessary and not my "subordination" to the other. If equity is necessary, we must have comparison and equality: equality between those that cannot be compared. And consequently, the word "justice" applies much more to the relationship with the third party than to the relationship with the other. But in reality, the relationship with another is never uniquely the relationship with the other: from this moment on, the third is represented in the other; that is, in the very appearance of the other the third already regards me. And this, nevertheless, makes the relation between justice and the responsibility with regard to the other extremely narrow. Your distinction is in any case just, at the same time that the proximity between these terms is true. The ontological language employed in *Totality and Infinity* is not at all a definitive language. The language in *Totality and Infinity* is ontological because it wants above all not to be psychological.[2] But in reality, it is already a search for what I call "the beyond being," the tearing of this equality to self which is always being—the *Sein*—whatever the attempts to separate it from the present. So too for the word "justice," we must establish the difference to which you point.

AUDIENCE If I am vulnerable, as you emphasize in your books, how can I be responsible? If one suffers, one can no longer do anything.

E.L. By vulnerability, I am attempting to describe the subject as passivity. If there is not vulnerability, if the subject is not always in his patience on the verge of an already senseless pain, then he posits himself *for himself.* In this case, the moment at which he is substance is not far away; the moment at which he is pride, at which he is imperialist, at which he has the other like an object. The endeavor was to present my relationship with another not as an attribute of my substantiality, not as an attribute of my hardness as a person, but on the contrary as the fact of my destitution, of my deposition (in the sense in which one speaks of the deposition of a sovereign). It is only then that a veritable abnegation, a substitution for the other, may take on meaning in me. You say, in suffering one can no longer do anything. But are you sure that suffering stops at itself? When one suffers because of someone, vulnerability is also to suffer for someone. It is this transformation of the "by" into the "for" that is in question; it concerns this substitution of the "for" for the "by." If one does not posit this, then you are immediately in a world of revenge, of war, of the preferential affirmation of the I. I do not contest that we are always, in fact, in this world, but this is a world wherein we are altered. Vulnerability is the power to say "*adieu*" to this world. One says "*adieu*" to it in growing old. Time endures in the form of this *adieu* and this *à-Dieu* [unto God].

AUDIENCE And yet, when one suffers, when one lets evil come as it will, how can one be responsible? My question comes back to the fourth written question: "Does the notion of 'substitution' also offer some space for the idea that it is sometimes necessary to oppose the other for his good or for the good of the third party?"

E.L. If there was only the other facing me, I would say to the very end: I owe him everything. I am for him. And this even holds for the harm he does me: I am not his equal, I am forevermore subject to him. My resistance begins when the harm he does me is done to a third party who is also my neighbor. It is the third party who is the source of justice, and thereby of justified repression; it is the violence suffered by the third party that justifies stopping the violence of the other with violence. The idea that I am responsible for the harm done by the other—an idea rejected, repressed although psychologically possible—brings us to the meaning of subjectivity. It is attested by this sentence of Dostoevsky, which I always cite, it is Alyosha, I believe, who says it, "Each of us is guilty before all, for all and for everything, and I more than the others." In the second part of the sentence the I [*moi*] has ceased to consider itself as a particular case of the I [*Moi*] in general. It is the unique point that supports the universe ("supports" in the two senses of the term: he who endures the unendurable, and he who upholds it). Evidently, this I is immediately overtaken by its general concept. It is necessary that it escape again. The I [*moi*] as I [*moi*] is the I [*moi*] who escapes his concept. And it is this situation that I have called vulnerability, absolute culpability, or rather, absolute responsibility. The I, when one has reflected upon it psychologically, is already an I [*moi*] equal to the other I's [*moi's*]. The concept of the I always catches up with me.

The idea of substitution signifies that *I* [*je*] substitute myself for another, but that no one can substitute himself for me as me. When one begins to say that someone can substitute himself for me, immorality begins. And, on the other hand, the I as I, in this radical individuality which is not a situation of reflection upon oneself, is responsible for the harm that is done. Very early on I utilized this notion, speaking of the dissymmetry of the interpersonal relation. The I is persecuted and is, in principle, responsible for the persecution that it suffers. But, "happily," it is not alone; there are third parties and one cannot allow that third parties be persecuted!

M. FRESCO Do you consider that a philosophy is always, by way of its origin, based on an option or a fundamental intuition that one can no longer ground? What are the consequences of that for this philosophy and for all philosophy? I have in mind the difference between the Greco-Latin tradition and the Judeo-Christian tradition. In the latter, the relationship between the I and the other has been conceived in a manner completely different from that of the pagan tradition. In the pagan tradition, it is the I, instead, who is in the center and the other who only exists in relation to him, while in the Judeo-Christian tradition, of which you are a part, it is, rather, the other who is at the center and, although the I may have to assume absolute responsibility, it is he, nevertheless, who exists in relation with the other, who is central. Therefore, if there is no possible tie between these two fundamental options, what conclusion should one draw from this observation?

E.L. This word "central" is a vague term. Of what consists this centrality? You ask me, is there not a first option? I would say, sooner, there is a first question. I will tell you why I prefer the term "first question": because the question can be posed beyond that which is ensured a response. The question is already a relation, there where there is no place for a response; there where a response does not suffice—where it would shrink what is in question. Our theoretical questions are already the extenuated form of that which is the question, of that which is searching or Desire. And I would agree with you that this reveals a great difference. Western philosophy is a philosophy of the response: it is the response that counts; it is the result, as Hegel says. Whereas it is the question that is the thing . . . I don't even dare say the first thing, because the idea of priority is a Greek idea—it is the idea of the principle. And I do not know if we must speak of priority when we want to speak of the question as a thinking more thoughtful than the doxic proposition of the response. I do not know if we should speak of priority when we speak of the question as searching and Desire, of searching in the sense in which the Bible speaks of the search for God and in which "God *found*" is still expressed as God *sought* (cf. Isaiah 65:1; we must pay attention to the Hebrew text, where this is visible). This is not at all a situation in which *one* poses the question; it is the question that takes hold of you: there you are brought into question. All these situations are probably different in the Greek way and in the way that is very deeply inscribed in the biblical tradition. My concern everywhere is precisely to translate this non-Hellenism of the Bible into Hellenic terms and not to repeat the biblical formulas in their obvious sense, isolated from the context that, at the level of such a text, is *all* the Bible. There is nothing to be done: philosophy is spoken in Greek. But we must not think that language models meaning. The Greek language—the language according to syntax—probably permits us to present the meaning. In my opinion, everything that occurs in linguistics today lies in the extension of the Greek tradition: *viz.*, the idea that it is language itself that is the event of meaning, the fundamental event. There we touch upon ultimate questions, assuming that there be ultimate questions: priority and ultimacy are terms of Greek philosophy. But I realize that I have not responded directly to your question on the *I* and the *other*. I have the impression, nevertheless, of having spoken of it in a certain sense, in responding to the preceding question.

H. PHILIPSE What is the relationship between religion and philosophy, and between your religion and your philosophy?

E.L. Religion knows much more about this. Religion believes it knows much more. I do not believe that philosophy could console. Consolation is a function entirely different, it is religious.

H.P. Is philosophy a diversion for you, as it was for Pascal?

E.L. If the undivertable can be a diversion, and if a diversion can be undivertable.

H.P. Is the philosophical attitude—which is in essence a skeptical attitude—not in contradiction with the attitude of faith?

E.L. "Skeptical" only means the fact of examining things, the fact of posing questions. I do not at all think that a question—or, at least, the original questioning—is only a deficiency of answers. Functional and even scientific questions—and many philosophical ones—await only answers. Questioning *qua* original attitude is a "relation" to that which no response can contain, to the "uncontainable"; it becomes responsibility. Every response contains a "beside the point" and appeals to an un-said [*dé-dit*].[3]

THEODOR DE BOER I would like to ask you a question on method, to which you have attended in a number of places in your work. How can one express in discourse the metaphysical relation to the Other? In the preface to *Totality and Infinity*, you refer to Husserl's transcendental method. You assert that you have followed the intentional analysis that goes back to the origin prior to every origin, to the most radical foundation of theory and practice. In your recent book,[4] I have found two new ideas concerning this problem of method. On page 228, you speak of the exaltation of language that is, perhaps, philosophy itself, and on page 182 you speak of a prereflexive iteration ("in the Saying of this very Saying"). One could thus conclude that there are, as it were, three paths leading from ontology to metaphysics: transcendental reduction, exaltation, and iteration. What I want to ask you today concerns, above all, some passages in *Otherwise than Being or Beyond Essence*, in which you say that, at a given moment, ontological categories are transformed into ethical terms (p. 115) and that the tropes of ethical language are adequate to the structure that you wish to express (p. 121). Language is able to equal the paradox of the metaphysical description (cf. p. 193, n. 35).[5] I would like to know whether the citations above represent an element radically new in your thought or not. Does ethical language not render superfluous the difficult problems of the paths toward metaphysics, and of the reduction of ontological language? Such that these paths are so many aporias or dead-end routes. Do you not give ontology too much credit with the central position that you give to the problem of the ineffability of the metaphysical dimension? You say that language translates as well as it betrays.[6] If ethical language is adequate to metaphysical problems, the reverse does not hold true for ethical language. And does this not signify that the exploration of ethical language could offer new possibilities for expressing the relation with the Infinite?

E.L.   These are fundamental questions. What is said in the preface of *Totality and Infinity* remains true, all the same, to the end for me with respect to method. It is not the word "transcendental" that I would retain, but the notion of intentional analysis. I think that, in spite of everything, what I do is phenomenology, even if there is no reduction, here, according to the rules required by Husserl; even if all of the Husserlian methodology is not respected. The dominant trait, which even determines all those who no longer call themselves phenomenologists today, is that, in proceeding back from what is thought toward the fullness of the thought itself, one discovers—without there being any deductive, dialectical, or other implication therein—dimensions of meaning, each time new. It is this analysis that seems to me to be the Husserlian novelty, and which, outside of Husserl's own methodology, is a lasting acquisition for everyone. It is the fact that if, in starting from a theme or an idea, I move toward the "ways" by which one accedes to it, then the way by which one accedes to it is essential to the meaning of the theme itself: this way reveals to us a whole landscape of horizons that have been forgotten and together with which, what shows itself no longer has the meaning it had when one considered it from a stance directly turned toward it. Phenomenology is not about elevating phenomena into things in themselves; it is about bringing the *things in themselves* to the horizon of their appearing, that of their phenomenality; phenomenology means to make appear the appearing itself behind the quiddity that appears, even if this appearing does not encrust its modalities in the meaning that it delivers to the gaze. This is what remains, even when intentionality is no longer considered as theoretical, even when it is no longer considered as an act. Out of the thematization of the human, new dimensions are opened that are essential to reflected meaning [*sens pensé*]. All those who think in this way and seek these dimensions in order to find this meaning are doing phenomenology.

And now the rest. It is in the ethical situation that, according to me, a certain unity is achieved. This is the unity of what remains disparate, or seems constructed or dialectical, in the ontological statement which, moreover, must struggle against the ontic forms of all language. In this sense, the language that translates this unity speaks in a manner more direct; but, inversely, the range or, if you wish, the context of this language, is inseparable from this progression from ontology. Ethics is like the reduction of certain languages. In this respect, it is more adequate; but I will also say that the Saying must be accompanied immediately by an unsaying, and the unsaying must again be unsaid in its manner, and there, there is no stopping; there are no definitive formulations. It is for this reason that, in the book to which you are referring, I call my conclusion "Otherwise Said."

And finally, something about which you do not question me—but perhaps to which your word "exaltation" alludes; something that will illustrate in what sense, in these developments, it is possible to associate ideas in a new manner, to detach the concepts one by one in a new manner— hence the term "emphasis," one I use a lot at this moment. The transcendental method consists always in seeking the foundation. "Foundation" is, moreover, a term from architecture, a term made for a world that one inhabits; for a world that is *before* all that it supports, an astronomic world of perception, an immobile world; rest *par excellence*; the Same *par excellence*. An idea is consequently justified when it has found its foundation, when one has shown the *conditions* of its possibility. On the other hand, in my way of proceeding, which starts from the human, and from the approach of the human who is not simply that which *inhabits* the world, but which *ages* in the world, which withdraws from it in a way other than by opposition—which withdraws from it through the passivity of aging (a withdrawal that, perhaps, confers its meaning upon death itself, rather than having it [death] thought from the standpoint of negation, which is a judgment)—there is another sort of justification of one idea by the other: to pass from one idea to its superlative, to the point of its emphasis. You see that a new idea—in no way implicated in the first—

flows, or emanates, from the overbid. The new idea finds itself justified not on the *basis* of the first, but by its sublimation. An example altogether concrete: in a certain sense, the real world is the world that is posited, its manner of being is the thesis. But to be posited in a truly superlative manner—I am not playing on words—is this not to be exposed, to posit oneself to the point of appearing, *to affirm* oneself to the point of becoming language? And there we pass from a structure rigorously ontological, toward subjectivity at the level of the conscience to which being calls. Another example: when I say that passivity consists in surrendering, in suffering beyond all passivity, through a passivity that does not take charge of itself [*qui ne s'assume pas*], I end in the fission of oneself. Our Western "passivity" is a receptivity followed by a taking charge [*assomption*]. Sensations are produced in me, but I grasp myself from these sensations and I conceive them. We are dealing with a subject who is passive when he does not give himself his contents. To be sure. But he receives them. He surrenders himself further when he expresses himself; whatever are the refuges of the *Said* [*Dit*]—its words and its sentences—the *Saying* [*Dire*] is an opening, a new degree of passivity. Prior to discourse, I am clothed in a form; I *am* where my being hides me. To speak is to break this capsule of the form and to surrender oneself. I am treating emphasis, as you see, as a method [*procédé*]. I think I have found, there, the *via eminentiae*. It is, in any case, the manner by which I pass from responsibility to substitution. Emphasis signifies at the same time a figure of rhetoric, an excess of expression, a manner of overstating oneself, and a manner of showing oneself. The word is very good, like the word "hyperbole": there are hyperboles whereby notions are transmuted. To describe this mutation is also to do phenomenology. Exasperation as a method of philosophy!

That is what I would respond as far as method is concerned. I will tell you also that I know nothing more about it. I do not believe that there is a transparency possible in method. Nor that philosophy might be possible as transparency. Those who have worked on methodology all their lives have written many books that replace the more interesting books that they could have written. So much the worse for the philosophy that would walk in sunlight without shadows.

These are the reflections by which I would defend the claim that my method is, all the same, an "intentional analysis" and that ethical language seems to me closer to the adequate language and that, for me, ethics is not at all a layer that covers over ontology, but rather that which is in some fashion more ontological than ontology; an emphasis of ontology.

This also responds to the written question that I will read: "In 1972—thus prior to *Otherwise than Being or Beyond Essence*—Professor Dr. Theodor de Boer wrote an article on your work under the title, 'An Ethical Transcendentalism.' If the transcendental condition is explained not as a fact but as a foregoing value—in Dutch *voor-waarde*—do you consent to this characteristic?" Well, I am absolutely in agreement with this formula, provided that "transcendental" signifies a certain priority: except that ethics is before ontology. It is more ontological than ontology; more *sublime* than ontology. It is from there that a certain equivocation comes—whereby ethics seems laid on top of ontology, whereas it is before ontology. It is thus a transcendentalism that begins with ethics.

J. G. BOMHOFF Cannot moral experience be translated as an experience of the other as identical to oneself? In my view, this corresponds to the imperative, which is in any case biblical: "Love your neighbor as yourself."

E.L. First, the term "moral experience": I try to avoid it. Moral experience supposes a subject who is there; who, first of all, *is* and who, at a certain moment, has a moral experience, whereas it is in the way in which he is there, in which he lives, that there is this ethics; or more precisely, the dis-inter-estedness un-does his *esse*. Ethics signifies this.

Concerning the biblical text—but here we are in the midst of theology —I am much more perplexed than the translators to whom you refer. What does "as yourself" signify? Buber and Rosenzweig were here very perplexed by the translation. They said to each other, does not "as yourself" mean that one loves oneself most? Instead of translating this in agreement with you, they translated it, "love your neighbor, he is like you." But if one first agrees to separate the last word of the Hebrew verse, *kamokhah*, from the beginning of the verse, one can read the whole thing still otherwise. "Love your neighbor; this work is like yourself"; "love your neighbor; he is yourself"; "it is this love of the neighbor which is yourself." Would you say that this is an extremely audacious reading? Yet the Old Testament supports several readings and it is when the entirety of the Bible becomes the context of the verse that the verse resounds with all its meaning. This is the interminable commentary of the Old Testament. A Dominican father, for whom I have much admiration and who knows Hebrew admirably, said one day before me: what one takes for an infinite interpretation of the letter of Scripture is simply a reading that considers the entirety of the book as the context of the verse. It is not at all the two or three verses that precede or follow the verse on which one comments! For the absolute hermeneutic of a verse, the entirety of the book is necessary! Now, in the entirety of the book, there is always a priority of the other in relation to me. This is the biblical contribution in its entirety. And that is how I would respond to your question: "Love your neighbor; all that is yourself; this work is yourself; this love is yourself." *Kamokhah* does not refer to "your neighbor," but to all the words that precede it. The Bible is the priority of the other [*l'autre*] in relation to me. It is in another [*autrui*] that I always see the widow and the orphan. The other [*autrui*] always comes first. This is what I have called, in Greek language, the dissymmetry of the interpersonal relationship. If there is not this dissymmetry, then no line of what I have written can hold. And this is vulnerability. Only a vulnerable I can love his neighbor.

H.H. When another does me harm, he harms himself as well, generally. You say, it is up to me to substitute myself for him, and it is immoral to demand that he substitute himself for me. Two questions then: Is it not true that, in certain cases, substitution can imply that I must oppose the other for his own good? And the second question: Cannot this substitution of another for me sometimes be, rather than an immorality, an a-morality in the sense of what is more sublime than morality; in brief, can it not be a gratitude?

E.L. Substitution for another means, in the ultimate shelter of myself, not to feel myself innocent, even for the harm that another does. I would go much further. "Ultimate shelter" is not a sufficient formula. It can make us believe that the I has a capsule. In order to explain the notion of substitution, it is necessary that I say more, that I use hyperbole: the individuation of the I, that by which the I is not simply an identical being, or some sort of substance, but rather that by which it is ipseity; that by which it is unique without drawing its uniqueness from any exclusive quality, all this is the fact of being designated, or assigned, or elected to substitute itself without being able to slip away. By this unavoidable summons, to the "I" [*Moi*] in general, to the concept, he who responds in the first person is torn loose: it is I [*moi*], or even straightaway in the accusative, "here I am."[7]

It is from this idea that I have even understood better certain pages of Heidegger. (You know, when I pay homage to Heidegger, it is always costly to me, not because of his incontestable brilliance, as you also know.) In §9 of *Sein und Zeit*, the *Dasein* is posited in its *Jemeinigkeit* ("Mineness").[8] What does this *Jemeinigkeit* signify? *Dasein* signifies that the *Dasein* has to be. But this "obligation" to be, this manner of being, is an exposition to being that is so direct that it thereby becomes mine! It is the emphasis of this rectitude that is expressed by a notion of *first property*, which is *Jemeinigkeit*. *Jemeinigkeit* is the extreme measure of the way in which the *Dasein* is subject to ess*a*nce. Heidegger says a few lines below: it is because the *Dasein* is *Jemeinigkeit* that it is an *Ich* [an I]. He does not at all say that the *Dasein* is *Jemeinigkeit* because it is an *Ich*; on the contrary, he goes toward the *Ich* from the *Jemeinigkeit*, toward I [*moi*] from the "superlative" or the emphasis of this subjection, from this being-delivered-over-to-being [*être-livré-à-être*], of this *Ausgeliefertheit*. The *Dasein* is so delivered over to being that being is its own. It is from the impossibility of my declining this adventure that this adventure is properly mine, that it is as *eigen* [own] that the *Sein* [Being] is *Ereignis* [Event]. And everything that will be said of this *Ereignis* in *Zeit und Sein* is already indicated in §9 of *Sein und Zeit*. Being is that which becomes my-own, and it is for this that a man is necessary to being. It is through man that being is "properly." These are the most profound things in Heidegger. This section, with the progression that goes from *Jemeinigkeit* to the *Ich*, has been much erased by the translation of *Eigentlichkeit* as "authenticity." One has erased, precisely, this element of *Eigentlichkeit* in authenticity: a principle of all *Eigentum*[9] (we can possess something because there is *Jemeinigkeit*)—but above all, "the event of being," or ess*a*nce—as the in-alienable.

This reading of Heidegger was motivated by the idea that the human I, the oneself, the uniqueness of the I, is the impossibility of slipping away from the other.[10] As long as there is no other, one cannot speak of freedom or of nonfreedom; there is not yet even identity of the person, which is an identity of the "undiscernable," internal to what is unique by dint of not being able to evade the other. The not-being-able-to-slip-away is precisely this mark of uniqueness in me: the first person remains a first person, even when it slips away empirically. *Se dérober* [to slip away, or to evade] is a pronominal verb: when I evade my obligations in respect to the other, I still remain I. I am not alluding here to the sentiment of sin in order to say that it is in this sense of sin that one certifies that one *is for the other*. I would say: one is delivered up [to the other] because one is I. In this sense, the I is absolutely inconstructible conceptually. To be sure, in knowledge there is a return of the I to oneself, but if there is, in the current of consciousness, a center toward which the return is possible, the core [*nœud*] of this return originates in another plot. It is through ethics, through the emphasis of my obligation, that I am I.

This is how I would respond to your question. In this sense, your objection is absolutely fair at the psychological level, or at the level of inter-human relations, but it leads me to state what comes to pass—meta-physically—beneath this substitution, which you are right to examine also in the sense of ethical conduct, of daily conduct.

As to the objection which one might raise here, that this idea of responsibility implies a certain paternalism: "You are responsible for the other and it is indifferent to you that the other might have to accept your responsibility." I respond: what the other can do for me is his affair. If it were mine, then substitution would only be a moment of the exchange and would lose its gratuity. My affair is my responsibility, and my substitution is inscribed in my I [*moi*], inscribed as *I* [*moi*]. The other can substitute himself for whomever he will, except me. It is probably even for this reason that we are numerous in the world. If, instead of substituting myself for another [*autrui*], I expect that an other [*un autre*] substitute himself for me, then this would be a doubtful morality, but moreover, it would destroy all transcendence. One cannot be replaced for substitution, as one cannot be replaced for death.

H.H. But then one could pose question number 9 to you. "You reject the idea of a pardon accorded by God, and you consider this as an important difference between your Jewish conception and the Christian conception. Could one not build a bridge between these two conceptions by way of the thought, often pronounced in the Bible, that the pardon of God in no way denies the Torah, but on the contrary, invites us to obey it? How, in this perspective, shall we judge your concepts 'inspiration' and 'witnessing?'"[11]

E.L. There is not a single thing in a great spirituality that would be absent from another great spirituality. The idea of grace is not at all an idea rejected by Jewish spirituality. Let us note in passing that, in order to characterize Jewish spirituality, it is not enough to evoke the Old Testament; that which is read according to rabbinical thought in the Old

Testament is Jewish. Now, in rabbinical thought, to obtain grace it is absolutely necessary that there be a first gesture coming from man. Even in Maimonides. Maimonides, who was nevertheless imbued as much by Greek thought as by Talmud, said in one of the texts of his Rabbinical Code [*Mishneh Torah*] on repentance—on which I had occasion to comment just recently before Christians: the first gesture calling forth pardon is in my freedom and owed by me, and it is once this first gesture is accomplished that the heavens come to my assistance. One will come to your assistance and will give you more than the part equal to what you have done. I suppose that you know some Hebrew. We divide in two parts the famous formula, "*Im Shamo'a, Tishm'a,*" which means in simple Hebrew, "if you listen." First "*Im Shamo'a*": "*if* you listen," or "if you obey"; "*Tishm'a*": "you will understand much more." This reduplication, characteristic of the Hebrew verb, is thus understood according to all the freedom of the rabbinical commentary, which nevertheless, in its apparent literal strictness [*acribie*]—even against grammar—searches for the spirit of the whole. But here we are in the midst of theology!

The notion of original sin likewise exists in rabbinical thought; however, sin does not comprise a condemnation that could go to the point of making impossible the first gesture of freedom in repentance. These texts of Maimonides are explicit on this point. I recall that my Christian audience was astonished by this absolute free will. It seemed to them psychologically aberrant. Yet they added, "fundamentally, we also hold both ends of the chain; thus it can not be absolutely aberrant." Gershom Scholem, who was a historian of religion (without counting himself among religious men), showed that in Jewish mysticism the faithful, in his approach to God, is like the moth that circles around the fire; it comes very close, but it never enters the fire. It always preserves its independence with regard to the fire around which it circles. All of Jewish mysticism is like this moth that does not burn its wings. But I am relating to you facts from the history of Jewish thought; this is not philosophy.

Perhaps now is the time to read the written question concerning the notion of the infinite. "How must we understand the adjective 'infinite'? Is this, originally, a noun or an adverb? In other words: 'is' the infinite 'something,' or is it only a 'how,' notably the 'how' of alterity: infinitely other?"

I think that the infinite is the domain where these distinctions disappear. This is not a rhetorical answer. I think that if the infinite was *an* infinite, under which there would be substance, an *Etwas überhaupt* [something in general] (which would justify the substantive term), it would not at all be the absolutely other, it would be an other "same." And there is no atheism in this way of not taking God for a term. I think that God has no meaning outside the search for God. It is not a question of method, nor is it a romantic idea. The "In" of the In-finite is at once the negation and the being affected of the Finite—the non- and the *in-* — human thought as a search for God, Descartes's idea of the Infinite in us.

H. VAN LUYK I would like to call your attention to one of the written questions. "Why can the reality of God be expressed only in terms of the past; why not also in terms of the future and of hope? We find both of these in the Bible. Besides, in the Bible, does the past not have an eschatological sense?"

E.L. A rapid answer. This is a question of points not yet presented in my writings published up to now. I have never sufficiently developed the theme of what is to come [*avenir*], or the future [*futur*], although in *Totality and Infinity* I evoked the messianic future.[12] There is in this book, nevertheless, a chapter relative to eroticism and to the son, and so to what is beyond the possible, which is the future.[13] This concerns the future according to the manner proper to me; which consists in treating of time from the starting point of the Other [*l'Autre*]. This is not faithful to a work of 1947, published under the title of *Time and the Other,*[14] but which is a "phenomenology" of time. It is according to its sense (if one can speak of sense without intentionality: without vision, nor even a focussing of vision) a patient waiting for God; a patience of im-measure (an unto-God, as I express myself now); but a waiting without an awaited. For this is a waiting for that which cannot be a *term* and which *always* refers from the Other [*l'Autre*] to another [*autrui*]. It is precisely the *always* of duration: length of time. The length of time is not the slowness of a river which flows, where time is confused with what is temporal. This is time as a relation—or as de-ference in the etymological sense of the term[15]—to "that" which cannot be re-presented (and which, for this reason, cannot even be expressed as "this," properly speaking); but which, in its difference [from the temporal], *cannot* be in-different to me. Or time as a question. Non-in-difference, a way of being dis-quieted by the difference, without the difference ceasing; it is a passivity or patience without assumption, because it is de-ference to what surpasses my capacity—a question! Thereby *infinitely* more than re-presentation, possession, contact, and answer; more than all this positivity—of the world, of *identity*, and of being—which dares to disqualify the subject, the search, the question, and the disquiet, as if questioning and searching were insufficient thoughts and "privations."

I do not know if one may speak here of hope, which has wings and does not resemble the patience in which the intentionality still so alive in hope is engulfed, in order to turn back into ethics. I have published little on these themes until now, outside of the very recent text in the *Nouveau Commerce* (nos. 30–31, 1975) entitled "God and Philosophy," and I apologize for approaching them from various sides at once, without a framework. You are thus quite right. I have not developed the theme of the future as broadly as that of the *immemorial past*. This is perhaps because of the consolation one expects from the philosophy of the future, whereas consolations are the vocation of religion. When I introduce the notion of prophetism, I am not interested in its oracular side. I find it philosophically interesting inasmuch as it signifies the heteronomy—and the trauma—of inspiration by which I define the spirit, against all the immanentist conceptions of it. This is the past in which I also never return to a creator God either, but rather toward a past more ancient than any remembrable past, and one where time is described in its diachrony, stronger than re-presentation, against any memory and any anticipation that synchronize this dia-chrony. It is, in effect, this illusion of the present, due to memory, which has always seemed to me more tenacious than an illusion because of anticipation. The anticipation of the future is very short. There is virtually no anticipation. The future is blocked from the outset; it is unknown from the outset and, consequently, toward it time is always diachrony. For the past, there is a whole sphere that is representable; there where the memory does not reach, history, or prehistory, reaches. Everything is torn from the past. But it is in the obligation for another which I never contracted—in which I have never signed any obligation, for never to man's knowledge have I struck a contract with another—that a writ was passed. Something already concluded appears in my relationship with another. It is there that I run up against the immemorial. This is an immemorial that is not representable; there reigns a true diachrony, there a transcendence comes to pass—not a transcendence that becomes immanent. All transcendences become immanent from the moment the leap over the abyss remains a possibility, even if this should be the leap of representation. For this reason, it appeared to me extremely interesting to search on that side . . . , for "that which was before being," for a "before" not synchronizable with what followed it. It is for this reason also that I often use the words "a time before time." The notion of creation also implies that. What commonly shocks us in the notion of creation is that which is interpreted there in the language of fabrication, or in the language of the present. Yet in this notion of a time before time something takes on a sense, starting from the ethical, and this sense is not a simple repetition of the present; for it is something that is not re-presentable. This is why the past has had such a predominant role in my work up until now.

H.L. Is it true that there is no philosophy of the future?

E.L. I do not know. And that proves nothing against the future. In what I just said there are perhaps possibilities for developments on the future.

H.L. And Bloch?

E.L. Of course there is a hope and, consequently, a utopian *anticipation* in Bloch. But Bloch is searching for a perceptible future. His hope is immanent and the utopia, provisional. My concern is not that of Bloch. I am looking to think about a transcendence that might not be in the mode of immanence, and which does not return to immanence: in the less is the more, which is not the containable.

H.L. Yet if it is possible to thematize transcendence as a time before time, why should it not be possible to thematize it as a time after time?

E.L. Do you think that these symmetries are obligatory? Time as patience in the waiting for the Infinite, turning into "substitution for another": is this a thematization? Moreover, is the past, which is "prior to time," or "which was never present," thematized in fraternity, wherein it signifies? The search for the Infinite, as Desire, accedes to God but does not lay hold of him; it does not thematize him as an end. Finality would be insufficient to describe the relationship with the Infinite! Meaning is not necessarily in vision, nor even in focusing of vision! The future, for Bloch, is the exclusion of all transcendence. His utopia's non-reality is a transcendence without an outside! But can one speak of transcendence when the *relation* with the utopian is still thinkable as realization and grasp? Be that as it may, I cannot fail to appreciate the greatness of this "immanentism with hope," whose advent is nevertheless its fulfillment, despite the equivalence of death and nothingness. There is in Bloch a way of not despairing over death without placing anything above *esse*. When one opens any fine book on death—even the very fine book of M. Jankélévitch[16]—one knows after a few lines that *there is nothing* to do: one will have to die one's death. In Bloch as well, there is nothing to do. One shall have to die. But there is much to do—one must do much— to rid death of anguish, without this being by diversion, in order to leave to death but an empty shell. For in a world entirely humanized, our being passes integrally into our work. The anguish of death, according to Bloch, would only be the melancholy of a work unaccomplished. This is the sadness of leaving a world that we have not been able to transform. We do not know this because we are, precisely, in a world still unfinished. If, at a certain moment, the human I, who belongs to the obscure sphere that subsists in an unfinished world, and who fears death, were to experience the completion of being—that is, that the I might be entirely I— then we have the world as more I than I myself: *Tua res agitur*.[17] Death will carry off what no longer counts! The world is mine and the true I is he who, in this "mine" of the world, has his ipseity as an I. The formal design much resembles the fashion in which the *personal* is deduced in Heidegger from the unavertable manner by which being has to be. In Bloch also, the fact that the world, which is foreign to us, becomes, according to his hypothesis, a world fulfilled by man, coincides with the consciousness of *tua res agitur*. In the intensity of this *tua* [*your*], the I arises, against which death can do nothing. Death can do something against the empirical being that I was. This may not be enough, perhaps, for you. But in any case, the altogether astonishing thing that he stated was the possibility of thinking the I starting from *Jemeinigkeit*.[18]

AUDIENCE What do you think in regard to the third written question? "Even if one agrees that Another cannot be understood within the categories of the Same, must one not admit that this comprehension, besides being the means by which to reduce the other to the same, could also be the condition by which to affirm the qualities peculiar to the other? In other words, can one do justice to the alterity of the other by not understanding him? Or, formulated still otherwise, do ethics and comprehension exclude one another?"

E.L. Ethics and comprehension are not on the same level. I substitute for comprehension not other relations, which would be *incomprehensions*, but rather that by which the comprehension of another alone begins to count for an I: it is not the knowledge of his character or his social position or his needs, but his nudity as the needy one; the destitution inscribed upon his face; it is his face as destitution, which *assigns me* as responsible and by which his needs can only count for me. I have told you that this counting-for-me is not a *vocative* that is a *reciprocal hello* and maintains me in my "for oneself." The vocative is not enough! Ethics is when I not only do not thematize another; it is when another *obsesses* me or puts me in question. This putting in question does not expect that I respond; it is not a question of giving a response, but of finding oneself responsible. I am the object of an intentionality and not its subject; one can present the situation that I describe in this way, although this manner of expressing oneself may be very approximate. That is, this expression erases all the novelty of this being-in-question, where subjectivity keeps nothing of its *identity* of a being [*identité d'être*], of its *for-oneself*, of its sub-stance, of its *situation*, except the new identity of him whom no one can replace in his responsibility, and who in this sense would be unique. This condition, or in-condition, is in no sense a theology or a negative ontology. It is described and expressed, albeit in paying attention to the expression; in unsaying what one says; in not supposing, notably, that the logical forms of propositions are encrusted in the significations ex-posed. It is necessary to take precautions, which is probably difficult. But one must not be silent. We are not before an ineffable mystery. And there are no worse waters than standing waters.

H.H. *Hora est.* By these words the beadle interrupts the discourse of he who defends his doctoral thesis, to indicate that it is time to finish. We are very grateful that you have had the patience for this dialogue with us. It is very impressive how, at each question, you have gone to the bottom of things and how you arrive at dispensing justice for the sake of the other who is different. We are very happy that our old university awards you a doctorate.

E.L. Thank you very much; I was very happy to defend my thesis.

§ Hermeneutics and Beyond

That the thought awakened to God might believe that it goes *beyond* the world or listens to a voice more intimate than intimacy, the hermeneutic that interprets this life or this religious psyche cannot assimilate it to an experience which this thought thinks precisely that it surpasses. This thought aspires to a *beyond*, to a *deeper than oneself*—aspiring to a transcendence different from the *out-of-oneself* that the intentional consciousness opens and traverses. What does this surpassing signify? What does this difference signify? Without making any decision of a metaphysical character,[1] we would like only to ask here how this transcendence, in its noetic structure, breaks with the *out-of-oneself* of intentionality. This demands a foregoing reflection upon the mode proper to intentionality in its reference to the world and to being.

1. We shall take as our point of departure the Husserlian phenomenology of consciousness. Its essential principle—which, in large measure, one can consider as the converse of the formula "all consciousness is consciousness of something"—states that being commands its modes of *being given*; that being orders the forms of knowledge that apprehend it, and that an essential necessity attaches being to its modes of appearing to consciousness. These formulas could certainly be understood as affirming *a priori*, or even empirically, a certain *state of affairs*, as one "eidetic" truth among eidetic truths, if these formulas did not concern that which, bearing on the correlation being/knowledge, assures the possibility of all truth, every empiric [*empirie*], and every eidetics; that upon which *appearing* depends as exhibition, and consciousness as knowledge. The re-

lationship between consciousness and the reality of the real is here no longer thought of as an encounter of being with a consciousness that would be radically distinct from it and subject to its own necessities, reflecting faithfully or unfaithfully the being encountered, according to "psychological laws" of some sort, and ordering images into a coherent dream within a blind soul. The possibility of such psychologism is henceforth ruined, even if the difference between being and the subjectivity to which being appears ties the psyche, which is consciousness or knowledge, into an *ipseity*.

2. It is necessary, consequently, to think the Husserlian formulas beyond their formulations. Consciousness finds itself promoted to the rank of an "event" that in some manner unfolds in *appearing* [*apparoir*]—or in manifestation—the energy or the ess*a*nce of being, and that which in this sense becomes a psyche. The ess*a*nce[2] of being would be equivalent to ex-*position*. The ess*a*nce of being, understood as exposition, refers on the one hand to its position as a being, to a consolidation on an unshakable terrain which is the earth beneath the vault of the sky, that is, to the *positivity* of the here and now, to the positivity of presence. The positivity of presence is the resting of the identical. It is, moreover, by way of this positivity—as presence and identity, or presence or identity—that the philosophical tradition almost always understands the *ess*a*nce of being*. And it is back to the *ess*a*nce of being* in its identity that the intelligibility or rationality of the *grounded* and the identical bring us. On the other hand, exposition refers being to exhibition, to appearing [*apparaître*], to the phenomenon. From position or ess*a*nce to phenomenon, one is not describing a simple degradation but an emphasis.

In becoming re-presentation, presence in this representation is exalted, as though ess*a*nce as consolidation upon a foundation went to the point of thetic affirmation in a consciousness; as though its position's "energy" gave rise, outside of all causality, to the activity of consciousness, to an experience proceeding from the I [*Moi*], unfolding as psychic life, external to this energy which is the very energy that the being puts into being. To return to a Hegelian formula (*Logic II*, 2),[3] is not the process of knowing here "the movement of being itself"? By way of the synthetic and inclusive activity (although marking its difference by its ipseity as an I "transcendent in its immanence") the transcendental apperception confirms presence: presence comes back to itself in the re-presentation and

fills itself or, as Husserl would say, identifies itself. This *life* of presence in
re-presentation is certainly also *my* life, but in this life of consciousness,
presence makes itself an event or a duration of presence. A duration of
presence, or a duration as presence: in duration any loss of time, any
lapse, is retained or it returns as memory; it is "rediscovered" or "recon-
stituted" and adheres to a *unity* [*ensemble*] through memory or historiog-
raphy. Consciousness as reminiscence glorifies, in the representation, the
ultimate vigor of presence. *The time of consciousness lending itself to representation is the synchrony that is stronger than diachrony.* This synchronization is one of the functions of intentionality: re-presentation. This is the
reason for the persistence of the celebrated formula of Brentano throughout all of Husserl's phenomenology: the fundamental character of representation within intentionality. Psychic life is representation, or has representation for a ground. In any case, in all its modalities, it can be transformed into a doxic thesis. Consciousness makes and remakes *presence*; it
is the *life* of presence. This is a consciousness that has already been forgotten for the benefit of the *present beings*: it withdraws itself from appearance [*l'apparaître*] to give room to these beings. The immediate, prereflective, nonobjectified, lived, and from the start anonymous or "mute"
life of consciousness is this *letting appear* by way of its retreat; this disap-
pearing of immediate consciousness in the letting appear of present beings. This is a consciousness in which identifying intentionality is turned
teleologically toward the "constitution" of ess*a*nce in truth, but which the
energy or entelechy of ess*a*nce commands according to its own modes,
and in a truly *a priori* fashion. The energy thus unfolds as *turned back*
into the working consciousness, which fixes the being in its theme and
which, when experienced, forgets itself in this fixation. The reference to
consciousness is effaced in its effect:

> Precisely because it is a question of a *universal and necessary reference* to the
> subject, which belongs to every object to the degree to which, as object, it is
> accessible to those who experience, this reference to the subject *cannot enter
> into the content proper* to the object. Objective experience is an orientation of
> experience toward the object. In an inevitable way, the subject is there, as it
> were, *qua* anonymous. . . . Every experience of an object leaves the I behind
> it; experience does not have the I before it.[4]

Within consciousness is "experienced" and identified the firmness, the
positivity, the presence—the being [*l'être*]—of the *primordially* thema-

tized being [*l'étant*], and it is as prereflective consciousness, anonymous from the outset, that consciousness hides and remains absent in any case from the "objective sphere" that it fixes.

The transcendental reduction's permanent effort amounts to bringing "mute consciousness" to the word and not taking the exercise of constituting intentionality, once brought to the word, for a being, posited in the positivity of the world. The life of consciousness excludes itself from the world and, precisely as excluded from the positivity of the world, as "mute subject," it permits the world's beings to affirm themselves in their presence and their numerical identity.

Thus, in the transcendental idealism of Husserlian phenomenology, we are beyond any doctrine in which the interpretation of being starting from consciousness would still preserve some sort of restrictive sense of the *esse-percipi*, and signify that being *is merely* a modality of perception, and in which the notion of the *in itself* would lay claim to a solidity stronger than what could ever proceed from an accord between identifying thoughts. On the contrary, all of Husserl's work consists in understanding the notion of the *in itself* as an abstraction, when it is separated from the intentional play in which it is experienced.

3. But the affinity between presence and representation is closer still. Ess*a*nce appears to the life of an I which, as monadic ipseity, distinguishes itself from it; it is to life that ess*a*nce *gives* itself. The transcendence of things in relation to the lived intimacy of thought—that is, relative to thought as *Erlebnis*; relative to experience (which the idea of a "still confused" and nonobjectifying consciousness does not exhaust)—the transcendence of the object, of an environment, just like the ideality of the thematized notion, is opened but also crossed by intentionality. Intentionality signifies distance as much as accessibility. It is a way for the distant to give itself. Already per*ception* grasps; the concept—the *Begriff*[5]—preserves this sense of holding. Whatever be the efforts demanded by the appropriation and utilization of things and notions, their transcendence promises possession and enjoyment, which consecrates the equality experienced between thought and its object in thought, as the identification of the Same, as satisfaction. Astonishment, as a disproportion between *cogitatio* and *cogitatum*, wherein knowledge looks for itself, dies out in knowledge. For the real, this way of standing within intentional transcendence "on the scale" of the lived experience and, for thought, this way

of thinking at its level and thus enjoying, signifies immanence. Intentional transcendence sketches out something like a scheme [*plan*] in which the adequation of the thing to the intellect is produced. This scheme is the phenomenon of the world.

Intentionality, as an identification of the identical *qua* stable, is sight aiming [*visée visant*], straight as a ray, at the fixed point of the goal. It is a spirituality accorded to the ends, to beings, to their position on solid ground. It is a spirituality accorded to the founding firmness of the earth, to the foundation as ess*a*nce. "In evidence . . . we have the experience of a being and of its manner of being."[6] Here, position and positivity confirm themselves in the doxic thesis of logic. This is the presence of what can be rediscovered, which the finger designates and the hand grasps; a "maintenance" [*maintenance*] or a present in which thought, thinking according to its measure, *rejoins* that which it thinks. This is the thought and psyche of immanence and satisfaction.

4. Does the psyche exhaust itself in deploying the "energy" of ess*a*nce, of the positing of beings?

To state such a question is not to expect that the *in itself* of beings might have a sense stronger than that which it obtains from the identifying consciousness. It is to ask oneself whether the psyche does not signify *otherwise* than by this "epic" of ess*a*nce which exalts in it and lives. It is to ask whether the positivity of *being*, of identity, of presence are the ultimate affair of the soul—and consequently whether knowledge is such an affair. Not that there would be grounds for expecting that affectivity or the will might be more significant than knowledge. Axiology and practice, as Husserl teaches, still rest on re-presentation. They therefore concern beings and the being of beings and do not compromise, but rather presuppose, the priority of knowledge. To ask oneself whether the psyche is limited to the confirmation of beings in their position is to suggest that consciousness—finding itself the *same*, identifying itself even in the exteriority of its intentional object, remaining immanent even in its transcendences—breaks this equilibrium of the *steady soul* and the soul thinking according to its scale, in order to understand more than its capacity. It is to suggest that its desires, its questions, its searching, rather than measuring its gaps and its finitude, are awakenings to Im-measure [*Dé-mesure*]. It is to suggest further that in its temporality, which disperses consciousness into successive moments—which nevertheless are synchronized in retention and protention, in memory and anticipation, and in the historic narrative and prevision—an alterity can undo this simultaneity and this assembly of the successive into the presence of representation, and that consciousness finds itself concerned with the Immemorial. Our wisdom pushes us to take seriously only the transcendence of intentionality, which nevertheless converts itself into immanence in the world. The thought awakened to God—or eventually devoted to God—interprets itself spontaneously in terms, and according to the articulations, of the noetico-noematic parallelism of the perception of meaning and of its being fulfilled.[7] The idea of God and even the enigma of the word "God"—which we find, fallen from who knows where or how and already circulating, e-normous,[8] in the guise of a noun, among the words of a language—inserts itself for current interpretation into the order of intentionality. The de-ference to God—which would lay claim to a difference other than that which separates the thematized or the represented from the lived, and would invoke another intrigue of the psyche—is recuperated in intentionality. One resorts to the notion of a horizontal religion, abiding on man's earth, and which ought to be substituted for the vertical one which departs for the Heavens in order to refer to the world; for it is starting from the world that one continues to think about men themselves. A substitution that can seem like a simple confusion: by what right, in effect, should the man seen at my side come to take the place of the "intentional object" corresponding to the word "God" that names or calls to it? But this confusion of terms, in its arbitrariness, translates perhaps the logical necessity of fixing the object of religion in conformity with the immanence of a thinking that aims at the world and which, in the order of thought, should be the ultimate and the unsurpassable one. To postulate a thinking structured otherwise would issue a challenge to logic and announce an arbitrary element in thought—or in the reflection upon this thought—more tolerable than this substitution of objects. Philosophical atheism, but also philosophical theism, refuse to accept even the originality of the psyche staking a claim beyond the world. They refuse to accept even the irreducibility of its noetic contours. In the remark about the *beyond*, one suspects an emphatic metaphor for intentional distance. Even if, in this suspicion, one risks having forgotten that the "movement" beyond is the metaphor and emphasis themselves, and that metaphor is language and that the expression of a thought in a discourse is not equivalent to a reflection in the indifferent milieu of a mirror, nor indeed to some adventure disdainfully called "verbal" whose stating presupposes, in the experience of significance, relations other than those of intentionality, which concern precisely, in an unrecoverable mode, the alterity of an other. That is, even if one risks having forgotten that the elevation of meaning by the metaphor in what is *said* [*dit*] owes its height to the *transcendence* of the *saying* [*du dire*] to the other [*autrui*].[9]

5. Why is there saying? This is the first fissure visible in the psyche of satisfaction. One can certainly bring language back to a teleology of being by invoking the necessity of communicating in order to succeed better in human enterprises. One can take an interest, consequently, in the *said* [*dit*], in its diverse genres and their diverse structures, and explore the birth of communicable meaning in words and the surest and most efficacious means of communicating it. Thus one can again attach language to the world and to being, to which the human enterprises refer; and thus attach language again to intentionality. Nothing stands in the way of this positivist interpretation. And the analysis of language, starting from the *said*, is a respectable, considerable, and difficult work. It nevertheless remains true that the very relationship of the *saying* is irreducible to intentionality, or that it rests, properly speaking, upon an intentionality that fails. This relationship is established, in effect, with the other man whose monadic interiority escapes my regard and my hold. But this *deficiency of re-presentation turns into a relationship of a higher order*; or, more exactly, into a relationship where there only begins to appear the signification itself of a higher and an other order. The Husserlian "appresentation," which does not arrive at satisfaction or at the intuitive fulfillment of the re-presentation, is inverted—as a failed experience—into a *beyond experience*, into a *transcendence* whose rigorous *determination* is described by ethical attitudes and exigencies, and by responsibility, of which language is one modality. The proximity of the neighbor, rather than passing for a limitation of the I by another, or for an aspiration to the unity yet to be effected, becomes desire nourishing itself from its hungers, or, to use a used word, love, more precious to the soul than the full possession of oneself by oneself.

This is an incomprehensible transfiguration in an order where all sensible signification goes back to the appearance of the world (that is, to the identification of the Same, that is, to Being), or a new rationality—unless this be the oldest rationality, prior to the one that coincides with the possibility of the world—which consequently is not brought back to ontology. A different—or deeper—rationality and one that will not allow itself to be led into the adventure that, from Aristotle to Heidegger, theology ran when it remained a thought of Identity and Being which was fatal to the God and the man of the Bible, or to their homonyms. Fatal to the One if we believe Nietzsche; fatal to the other according to contemporary antihumanism. Fatal to the homonyms in any case. Any thinking that would not lead to establishing an identical—a being—in the absolute rest of the earth beneath the vault of the heavens, would be subjective, an affliction of the unhappy consciousness.[10]

Must the un-rest and the disquiet where the security of what is completed and grounded is put into question *always* be understood starting from the positivity of the response, the lucky find, *satisfaction*? Is the question *always*, as in functional language (or even in scientific language where responses open onto new questions, but onto questions that aim only at responses), a knowledge in the process of being made, a thought *still* insufficient about the *given* that could satisfy it by placing itself at the level of what is expected? Is the question henceforth the famous question alternating with the response in a dialogue that the soul would hold with itself, and wherein Plato recognized thought, solitary from the outset and moving toward coincidence with itself, toward self-consciousness? Must we not admit, on the contrary, that the request and the entreaty, which one could not dissimulate in the question, bear witness to a *relationship to another*, a relationship that does not remain within the interiority of a solitary soul, a relationship that, within the question, takes shape? Do these not attest to a relationship that takes shape in the question, as in its not ordinary but original modality? A relationship to the Other [*l'Autre*] who, precisely by virtue of his irreducible difference, escapes [*se refuse*] a thematizing and thus always assimilative knowledge. A relationship that thus does not become correlation. Consequently, this is a relationship that could not call itself a relationship, properly speaking, since between its terms there would lack even the community of synchrony, which as an ultimate community no relationship could deny to its terms. And yet to the Other—a relationship. A relationship and a nonrelationship. Does the question not signify that? The relationship to the absolutely other— to the un-limited by the same—to the Infinite; would not transcendence be equivalent to an original question? A relationship without a simultaneity of terms; unless time itself endures in the form of this relation-nonrelation, in the form of this question. This is a time to be taken in its dia-chrony and not as the "pure form of sensibility": the soul in its diachronous temporality, where retention does not annul the lapse, nor the protention absolute novelty. The soul, in the passive synthesis of aging and of its ad-vent, in its life, would be the original question, even the unto-God itself [*l'à-Dieu même*]. Time as a question: an un-balanced relationship to the Infinite, to that which could not be comprehended: neither encompassed, nor touched, a tearing of the correlation and beneath the parallelism and the noetico-noematic balance, beneath the emptiness and the filling up of the signitive, a question or an original "insomnia," the very awakening into the psyche. *But also the manner by which the Unequalable concerns the finite and which is perhaps what Descartes called the Idea of the Infinite in us.* Proximity and religion: it is all the novelty that love comprises compared to hunger; Desire compared to need. This proximity is better to me than any internalization and any symbiosis. A rending beneath the rectilinear uprightness of the intentional focus that the intention supposes and from which it derives in its correspondence with its intentional object, although this original *vigil*, this insomnia of the psyche, lends itself to the measure given it by its own derivations, and risks being expressed in terms of satisfaction and dissatisfaction as well. An ambiguity, or an enigma of the spiritual.

The transcendence toward God is neither linear like the focus of intentionality nor teleological so as to end at the punctuality of a pole and thus stop at beings and substantives. Neither is it even initially dialogical, naming a "you" [*tu*]. Is this transcendence toward God not already produced by ethical transcendence, so that desire and love might be made more perfect than satisfaction?[11] It would be advisable nevertheless to ask here whether it is a question of a transcendence toward God or a transcendence out of which a word such as "God" alone reveals its meaning. That this transcendence be produced from the (horizontal?) relationship with the other means neither that the other man is God, nor that God is a great Other.

A desire that makes itself perfection? The philosophy [*la pensée*] of satisfaction has judged otherwise. And this is, to be sure, good sense itself. Diotima disqualified love in declaring it a demigod, on the pretext that as aspiration it is neither fulfilled nor perfect. Certainly this good sense is infallible in our relation to the world and to the things of the world for eating and drinking. To contest it in the order of the world is a sign of unreason. It is infallible from Plato to Hegel, who spoke with irony of the beautiful soul! But when Kierkegaard recognizes in dissatisfaction an access to the supreme, he does not fall back, despite Hegel's warnings, into romanticism. He no longer departs from experience, but from transcendence. He is the first philosopher who thinks God without thinking of Him from the starting point of the world. The proximity of the other is not some sort of "detachment of being relative to oneself," nor is it "a degradation of coincidence," according to the Sartrian formulas. Desire, here, is not pure privation; the social relationship is worth more than the enjoyment of oneself. And the proximity of God devolved to man is, perhaps, a destiny more divine than that of a God enjoying His divinity. Kierkegaard writes,

> In the case of worldly goods, to the degree to which man feels less need for them, he becomes more perfect. A pagan who knew how to speak of worldly goods said that God was happy because He had need of nothing and that after Him came the wise man, because he had need of little. But in the relationship between man and God the principle is inverted: the more man feels the need for God, the more he is perfect.

Or again, "One must love God not because He is the most perfect, but because one needs him." Or "A need to love—supreme Good and supreme felicity."

Here we find the same reversal of absence into supreme presence in the order of knowledge. "If I have faith," writes Kierkegaard, "I cannot come to have an immediate certainty of it; for to believe is precisely this dialectical wavering which, although ceaselessly in fear and trembling, never despairs; faith is precisely this infinite preoccupation with the self which holds you awake and ready [*éveillé*] to risk everything, this internal preoccupation with knowing whether one truly has faith." This transcendence is possible only by way of un-certainty! In the same spirit, it is a breaking with the "triumphalism" of common sense; in that which is a failure relative to the world there exults a triumph. "We will not say that the man of goodness will one day triumph in another world, or that his cause will prevail one day here below; no, he triumphs in the midst of life, he triumphs in suffering from his living life, he triumphs on the day of his affliction."

According to the models of satisfaction, possession commands seeking, enjoyment is worth more than need, triumph is truer than failure, certitude is more perfect than doubt, and the answer goes farther than the question. Seeking, suffering, questioning would be simple diminutions of the happy find, of enjoyment, happiness, and the answer; insufficient thoughts of the identical and the present, indigent cognitions or cognition in the state of indigence. Once again this is good sense. This is also common sense.

But can the hermeneutic of the religious life forego im-balanced thoughts? And does not philosophy itself consist in treating "mad" ideas with wisdom, or in bringing wisdom to love? The knowledge, the answer, and the result would belong to a psyche still incapable of thoughts in which the word *God* takes on meaning.

§ The Thinking of Being and the Question of the Other

1. What is meant by the intelligibility of the intelligible, the significa-tion of meaning; what does reason signify? There lies, without a doubt, the preliminary question of the human being enamored of meaning; the preliminary question of philosophy. Or the very question of philosophy, which is probably the preliminary in itself.

That meaning might have its "place" in what appears, in the truth, and consequently in the knowledge or understanding of being—this is already a response to this question about the meaning of meaning, already a cer-tain philosophy. Is it the only meaningful philosophy? The ultimately theoretical aspect of philosophical discourse would confirm *after the fact* this kinship of meaning and knowledge. And the preliminary question about the meaning of meaning, which as a question is taken for an artic-ulation of theoretical thought, should justify this priority or this privilege of the theoretical, arising as if bent over its own cradle.

And, to be sure, the theoretical is not rational by accident. If it is an adventure of the intelligible, then this adventure could not be gotten around.[1] Yet that philosophical discourse would show itself *ultimately* as theoretical does not imply its independence with respect to another regime of significations and does not efface its submission to this regime. In the same way, the interpretation of the question as a modality of the theoretical lets itself be put in question in its turn, even if theory cannot fail to make its appearance *in* the question, nor fail to become aware of the question itself, which calls to it.[2]

It remains the case that the philosophy passed on to us—which, de-spite its origin in Greece, is the "wisdom of the nations," for there is an agreement between the intelligibility of the cosmos in which are posited both solid and graspable beings, and the good practical sense of men having needs to satisfy—makes all significance, all rationality, go back to being. It goes back to the "gesture" of being[3] carried out by beings, inasmuch as they assert themselves as beings, and to being, inasmuch as it asserts itself as being, to being *qua* being, to the ess*a*nce of being. We write "ess*a*nce" with an "a," like "insist*a*nce," to give a name to the verbal aspect of the word "being."[4] This "gesture" is equivalent to this assertion, which as language resounds as a pro-position and is there confirmed to the point of appearing and of making itself into presence in a consciousness. The appearing-to-a-consciousness, as an emphasis of the assertion of being, was certainly one side of the idealist philosophy that did not intend to put into question and doubt the actuality of being, an actuality that, before asserting itself and being confirmed in judgment and in its "doxic thesis," signifies a position on a solid ground, the most solid of grounds, the earth. The affirmation of ess*a*nce supposes this rest; it supposes this substance, beneath all motion and all cessation of motion. It is a reign of a fundamental rest in the verb "to be," which the grammarians lightly call auxiliary. It states an activity that effects no change, neither of quality nor place, but in which, precisely, is fulfilled the very identification of identity, the nonrestlessness of identity, as the act of its rest.[5] This is an apparent contradiction in terms which the Greeks did not hesitate to think of as pure act! Beneath the agitation of the pursuit of beings and things reigns a rest as imperturbable as the very identity of the identical. That this rest reigns precisely beneath the vault of fixed stars, on firm ground, that something such as sovereignty without violence—yet this is already rational necessity!—might arise in deference to the stars, is infinitely astonishing. Astonishing and familiar, for it is the "mundanity" of the world. Through this rest, where everything has a place and is identified, everything takes place. The experience of nameable beings and of *esse* itself is the result of this profound and fundamental experience, which is also an experience of the fundamental, of the foundation, and of the profound which is the experience of ess*a*nce, an ontological experience of the firmness of the earth under the visible but intangible fixity of the starry sky; here is an experience of the fundamental asserting itself *emphatically*, precisely as experience. In this way, expressions such as *experience of identity* or *experience of being* qua *being* are tautologous.

Identity is henceforth a criterion of meaning. In our intellectual tradi-

tion, *being* and *knowledge of being* in its identity are the very theater of
the Spirit. According to the *Timaeus*, the circle of the *Same* includes or
comprehends the circle of the Other [*l'Autre*]. The eternity of the world
soul, to which the human soul is related, is therein the cyclical return of
the Same when the two circles reestablish their initial positions at the end
of the great year. But the geometry of the Copernican universe—and this
up to the interstellar voyages of today—preserves the identity of the
Timaeus's cosmos, while suppressing the transcendence of elevation.

The idealism of modern thought, which seems to privilege the activity of a synthesizing thought against the resting of being, does not dis-
miss this stability, that is, this priority of the world, this reference to as-
tronomy. We alluded to this earlier when we recognized in *what appears*
[*l'apparaître*]—and consequently in consciousness—the emphasis of being: the rationality of ess*a*nce depends upon the hyperbole of positivity
turning into "presence unto... ," of positivity making itself representation.
The firmness of rest is asserted to the point of exposing itself and appearing. The *esse* of being, itself, is ontology: comprehension of *esse*. The psyche as the pneumatics of representation unfolds as a synthetic activity of
transcendental apperception, and of the energy of presence that gives rise
to it. It does so even though it must attest to its distinction with regard
to being by way of its crystallization into ipseity, which is always "mine,"
and by way of its belonging to what Gabriel Marcel calls "the existential
orbit of being," a hyperbole of ess*a*nce entering into the role of a subjectivity. The ess*a*nce of the resting of being repeats itself in the positivity—
or the *thetic* quality—of thematization and synthesis.

Positivity—the resting upon an unshakable foundation; the holding,
firmly contained and graspable in the worldliness of the world—preserves
a value of virtue in a philosophy that is nevertheless mistrustful of posi-
tivism. Ideas and signs count only for their contents; they count only as
positive thoughts and languages. The negation that claims to deny being
is still, in its opposition, a position on a terrain upon which it is based.
Negation carries with it the dust of being that it rejects. This reference of
the negation to the positive in the contradiction is the great discovery of
Hegel, who would be the philosopher of the positivity that is stronger
than negativity. The rational privilege of identity, of the resting of being,
shows itself as the auto-foundation of self-consciousness: the immediacy
of a nameless singularization, which can only be pointed toward, returns
to the absolute rest of identity across the diverse figures of mediation.

Hegelian logic shall assert the identity of the identical and the nonidentical. Any overflowing of the Same by the Other passes henceforth for an incomplete thought, or as romantic. The two attributes will have the same pejorative signification: thoughts without a foundation, not rejoining the ess*a*nce of being. It is not metaphorically that the justification of all signification shall be named "foundation," that the systems will comprise structures and an architectonic, that objects will be grasped in their transcendental *constitution*. One can legitimately ask oneself—and this is one of the central problems of Husserl's *Formal and Transcendental Logic*[6]— whether formal logic, in its claim to the purity of the void, is possible, whether any *formal ontology* does not already sketch out the contours of a *material ontology*, and consequently, as we would put it, whether the very idea of form does not demand the stability of being and of the Same, and the "astronomical" order, and when all is said and done, the world that secures this order.

For Husserl, in the encompassing and synthetic activity of transcendental consciousness, rationality is equivalent to the confirmation of intentionality by the given; intentional activity is identification. A midday sun scours every horizon in which *the other* would be hidden. That which irreversibly goes away, or passes, is immediately caught hold of, is re-collected [*se sou-vient*] in memory, or returns, reconstructed by history. Reminiscence, from Plato to Husserl, is the ultimate vigor of the identity of being and, at the least, the normative program of ontology. And even in *the appearing* that is directly *situated*, directly *here*, directly a habitation of a place—such as the phenomenology and the etymologies of Heidegger and his disciples suggest—man in the world is ontology. His being *in the world*—even into death, which measures its finitude—is a comprehension of being. Rationality remains a gathering. In one of his last texts, *The End of Philosophy and the Task of Thinking*,[7] Heidegger goes back prior to presence but he finds in his "clearing"—"reconciliation," a "heart at peace," and the "Same."

2. The crisis of the philosophy that is handed down to us can only be expressed in its incapacity to respond to its own criteria of meaning. It would be due to the impossibility, which this philosophy confronts, of maintaining the accord between knowledge [*connaissance*] and itself. The crisis would be an internal bursting open of *meaning*, situated within knowledge and expressing the identity or the resting of being. Philosophy

runs up against the non-sense of meaning, if reason signifies the presence of being or representation: a manifestation of beings to a true knowing in which beings assert themselves "in the original," in which their identity as beings [*êtres*] or their presence as beings [*êtres*] is asserted. Philosophy first runs into the fact that the relation to being which it seeks to maintain is a repetition of the relation established in the sciences, engendered by philosophy. The sciences, in their universal communicability, have dissolved the credibility of the language of philosophy—structured as propositions as though it [philosophy] expressed some sublime perception or named substantives, and losing itself in innumerable and contradictory discourses. The death knell of the philosophy of being resounds in the *Te Deum*, triumphant in its fashion, of the irresistible sciences.

But philosophy has run up against its non-sense in its own ambitions and paths. It happens that beyond their immediate presence beings can appear, in some fashion, without remaining in their being. By way of the signs and the words that fix them, or assemble or call them, beings appear that have nothing of being but resemblance and pure semblance, where appearance is the ever possible reverse-side of their manner of appearing.[8] The ground of knowledge [*la raison du savoir*] should beware of certain games that bewitch the spontaneous exercise of cognition—games that bewitch cognition unbeknownst to it—without stopping or even running counter to its rational course. This is an insecurity of the rational that consequently puts in check an intelligibility where the sureness, the security of the foundation is reason itself. That there might be in philosophy a need for a vigilance distinct from good sense and from the evidence of the scientific research deeply concerned about presence, being, and satisfaction—such was the novelty of criticism. Therein lay an appeal to a new rationality. Is this new rationality or critique only a modality or a species of what was common to philosophy and to philosophy-engendered science? Is it only its hyperbole, only a lucidity under a stronger light? Post-critical thought [*le post-criticisme*] will certainly have interpreted it this way. One can also wonder, however, whether a *new* mode of signifying is not necessary to critical lucidity itself, which, in order to think according to its level in knowing, must also ceaselessly *awaken*: a vigilance that, before serving knowledge, is a rupture of limits and a bursting of finitude.

Be that as it may, beneath the critical ending of metaphysics is announced simultaneously a philosophy distinct from science, and the end of a certain rationality of the philosophy that reasons straight ahead of itself. A moment characterized by the denunciation of the transcendental illusion and of a radical malice within the good faith of knowledge; a malice within a reason that is nevertheless innocent of any sophism, and which Husserl called naïveté. In his phenomenology, to which critical thought leads, this amounts to denouncing the gaze directed upon being in its very appearing, as a way for the object in which the innocent gaze is absorbed in good faith to block up this gaze—as if the plastic forms of the object, which are sketched out in this view, lowered themselves over the eyes like lids: the eyes would thus lose the world in gazing at things. A strange denial inflicted upon vision by its object, and one that Plato already denounced in the myth of Gorgias when he spoke of men who have placed "before their souls a screen made up of eyes and ears and of the body in its entirety" (523 c–d). The faculties of intuition in which the whole body participates, the organs of the life of relatedness with the outside, would be precisely that which blocks up the view. This is a blindness against which, in our day, a phenomenological rationality is invoked: a new rationality of the reduced and constituting consciousness wherein appearing and being coincide. Every being must henceforth be understood in its origin from this privileged appearing within "transcendental consciousness," starting from this being-phenomenon, from this presence or this living present given to intuition, wherein every overflowing of real presence—every unreality or ideality—is signaled, measured, and described.

Derrida's *Speech and Phenomena* places precisely this privilege of presence in question.[9] The very possibility of the fullness of presence is contested. The latter would always be postponed, always "simply indicated" in the "meaning to say" (in the *Meinen*) which, for Husserl, referred entirely to intuitive fullness. This is the most radical critique of the philosophy of being, for which the transcendental illusion begins at the level of immediacy. Before the importance and intellectual rigor of *Speech and Phenomena* one might wonder whether this text does not cut across traditional philosophy, with a demarcation line similar to that of Kantianism; one might wonder whether we are not, anew, at the end of a naïveté, awakened from a dogmatism which slumbered at the bottom of what we took for a critical spirit. The end of metaphysics thought through to its end: it is not only the worlds behind our world that are without meaning, it is the world spread out before us that incessantly escapes. It is lived experience that is postponed in lived experience. The *immediate* is not only a call to mediation, it is a transcendental illusion. The signified, which is always to come in the signifier, never manages to take shape; the mediation of signs is never short-circuited. This is a view that corresponds with what is perhaps the profoundest discovery of psychoanalysis: the dissimulative essence of the symbol. Lived experience would be repressed by the linguistic signs creating the texture of its apparent presence: an interminable play of signifiers postponing forever—repressing—the signified.

Yet this is a critique that nevertheless remains faithful in some fashion to the gnoseological signification of meaning, precisely to the degree to which the deconstruction of intuition and the perpetual deferral of presence, which deconstruction shows, is thought exclusively from presence itself, which is treated as a norm. Herein, the Husserlian indicative reference, the *"Anzeige"*—which comprises no intrinsic signifier but rather connects two terms without any prefiguration,[10] even though this were in the "hollowness" of what is indicated in the indicator—cannot be expelled from any signification, and there it causes a scandal (even if this scandal were not to be frightening).

3. Does this indication, reduced to a rigorously extrinsic relation of the one referring to the other by a purely formal reference, have no other source than formal association? This purely formal reference would thus, from the point of view of the knowledge of being or from the ontological point of view, be the poorest of meanings, that of a conventional sign, an inferior intelligibility relative to vision and even to the intention (*meinen* means "to want to say"),[11] which tends toward its correlate in the manner that Husserl calls "signitive." Does this indication not bespeak a less empirical origin, that is, the schema of knowledge: a satisfaction of thought by being—though it might have to be abandoned? Does not the extraneousness of the terms—as the radical exteriority shown in pure indication, the difference—go back to a system of meaning, an intelligibility not reducible to the manifestation of a "content of being," or to a thought? One does not find oneself at the origin of exteriority when one registers it as a transcendental fact (*qua* form of sensibility), or an anthropological one, or as an ontological *datum*. As a relation within the exclusion of all relation, there would be exteriority where one term is affected by what does not lend itself to the *avatar* of a content, by what

does not lend itself to some sort of fall "within the limits" in order to fit their bounds precisely like an "intentional object," by what should not be called a "this," rigorously speaking. There would be exteriority where one term is affected by that which it cannot assume, by the Infinite. This is a being-affected [*affection*] by what does not enter into a structure. It is a being-affected by what does not form a *whole* with that which it affects, as would the "intentional object" that is assembled in a co-presence with the intention wherein it is seen or intended.[12] This is a being-affected by the absolutely other. The indication—as a relation of pure extraneity of the one to the other, without there being anything in common, nor any "correspondence" between them, a relation of absolute difference—is not the diminution of an intuition of some sort. It gets its intelligibility from transcendence itself, which is thus irreducible to intentionality and to its structures of a need to be satisfied. Is not the absolute difference of transcendence announced thus as non-in-difference, being-affected—and affectivity—radically distinct from the presentation of being to the consciousness of... ? A being-affected by the invisible— by what is invisible to the point of not letting itself be represented, or thematized, or named, or pointed out as a "something" in general like a this or a that and, consequently, "the absolutely non-incarnatable," that which does not come to "take form" [*prendre corps*], and which is unsuited to hypostasis—a being-affected beyond being and beings, and beyond their distinction or amphibology; the infinite eclipsing ess*a*nce. Being-affected or passivity: here is a consciousness that would not be consciousness of... , but rather a psyche holding its intentionality as one holds one's breath, and, by consequence, pure patience: a waiting that awaits nothing, or hope where nothing hoped for comes to incarnate the Infinite, where no pro-tention comes to thwart [*dé-jouer*] patience; a passivity more passive than any passivity of undergoing, which would again be a reception; patience and length of time; patience or length of time. In the deferral or the incessant differ*a*nce of this pure indication, we suspect time itself, but as an incessant dia-chrony: proximity of the Infinite, this is the *forever* and the *never* of a dis-inter-estedness and of the unto-God [*l'à-Dieu*]. This is a being-affected, but without touch [*tangence*]: affectivity. A proximity in the fear of the approach, a traumatism of the awaking. The dia-chrony of time as a fear of God.[13]

A proximity of God where sociality is sketched out in its irreducibility to knowledge [*savoir*], *better than* fusion and the completion of being in self-consciousness; a proximity where, in this "better than," the *good* begins to signify. A proximity that already confers a meaning to duration, to the patience of living; a meaning of the life purely lived, without reason for being. A rationality more ancient than the revelation of being.

4. The philosophy that has been handed down to us could not fail to name the paradox of this non-ontological significance; even though, immediately, it turned back to being as to the ultimate foundation of the reason it named. The placing of the Idea of the Infinite within the finite, surpassing its capacity, as taught by Descartes, is one of the most remarkable expressions of transcendence. To be sure, it is for Descartes the premise of the proof of the existence of God. And, thereby, the positivity of thematized and identical being is sought for the transcendence of the immeasurable [*démesure*], which affects the finite in a certain fashion. Under different terms, this relation of transcendence is shown—if only for an instant in its purity—in the philosophies of knowledge. It is the beyond being in Plato. It is the entry, "through the door," of the agent intellect in Aristotle. It is the exaltation of theoretical reason into practical reason in Kant. It is the search for recognition by the *other man* in Hegel, himself. It is the renewal of duration in Bergson, who has grasped there, perhaps, rather than in his conception of the integral conservation of the past, the very diachrony of time. It is the sobering of reason in Heidegger.

This way for thinking to think beyond the correlative that is thematized, this way of thinking about the Infinite without equaling it, and thence without coming back to itself, is a putting into question of thinking by the Other [*l'Autre*]. This putting into question of thinking does not mean that, in some manner or other, thought would have to question itself about its nature and its quiddity, but rather that thought is disquieted by, or awakes from, the positivity wherein it stands in the world.

In the philosophy that is handed down to us, the meaning that does not refer to what is established in the positivity of the solid earth beneath the celestial vault passes for something purely subjective, for the dream of an unhappy consciousness. The Questioning, and the Searching, and Desiring are the privations of the response, of possession, of enjoyment. One does not wonder whether the question, paradoxically unequal to itself, *does not think beyond*; whether the question, instead of carrying within itself only the hollowness of need, is not the very mode of the relationship with the Other, with the uncontainable, with the Infinite.

With God. Before being posed in the world and satisfied with responses, the question would be, by way of the demand or the prayer that it carries—by way of the wonder in which it is opened—a relationship-to-God [*relation-à-Dieu*], the original insomnia of thinking. The question would not be a modification, or a modality, or a modalization of *apophansis*,[14] like doubt or the consciousness of the probable or the possible. The question is original. The question is exactly the figure that takes, or the knot wherein is tied, the disproportion of the relation—without this impossible figure—of the finite to the Infinite. It is the "in" of the "infinite *in* the finite," which is also the *outside* more exterior than any exteriority, or the transcendence, or the infinite duration that neither arrives nor goes to its end.[15] Is it not of this thought—which is other than that which, as intentional consciousness, wills the correlate at its level, the rest and the identity of the astronomical positive—that Blanchot speaks when he says, paradoxically, "We foresee that the dis-aster is thought."[16] An intelligibility for which the unusual is not reduced to a negative theology. The transcendence of the Infinite is not recovered in propositions, though they were negative ones.

In effect, we have attempted elsewhere[17] to show how the transcendence of the Infinite turns into a relationship with another [*autrui*], my neighbor; how proximity signifies, from the face of the other man, the responsibility already assumed for him. We have attempted to show how, by this untransferable and inescapable responsibility—going to the point of substitution for the other man, potentially, all the way to the uncondition of a hostage—the subjectivity that says *I* takes on meaning in this responsibility of the first-come, of the first person torn from the comfortable place that he or she occupied as a protected individual in the concept of the *I in general* of the philosophies of self-consciousness. The question of the Other turns back into responsibility for another, and the fear of God—which is as foreign to fright before the sacred as it is to anguish before nothingness—turns into fear for the neighbor and for his death.

The "pure indication" of Husserlian analyses—the one evoking the other without any "hunger" for the other—which, in the element of the knowledge of being (which is that of the identification of the identical and the world) is a deficiency and nothing more, belongs to a wholly different element than does ontology, and signifies in another sense that, in ethics, will have its *hypotyposis*. This ethics is not understood as the corollary of a vision of the world, or as founded upon being, upon knowledge, upon categories, or upon existentials.

In the human, there is an intelligibility older than what is manifested as a comprehension of being, embraceable, and thus constitutable by consciousness, and which reigns as world. This is a signification by way of transcendence, older than what governs *esse*, even if, in its turn, the former lets itself be shown in the language it summons and gives rise to, in order to enter into propositions of an ontological and ontical form.[18] This is a meaning that would be paradoxical with respect to the meaning that agrees with the doxic thesis of propositions. In terms of knowledge, it would signify the infinite in the finite. But it is on the signification of this "*in*" that our analyses have attempted to shed light.

We have confronted, on the one hand, the evidence of that knowledge which is a mode of the resting of being where, in the equality of appearing and of being, its identity as being is identified and confirmed. On the other hand, we have confronted the patience of the infinite, where reason is an incessant disturbance of the Same by the Other [*l'Autre*], or the diachrony of Time; that which comes to pass, concretely, in my responsibility for another [*autrui*] or in ethics. We have asked whether the Other [*l'Autre*]—who refuses identification, that is, thematization and hypostasis, but whom the philosophy of the tradition attempted to recover in the patience of the concept through the methodology of history as self-consciousness—must not be understood wholly otherwise, in a putting in question of thought by the Infinite which thought could not contain; in the awakening [*l'éveil*]. This is a putting in question and an awakening which are reversed into the ethics of responsibility for the other; an incessant putting in question of the quietude or the identity of the Same. It is a susception more passive than any passivity, yet an incessant awakening, a waking up in the midst of awakening that, without this, would become a "mood" [*état d'âme*], a state of wakefulness, or wakefulness as a state.[19] A thought more thoughtful than the thought of being, a sobering up that philosophy attempts to say; that is, which it attempts to communicate, and this, if only in a language that ceaselessly unsays itself, a language that insinuates.

§ Transcendence and Evil

> I establish peace and am the author of Evil,
> I, the Eternal, do all that.
>
> —Isaiah 45:7

Thought and Transcendence

The attempt to place in doubt the very significance of words such as "transcendence" and "beyond" bears witness to their semantic solidity, since, at least in this critical discourse concerning them, we recognize what we are contesting. The reduction of the absolute meaning of these terms to a relative "transcendence" and "beyond" carried—by the force of who knows what drive—to the farthest and highest degree already causes "transcendence" and "beyond" to intervene in this superlative, or lends a transcendent power to certain of our psychological forces. And yet, in order for them to become truly thoughts, is not something lacking in the intelligibility of these notions? It is that in our philosophical tradition, the veritable thought is a thought that is true; a knowing; a thought referred to being, to being [*être*] in the sense of designating a being [*étant*], but also to being [*être*] understood as a verb, expressing the fulfillment by beings of the task or the destiny of being without which we could not recognize the being [*l'étant*] as a being [*étant*].

In distinguishing idea and concept, reason and understanding, Kant was, to be sure, the first to separate thinking from knowing, and thus to discover meanings that did not rejoin being or, more precisely, meanings not subject to the categories of the understanding, and not subject to the reality that, in fact, is correlative to these categories. But this distant thought of being, which is not reduced to senselessness for all that, is again understood by Kant as devoid of the things in themselves toward which it aims. It is still measured against the being that it lacks. The ideas thus have a dialectical status, in the pejorative sense that Kant gives to this adjective; the transcendental illusion played out in this thought is the drama of an aspiration toward being. Everything always comes to pass as if the appearing and the cognition of being were equivalent to rationality and to the "spirit"; as though the signification of meaning—intelligibility—was due to the manifestation of being, and was ontology, if only in the guise of intentionality—that is, of a will or of a nostalgia for being. To be sure, through these reboundings of ontology, Kant had the audacity to draw a more radical distinction between thinking and knowing. He discovered in the practical use of pure reason an intrigue irreducible to a reference to being. A good will, utopian in some fashion, deaf to information, indifferent to the confirmations that could come to it from being (and which make a difference to the technique and the hypothetical imperative, but do not concern practice or the categorical imperative), proceeds from a freedom situated above being and prior to knowledge and ignorance. And yet, after an instant of separation, the relation with ontology is reestablished in the "postulates of pure reason," as though it were awaited in the midst of all these audacities: in their way, the ideas rejoin being in the existence of God, guaranteeing either (according to the letter of the critique) the agreement of virtue and happiness or, according to Hermann Cohen's reading, the agreement of freedom with nature and the efficacy of a practice decided without knowledge. The absolute existence of the Ideal of pure reason, the existence of the Supreme Being, is finally of importance in an architecture wherein the concept of freedom ought to have been the keystone.

This capacity of the idea to equal the given, its obligation to justify its emptiness, this tendency to refer to being (even if other than intuitive, but always to being)—does this necessity for thought to belong to cognition [*connaissance*] remain the measure of all intelligibility? Is the thought going toward God tied to this measure, at the risk of passing for a thought in decline, that is, for a privation of knowledge? Can we not show that, far from confining ourselves to the pure denial of norms of knowledge, the thought going toward God (and which goes there otherwise than one goes to what is thematized) entails spiritual [*psychique*] and original modes beyond those that a world of laws without play demands with its relations of reciprocity and compensation, and its identifications of differences? Can we not show, in this thought, modalities of the disturbance of the Same by the Other, proper and original modalities of the unto-God [*à-*

Dieu], where the ontological adventure of the soul is interrupted, and where, before Glory, the idea of being is *eclipsed* (perhaps fallen, precisely, in God, to the rank of a simple attribute), and where in dis-inter-*estedness*, the alternation between the real and the illusory is dimmed?

Transcendence and Phenomenology

How and where is there produced, within the psyche of experience, the major break capable of accrediting an *other* as irreducibly other [*autre*] and, in this sense, as *beyond*, even though in the tissue of the thematized thinkable every rending preserves or renews the texture of the Same? How can a thought go *beyond* the world that is precisely the way by which the being that it thinks is assembled, whatever the heterogeneity of its elements and the variety of their modes of being? How can the transcendent signify "the wholly other," easy to say, certainly, but which the common fund of the thinkable and of discourse restores to the world and as a world? It is not enough that, in what is thinkable, a difference is revealed or a contradiction opened such that there gapes an interval corresponding to transcendence or even to a nothing, before which the dialectical and logical resources of thought would be used up in impotence. How does a *nothingness* [*un néant*] take on meaning that is not merely the negation of the negation, which "preserves" (*aufhebt*) the being that it denies? How does the difference of an alterity that does not rest upon some common fund take on meaning?

I think that, on these two points, Husserlian phenomenology has opened new possibilities. It affirms the rigorous solidarity of everything intelligible with the psychic modalities *by* which and *in* which it is thought —not that simply any meaning is accessible to simply any thought. These modalities of the psyche comprise, to be sure, intentional implications— repressed or forgotten intentions—but they are irreducible essences, *origins* (whatever be the reductive ambitions of the phenomenology called "genetic"). Husserlian phenomenology is, all things considered, an *eidetics of pure consciousness*. It is, on the one hand, confidence in the idea of the irreducible structure of the psyche—irreducible to some sort of mathematical or logical order, and this by an irreducibility more original than any mathematics and any logic, which thus lends itself only to description. Phenomenology is the idea of the essences of the psyche, not constituting a "definite multiplicity" (*definite Mannigfaltigkeit*). It is, on the other hand, the reference of meaning to the donation of meaning—to the *Sinngebung*—which animates these irreducible thoughts. Phenomenology teaches us therefore not to clarify a meaning, thought uniquely or principally from its relations with other objective meanings, at the risk of relativizing all meaning and confining all signification within the *system* without egress. Phenomenology has taught us to make explicit or to elucidate a meaning starting from the *irreducible psyche* wherein it is given. It has taught us thus to seek out meaning in its origin, to seek out the original meaning. This method, born of a philosophy of arithmetic and of logical investigations, affirms the primacy—the principality—of the nonformal!

In this perspective we understand the novelty of the Heideggerian approach, which goes, for example, to nothingness from out of lived anguish, a modality of the psyche leading farther than did negation. However, for the notions of the *other* [*autre*] and the difference-without-common-ground, contemporary thought seems equally indebted to a Heideggerian concept developed from anguish: to that of the *ontological difference*. Indeed, the difference between being and beings presupposes, in effect, nothing more in common between them than the paper upon which the words designating them are inscribed, or the air in which the sounds serving to pronounce them vibrate. The difference between being and beings is *the* difference. Consequently, it is not astonishing that this difference exerts a fascination upon those philosophers who, after the Nietzschean remark about the death of God—and outside of all onto-theology—dare to take interest in the meaning of transcendence, guided doubtless by the conviction that the domain of the *meaningful* is limited neither to the *seriousness* of the sciences and the works attached to thematized being, nor to the *play* of the pleasures and arts, which escapes from being but preserves its memory, and draws pleasure from its images and entails certain stakes.

One may certainly wonder whether being, in Heidegger's sense of the word as that which transcends a being but gives itself to all beings, remains beyond the world that it makes possible, and whether it permits us to think of a transcendent God from beyond being. One may wonder whether the neutrality, which offers itself to the *thinking of the being* transcending *beings*, can be suitable for, and sufficient to, divine transcendence. The fact remains that the *ontological difference* serves philosophers as the model of transcendence and that, even when repudiated in research related to religious thought, it is frequently invoked. It is sufficient to recall the profound and subtle essay of Jean-Luc Marion[1] on the divinity of God: a courageous attempt at a breakthrough; an attempt still isolated, among philosophers, to understand God no longer primordially from being. While recognizing his debt toward Heidegger, and while setting his own itinerary in exploring the Heideggerian paths, the author finally sets himself "at a distance from the ontological difference" (214).

Another young thinker, Philippe Nemo, recently wrote a book on the suffering of Job. This work was written with the same attention paid to transcendence and starting from a certain modality of the psyche—from a certain remarkable experience—which interrupts the world (even if psychology, which as science, that is, as thematization, recovers itself from this interruption and always has time for this recovery of self, and takes this interruptive phenomenon as one psychological state[2] among others accessible to theory and to treatment). This book is an exegesis of a biblical text.[3] The *ontological difference* seems, here again, to have been the chief encouragement for the work. Yet this is a description of lived experience justifying itself by the phenomenon, even if it is suggested by the verses of the book that is commented upon. The rupture of the same is approached in Nemo's work from a psychic content endowed with an exceptional signification; what it contains that is extreme is not sought in some sort of superlative, but in the simple *datum* of an experience. We would very much like to emphasize this phenomenology and judge it for itself, forgetting the exegetical intentions from which it proceeds, despite the great finesse and scrupulousness of that hermeneutic. But we do not intend to take a position, here, on the truth of the ultimate meaning this work lends to the book of Job. The philosophical language used by the author to whom we are responding seems perfectly justified by the philosophical perspective opened by this work, which is not an exercise in piety.

The Excess of Evil

In order to describe evil such as it would be experienced in the suffering of Job, Philippe Nemo first insists upon the anguish that would be its underlying event. In agreement with Heidegger, anguish is interpreted as an unveiling of nothingness, as being-unto-death [*être-à-la-mort*], as the fact of a world that slips away and isolates man, and that of man who closes himself to words of consolation which still belong to the resources of the world that is coming undone.

Thus understood, anguish could not pass for a simple "mood" [*état d'âme*], "for a form of moral affectivity," for a simple consciousness of finitude or a moral symptom preceding, accompanying, or following a pain that, unthinkingly no doubt, one would call physical. Anguish is the sharp point at the heart of evil. A malady, a disease of living flesh, aging, corruptible; a declining and a rotting. These would be the modalities of anguish itself. By these and in these—the dying that is lived in some way and the truth of this death, unforgettable, unexceptionable, irremissible, in the impossibility of hiding it from oneself—lies non-dissimulation it-self and, perhaps, disclosure and truth *par excellence*; what is, of itself, open; the original insomnia of being; a gnawing away of human identity that is not an inviolable spirit weighed down with a perishable body but *incarnation*, in all the gravity of an identity that is altered in itself. Here we are inside and already beyond the Cartesian dualism of thought and extension in man. The taste and the odor of decay would here not be added to the spirituality of a tragic knowledge, nor to some sort of pre-sentiment or expectation, albeit desperate, of death. Despair despairs like a disease of the flesh. Physical pain or evil [*mal physique*] is the very depth of anguish and consequently—Philippe Nemo shows this through the verses of Job—anguish, in its carnal acuteness, is the root of all social misery, of all human dereliction; of humiliation, solitude, persecution.

But in the analysis offered us here, this conjunction of evil and anguish does not receive the meaning to which we have become accustomed by the philosophers of existence, and of which Heidegger—at least the Hei-degger of *Sein und Zeit*—has traced the model most clearly. What is es-sential to anguish consisted, then, in opening the horizon of nothingness, more radically negative than that of negation, incapable of causing the forgetting of the being that it denies. The death which anguish under-stood is announced as pure nothingness. Now, what appeared to us strongest and most novel in Nemo's book is the discovery of another di-mension of meaning in the conjunction of anguish and evil. To be sure, evil will signify an "end" of the world, but an end that, in a very signifi-cant fashion, leads beyond; elsewhere than to being, certainly, but also elsewhere than to nothingness, to a *beyond* that neither negation nor the anguish of the philosophers of existence conceived. Evil is neither a world, nor a species, nor some sort of perfection of negation. Why then this insis-tence upon anguish at the depths of evil? We will return to this question.

In evil's malignancy, it is excess. Though the notion of excess evokes from the first the quantitative idea of intensity—by its degree surpassing all measure—evil is excess in its very quiddity. Here is a very important remark: evil is not excess because suffering can be strong and thus go beyond what is bearable. The rupture with the normal and the normative, with order, with synthesis, with the world, already constitutes its qualitative essence. Suffering, as suffering, is but a concrete and quasi-sensible manifestation of the nonintegratable, or the unjustifiable. The "quality" of evil is this *non-integratableness* itself, if we may use such a term. The concrete quality is defined by this abstract notion of evil. Evil is not only the non-integratable, it is also the non-integratableness of the non-integratable. It is as if, opposed to synthesis—though it be the purely formal synthesis of the Kantian "I think," and capable of joining together the *given*, however heterogeneous that might be—were found the non-synthesizable, in the form of evil, as still more heterogeneous than any heterogeneity subject to the embrace of the formal, exposing heterogeneity in its very malignancy. As though Bergson's teaching, in *Creative Evolution*, on disorder as an order that is other, were contradicted by evil, like an irreducible derangement. Quite remarkably, that which is purely quantitative in the notion of excess is shown in the form of a qualitative content characteristic of the malignancy of evil, as the quiddity of a phenomenon. In the appearing of evil, in its original phenomenality, in its *quality*, there is announced a *modality* or a manner: it is the not-finding-a-place, the refusal of any accommodation with... , a counter-nature, a monstrosity, the disturbing and foreign in itself. *And in this sense transcendence!* Within the pure quality of the phenomenon of evil, the intuition that consists in catching sight of the *how* of the rupture of immanence is a view that appears to us as rich intellectually as the rediscovery, at the beginning of phenomenology, of intentionality, or the brilliant pages on *Zuhandenheit* and *Stimmung* in *Sein und Zeit*.[4] But these are, perhaps, private impressions that belong only to the lesser, and anecdotal, history of phenomenology!

   The exteriority or transcendence in evil does not receive its meaning in opposition to psychic "interiority." It does not borrow its meaning from some sort of prior correlation of exteriority and interiority that would make possible the illusion of multiple worlds behind the world, accumulating nevertheless in the same space. It is in the *excess* of *evil* that the prefix *ex-* signfies in its original sense, as exceeding [*excession*] itself, as the *ex-* of all exteriority. No categorial *form* could invest it, none could hold it within its framework. The "wholly other," beyond the community of the common, is no longer a simple term! It is the *other*, an "other scene," as Nemo calls it, because it is more foreign to the consciousness of being-in-the-world than the scene of the unconscious, which is simply other, a fold of provisional alterity and one that psychoanalysis knows how to unfold within the world.

That transcendence be the unjustifiable, whose concrete event would be the malignancy of evil, is perhaps the entire meaning of the derisory theodicy of the friends of Job. Their idea of justice would proceed from a morality of reward and punishment, from a certain already technological order of the world. Moreover, is not every attempt at a theodicy simply a way of thinking of God as the reality of the world?

Does not the evil in which Philippe Nemo distinguishes anguish get its sense of excess and transcendence independently of anguish? Does it not obtain that signification by way of the unjustifiable, which is the malignancy of evil, or by the resistance that it opposes to theodicy, rather than by way of its being-unto-death which anguish anticipates? We have already pondered this. But is it so certain, after all, that the essence of death, which is fulfilled in anguish, must be thought, according to the description of *Sein und Zeit*, as nothingness? Is the secret about death not phenomenologically inherent in death and the anguish of dying? Is it not a modality, or the anticipated sharpness [*acumen*], of suffering—and not the solution to the dilemma: to be or not to be?[5]

The You

Evil's content would not be exhausted by the notion of excess.[6] Guided by exegesis—but laying claim to an intrinsic significance—the analysis, in a second moment, discovers an "intention" there: evil reaches me as if it sought me, evil strikes me as if there were an aim underlying the bad destiny that pursues me, "as if someone were dead set against me," as if there were malice, as if there were someone. Evil, of itself, would be an "aiming at me." It would reach me in a wound from which a meaning arises and a *saying* is articulated, recognizing this someone who is thus revealed. "Why do you [*pourquoi toi*] make me suffer and not reserve for me, rather, an eternal happiness?" A first saying, a first question or first lamentation or first prayer. In any case, this is the summons of a You [*Toi*] and the glimpse of the Good behind Evil. A first "intentionality" of transcendence: someone is searching for me. A God who causes pain, but God as a You [*Toi*]. And, by the evil in me, my awakening to myself. "A waking of the soul in the excess of evil," says Nemo. From his state of subjectivity in the world, from his being-in-the-world, the I is awakened to the condition of the soul that summons God. This idea of suffering as persecution and election in persecution, and of the setting apart and the distinction in pain, is certainly not as communicable from a phenomenology, nor as universal, as the idea of the excess in evil. We have reason to think that it is inspired by more than the peculiarities of the book of Job.

That the original "intentionality" of the relationship between beings might be a relationship with God, that it might come from God; that this relation could not be described in a neutral and formal fashion; that it might from the outset be qualified as a "to cause me pain," like a maliciousness in the somber paradox of the wickedness of God; that the original—that the principal—be neither the general, nor the formal, but the *concrete and the determinate* (not to be taken in an empirical sense), is striking enough here, and remains consistent with the spirit of the analysis that was able to discover transcendence and excess in the concreteness of evil. Yet, at the same time, the "element" in which "first philosophy" moves is no longer the impersonal, the anonymous, the indifferent, the neutral unfolding of being approached—even in the humanity that it encompasses—as a world of things and laws, or as a world of stones, a world bearing every intervention and as if liable to *satis*-fy whatever desire by way of the intervention of technology. The latter supposes only the legality of things, their equality to our desires, and the ruse of thought. The first metaphysical question is no longer Leibniz's question—"Why is there something rather than nothing?"—but "Why is there evil rather than good?" (Nemo, 155). This is the deneutralization of being or the beyond being. The ontological difference is preceded by the difference of good and evil. *The* difference is the latter; it is that which is the origin of the meaningful [*sensé*]: "that which concerns the alternative of the good and of extreme evil has meaning for a soul in waiting" (Nemo, 212).[7] Meaning begins, therefore, in the relation of the soul to God, starting from its being awakened by evil. God hurts me to tear me from the world as unique and ex-ceptional: as a soul. Meaning implies this transcendent relation as "the alterity of the other scene," which is no longer a negative concept. "The meaning of the alterity of the other scene," writes Nemo (212), "is good and evil insofar as they exceed the world and orient it. The 'difference' that exists between one scene and the other is the difference of good from evil. Any other 'difference' is internal to the world."

We would put this as the priority of the ethical relative to the ontological, although Philippe Nemo need not care for this formula in order to qualify his path. In effect, despite a notion of difference that is not ontological, the discovery of the You, summoned in evil, is interpreted by way of recourse to being. "God who appears in the You has, as His being, to be a You." The You in God is not an "otherwise than being," but a "being otherwise." The reflection on the You does not venture to the point of thinking in him a beyond of being. This reflection subordinates itself to ontology, recoiling before its supreme infidelity to the philosophy that was handed to us, for which a being, and the being of beings, are the ultimate sources of the meaningful. To keep oneself in relation with the You, who in God *eclipses* being, would be pejoratively interpreted as a manner of taking pleasure in illusion. One will not dare think[8] that the human psyche, in its relation to God, ventures all the way to significations of the beyond of being and nothingness, beyond reality and illusion; all the way to dis-inter-*estedness*.[9]

Theophany

Evil as excess, evil as intention: there is a third moment in this phenomenology: evil as hatred of evil. A last reversal of the analysis: evil strikes me in my horror of evil and thus reveals—or is already—my association with the Good. The excess of evil by which it is in surplus to the world is also the impossibility of our accepting it. The experience of evil would thus also be our waiting for the good—the love of God.

This reverting of evil and of the horror of evil into an awaiting of the Good, of God, and of a beatitude on the measure, or the beyond-measure, of the excess of evil presented in the last pages of this beautiful and suggestive book, poses a number of questions. Is this horror of evil—in which, paradoxically, evil is given—the Good? Here it cannot be a question of a passage from Evil to the Good by an attraction of contraries. That would be an additional theodicy. Does not the philosophical contribution of this entire biblical exegesis consist in being able to go as if beyond the reciprocal call of terms that negate each other, beyond the di-

alectic? Evil, precisely, is not any species of negation. It signifies the excess, refusing every synthesis where the wholly-otherness [*tout-altérité*] of
God shall come to be shown. Also present to Nemo is the Nietzschean
warning against the spirit of resentment. He would not want, at the end
of his hermeneutic, a good that would only signify a redemption of evil
or a vengeance that would also be equivalent to a return of the technical
spirit in the suffering of evil. From this comes, in the description of the
anticipation of the Good, the formulation, to our mind quite profound,
of a thought that would think more than what it can think: "the soul,"
writes Nemo (231), "knows henceforth that the end that it intends, the
beatific encounter with God, surpasses infinitely that which it intends."
The soul that, awakened by evil, finds itself in relation to the beyond of
the world, does not return to the manner [*facture*] of a being-in-the-world,
of an empirical or transcendental consciousness *equaling* its objects, *adequate* to being, making itself equal to the world in its desires promised to
satis-faction. The soul beyond satisfaction and reward awaits an awaited
which infinitely surpasses the awaiting. There lies, no doubt, the "psychic
modality" of transcendence and the very definition of the religious soul,
which would not be a simple specification of consciousness. The notion
of the "game" that by opposition to technique designates for our author
the relationship of the soul to God is nevertheless not deduced from this
disproportion between the awaiting and the awaited. "Only the excess of
beatitude," he writes, "will respond to the excess of evil." Now, it is not
certain that the excess is said in the same sense in the two parts of this
proposition. The excess of evil does not signify an excessive evil, whereas
the excess of beatitude remains a superlative notion. If it were necessary,
in effect, to see an excess already in beatitude as such, then evil would not
be able to have the privileged meaning around which all of Nemo's book
is constructed. Transcendence could then follow paths less tortuous.

Does not the movement leading from the "horror of evil" to the discovery of the Good—which thus completes in a theophany the transcendence opened in the totality of the world by the concrete "content" of
evil—lead only to the opposite of evil and to a goodness of simple pleasure, however great this might be? Does not the Good, anticipated in this
"awaiting that intends infinitely more than this awaited," maintain a relationship less distant with the evil that suggests it, while differing from it
with a difference more different than opposition? In reading this commentary of the book of Job, which is so concerned about the texts and

their implications, so concerned about the said and the unsaid, so deli-
cate in its listening and its intelli-gence, one is astonished that there never
appears *in the foreground* the problem of the relation between the suffering of the I and the suffering that an I can feel before the suffering of the
other man. Even if we suppose that in this biblical text itself it is never a
question of this problem, would there not be in this very silence some secret indication? Is it really never a question of this problem? What about
the question, "Where wast thou when I laid the foundations of the
earth?" in Chapter 38, verse 4, at the beginning of the discourse attributed to God, which recalls to Job his absence at the hour of Creation?
Does this question address only the impudence of a creature who allows
himself to judge the Creator? Does this expound only a theodicy, wherein
the economy of a harmonious and knowingly arranged totality only har-
bors evil for the limited gaze of a part of this whole? Can one not hear in
this "Where were you?" a statement of deficiency that cannot have meaning unless the humanity of man is fraternally bound up with creation,
that is, responsible for that which has been neither his I nor his work?
Might this solidarity and this responsibility for any and all—which cannot be without pain—be spirit itself?

We are not going to propose "ameliorations" to Philippe Nemo, whose
thought is so personal, so new, and so mature. It is rather in the context
of his thought that there is illumined singularly an idea familiar and dear
to us, and often restated, and to which we willingly associate the light his
work brings to the paths of transcendence and to the manner by which
this light is borne. It is borne by recourse to a "material datum" of consciousness, to a "concrete content," rather than by reflection upon some
"formal structure." Thus is signified a "beyond" to the closed dimensions
sketched by the judgments of the intellect and reflected by the forms of
logic.[10] In effect, it is in the same way that transcendence appeared to us
to shine from the face of the other man: an alterity of the non-integratable, of that which does not let itself be assembled into a totality, or of
that which, in the assembly—unless it undergoes violence and powers—
remains in society and enters there as a face. This is a transcendence that
is no longer absorbed by my knowledge. The face puts into question the
sufficiency of my identity as an I, it compels me to an infinite responsibility toward another. An original transcendence signifying in the *concreteness, which is ethical from the outset*, of the face. Is there not a breakthrough of the Good, there, where the evil suffered by the other man

could reach me in the evil that pursues me? Is it not that this evil might touch me, as if, from the first, the other man appealed to me, placing in question my *resting upon myself* and my *conatus essendi*; is it not as if, before lamenting my trouble on earth, I had to respond for the other? *Does not the Good break through there, in evil, in the "intention" of which, so exclusively in my pain, I am the addressee?* Theophany. Revelation. This is the horror of the evil that addresses me becoming the horror of suffering in the other man. A breakthrough of the Good which is not a simple inversion of Evil, but an elevation. A Good that is not pleasant, which commands and prescribes. The obedience to prescription—and already that of listening and understanding, which are the first obediences—implies no other reward than this very elevation of the dignity of soul; and disobedience implies no punishment if not that of the rupture itself with the Good. A service indifferent to remuneration! No failure could release me from this responsibility for the suffering of the other man. This responsibility remains meaningful despite failure. It is wholly contrary to the calculative thoughts [*pensées techniques*] out of which, if we believe Nemo, evil calls us back to our lives as human souls.

Ambiguity

The knowledge of the world—thematization—certainly does not abandon the game. It attempts to reduce, and succeeds at reducing, the disturbance of the Same by the Other. Thematization reestablishes the order troubled by Evil and by the Other through the history into which it agrees to enter. Yet fissures reappear in the established order. Our modernity would not depend solely upon the certitudes of History and Nature, but upon an alternation: Recovery and Rupture; Knowledge and Sociality. This is an alternation where the moment of recovery is not more true than that of rupture; wherein laws have no more sense than the face-to-face with the neighbor. This does not attest to a simple flaw in synthesis, but would define time itself, time in its enigmatic diachrony: a tendency without an outcome, an intending without coincidence. It would signify the ambiguity of an incessant adjournment or the progression of holding and possession. But it also signifies the approach of an infinite God, an approach that is His proximity.

PART III

The Meaning of Being

§ Dialogue

Self-Consciousness and Proximity
of the Neighbor

The value that an entire series of philosophers, theologians and moralists, politicians, and even public opinion, attach to the notion, or to the practice—and, in any case, to the word—of dialogue, to the discourse that men facing each other hold between them, summoning one another and exchanging statements and objections, questions and answers, attests to a new orientation toward the idea that Western society has had of the essence of the meaningful and the spiritual. This is perhaps a result of the trials of the twentieth century since the First World War. It is thus not out of the question, in our time, to speak of a philosophy of dialogue and oppose it to the philosophical tradition of the unity of the I or the system, and self-sufficiency, and immanence. The work of Martin Buber and Franz Rosenzweig in Germany, that of Gabriel Marcel in France, and their influence in the world—but also the many remarkable works signed by less illustrious names—justify this manner of speaking.

Spirit as Knowledge, and Immanence

It is in the psyche, conceived as knowledge—to the point of self-consciousness—that the received philosophy situates the origin or the natural place of what is meaningful, and recognizes spirit. Does not all that occurs in the human psyche, and all that takes place there, end up by being known? That which is secret and unconscious, repressed or altered, is still measured or healed through the very consciousness that these things have lost, or which has lost them. All that is lived is expressed legitimately as *experience*. It is converted into "received lessons" that converge into a unity of knowledge, whatever their dimensions and modalities: contemplation, will, affectivity; or sensibility and understanding; or external perception, self-consciousness and reflection on self; or objectivizing thematization and familiarity with that which is not pro-posed; or primary and secondary qualities, kinesthetic and cenesthetic sensations. The relations with the neighbor, the social group, and God would again be collective and religious *experiences*. Even reduced to the indetermination of *living* and to the familiarity of pure *existing*, of pure being, the psyche *lives* this or that, *is* this or that, on the mode of *seeing* or of feeling, as if *to live* and *to be* were transitive verbs and *this* and *that* their direct objects. It is this implicit knowledge, doubtless, which justifies the wide use that Descartes makes of the term *cogito* in the *Meditations*. And this first person verb expresses well the *unity* of the I, where all knowledge is adequate to itself.

As knowledge, thought relates to what is thinkable, that is, the thinkable called being. Relating to being, thought is outside itself, but remains marvelously in itself, or returns to itself. The exteriority or alterity of oneself is taken up again into immanence. That which thought knows, or what it learns in its "experience," is at once the *other* and the *property* [*propre*] of thought. One learns only that which one already knows, and that which attaches to the interiority of thought in the manner of a memory that can be evoked or re-presented. Reminiscence and imaginings assure something like the synchrony and the unity of that which, in experience subject to time, is lost or is only to come.

As learning, thought entails a grasping [*saisie*], a *hold* on what is learned, and a possession. The "grasping" of learning is not purely metaphorical. Even before technical interestedness, this learning is already an outline of an incarnate practice, already "hands on" ["*mainmise*"]. Presence becomes main-tenance.[1] Can even the most abstract lesson dispense with any manual hold on the things of the "life world," the famous *Lebenswelt*? The being that appears to the I of cognition not only instructs it, but *gives* itself *ipso facto* to it. Already perception grasps; and the *Begriff* [concept] preserves this meaning of ascendancy. The "*giving* itself"—whatever the efforts that the distance "from the cup to the lip" requires—is on the scale of thought thinking; through its "transcendence," it promises to thought a possession and an enjoyment, a satisfaction, as though thinking thought to its measure through the fact of being able—as incarnate thought—to rejoin what it thought. The thinking and the psyche of immanence: self-sufficiency. This is precisely the phenomenon of the world: viz., the fact that an accord is assured in the grasping, between what is thinkable and the thinking; the fact that its appearing is also a *giving itself,* and that knowledge of the world is a satisfaction; as though this knowledge filled a need. Perhaps it is this that Husserl is expressing when he affirms a correlation—which is *the* correlation—between thought and the world. Husserl describes theoretical knowledge in its most perfected forms—objectivizing and thematizing knowledge—as filling the measure of the intention, or as empty intentionality filling itself.

The works of Hegel, into which all the currents of the Western spirit have come to flow, and in which all its levels are manifested, is at once a philosophy of absolute knowledge and of the satisfied man. The psyche of theoretical knowledge constitutes a thought that thinks to its measure and, in its adequation to what is thinkable, equals itself and shall be conscious of itself. It is the Same that finds itself anew in the Other.

The activity of thought *has reason* over every alterity and it is therein, ultimately, that its very rationality resides. Conceptual synthesis and synopsis are stronger than the dispersion and the incompatibility of what is given as other, as *before,* and as *after.* Dispersion and incompatibility refer back to the unity of the subject and of the transcendental apperception of the *I think.* Hegel writes, in the *Wissenschaft der Logik,* "It is to the deepest and most accurate views of the *Critique of Pure Reason* that the view belongs, which consists in recognizing the unity that constitutes the *essence of the concept* as an originally synthetic unity of apperception, as a unity of the *I think,* or the consciousness of self."[2] The unity of the *I think* is the ultimate form of spirit as knowledge, though it might be confounded with the being that it knows, and identified with the system of knowledge.

The unity of the *I think* is the ultimate form of spirit as knowledge. And to this unity of the *I think* all things are referred, constituting a system. The system of what is intelligible is, ultimately, a consciousness of self.

The Dialogue of Immanence

The *I think* in which being-in-act is constituted can be interpreted as coinciding with what it constitutes: the full self-consciousness of the *I think* would be the very *system* of knowledge in its unity of intelligibility.

The thinking thought that tends toward this order of reason will express itself consequently, despite the labor of its research and the genius of its invention, as a detour which the system of being takes to put itself in order. This is a detour that its terms and structures follow to arrange and secure themselves [*s'arrimer*]. Such is *spirit*, not only according to Hegel, where the process of knowing is "the movement of being itself" (*Logik*); nor merely according to our contemporary structuralist objectivism. In Husserlian phenomenology—despite the creative spontaneity conferred upon the transcendental Ego—the modes of knowledge are commanded, as the teleology of consciousness, essentially by the being [*l'être*] to which consciousness accedes. The spirit is the order of things—or the things in order—of which thinking thought would only be the recollection and the ordering. The possibility or hope that the *I think* would have, no longer to posit itself for itself over against the thinkable, to efface itself before the intelligible, would be its own intelligence, its rationality, and ultimate internalization.

An accord and a unity of knowledge in the truth. The thought ever thinking seeks these by diverse paths. It certainly resorts to words. But these are signs that thought gives to itself without speaking to anyone. In its work of assembly, thought may have to search for a presence of the thinkable beyond that which presents itself immediately, "in flesh and blood" (*leiblich da*)[3] or in images, or for the presence of a signified through a sign. It may have to search for what is not yet present to thought, but which is already no longer closed up in itself. That there be no thought without language does not signify, consequently, the necessity of an internal discourse. Thought divides itself in order to question itself and to respond, but the thread is again tied up. Thought *reflects* upon itself by interrupting its spontaneous progression, but it still proceeds from the same *I think*. It remains the same. It passes from one term to a contrary one that calls to it, but the dialectic in which it finds itself is not a dialogue or, at least, it is the dialogue of the soul with itself, proceeding by questions and answers. Plato defines thought in precisely this way. According to the traditional interpretation of the internal discourse, which goes back to this definition, the spirit thinking remains no less one and unique, despite its movements and its going and coming, whereby it can oppose itself to itself.

It is through the empirical multiplicity of thinking men that the language that is effectively spoken would circulate. Yet even there, this language is comprehended in its subordination to knowing. For each of the interlocutors, this language consists in entering into the thought of the other, in coinciding in *reason*, and in internalizing itself there. In opposition to the "interiority" of sly passions and the secret perfidy of subjective opinions, Reason would be the true inner life. Reason is one. It has no one left with whom to communicate; nothing is outside of it. And consequently, Reason is like the silence of inner discourse. The questions and the answers of such an "exchange of ideas" reproduce or stage anew those of a dialogue that the soul holds with itself. Thinking subjects would amount to multiple obscure points around which a clarity is created when they speak to and rediscover one another, in the same way that, in inner discourse, the thread of thought that had to question itself is retied. In this clarity, the obscure points of the various I's pale, fade, but are also sublimated. This exchange of ideas will hold ultimately within a single soul, in a single consciousness, in the *cogito* that Reason remains. One can call this conversation dialogue, wherein the interlocutors enter, the ones into the thought of the others; wherein the dialogue brings someone to reason [*faire entendre raison*]. One can call "sociality" the unity of the multiple consciousnesses that have entered into the same thought in which their reciprocal alterity is suppressed. This is the famous dialogue that is called to stop violence by bringing the interlocutors to reason, establishing peace in unanimity, and suppressing proximity in coincidence. The path of predilection of Western humanism. A nobility of idealist renunciation! To be sure. But it would only be possible in a Spinozistic universe of pure love of truth and intelligibility. An effacement before truth, but also a power of domination and a possibility of cunning: a knowledge of the other as of an object prior to any social existence [*socialité*] with that other. Yet consequently also a power acquired over him as over a thing and, through language, a power that ought to lead to the unique reason all the temptations of a deceitful rhetoric, of publicity and of propaganda. Yet we must above all wonder whether the elevation of this peace by the Reason relished by noble souls owes nothing to the prior non-indifference to the other man; whether it owes nothing to the social life with him which would be a relation to the neighbor, a relation other than the representation one can form of his being, other than the pure knowledge of his existence, his nature and his spirituality. We must ask ourselves whether the dynamism and exaltation of peace by truth derives uniquely from the suppression of alterity and not just as much from the very possibility of the Encounter with the other as other (perhaps thanks to a dialogue preceding reason), for which a common truth is the pretext.

Be that as it may, the great problem placed in the path of those who expect the end of violence starting from a dialogue that would only need to perfect knowledge is the difficulty, by Plato's own admission, of bringing to this dialogue opposed beings inclined to do violence to each other. It would be necessary to find a dialogue to make these beings enter into dialogue. That is, unless we suppose the prior unity of a sovereign and divine knowledge, or of a substance that thinks itself and that would have burst into a multiplicity of consciousnesses, sufficiently masters of themselves, limited in their horizons, opposed by their differences, and hostile to each other—yet which find themselves, from conflict to conflict, compelled or led to the dialogues that ought to permit, by degrees, the convergence of gazes starting from multiple points of view, all of which being necessary nonetheless to the plenitude of a thought rediscovering its lost sovereignty and *unity*, its *I think*, or its *system*.

The very birth of language could, consequently, be sought starting from knowledge. This birth would be logically and perhaps chronologically posterior to it. In the empirical multiplicity of beings existing as intentional and incarnate consciousnesses, each one would have knowledge and consciousness of "something" and of its own consciousness. However, it would arrive, by appresentative experiences and by *Einfühlung* [empathy], at an awareness of other consciousnesses; that is, at a knowledge that each consciousness other than itself had, of the same "something," of it itself, and of all the other consciousnesses. In this way communication would be established: the signs of language would be born from all the expressive manifestations of bodies signifying in appresentation. The Husserlian theory of the constitution of intersubjectivity can be considered a rigorous formulation of the subordination of language to knowledge, reducing to the lived *qua experience* every modality independent of meaning to which dialogue could lay claim. In a characteristic and remarkable text of his *Krisis*, Husserl goes to the point of claiming "to take lodging in the internal discourse, the discourse which goes toward all the others." "That which I am there stating scientifically," he writes, "is said from me to me, but at the same time, in a paradoxical fashion, I say it to all the others inasmuch as they are implicated transcendentally in me and the ones in the others."[4]

The Hegelian way of deducing the multiplicity of consciousnesses, recognizing each other mutually and thus communicating among themselves, from a march toward absolute knowledge in the celebrated pages of the *Phenomenology of Spirit*, again proceeds from this priority of knowledge over dialogue. But it is—in an ontological context quite different from that of Husserlian phenomenology—a speculative effort to found, in thought, the opposition of this multiplicity, while even the necessity to resort to this grounded moment signifies the impossibility of language's staying within the dimensions of the *cogito*.

Dialogue and Transcendence

Contemporary philosophy of dialogue insists upon a wholly other dimension of meaning that opens in language: upon the interhuman relation or the original sociality produced in dialogue. This would have a signification by itself and would constitute a spiritual authenticity of its own. The multiplicity of thinking beings, the plurality of consciousnesses, is not a simple fact—some sort of contingency, or a purely empirical "misfortune"—like the effect of some fall or ontological catastrophe of the One. The social existence that language establishes between souls is not compensation for a unity of thought that would have been lost or missed. Quite the contrary, beyond the sufficiency of the being-for-itself another possibility of excellence is shown in the human dimension that is not measured by the perfection of the consciousness-of-self. In effect, early in his work, Gabriel Marcel denounced in his *Journal Métaphysique* what he called "the eminent value of *autarchy*," or the sufficiency unto oneself, in order to affirm that "only a relation of a being to a being can be called spiritual."[5]

In the new reflection, the sociality of language is no longer reducible to the transmission of types of knowledge among the multiple I's and to their confrontation, in which this knowledge is raised to the universal intelligibility into which these thinking I's would be absorbed, or sublimated, or united in order to "finally suffice unto themselves" by way of this unity of Reason. For Marcel, the relationship among thinking beings would have a meaning: sociality. It would have this meaning in the summons of a You by an I, in what Buber calls by the primary word "I-Thou," which would be the principle and the basis—uttered or implicit—of all dialogue. This word would be radically distinguished from the other primary word, "I-It."[6] The latter would express the knowledge of an I investing an "object" in its neutrality submissive to the act of knowledge that assimilates it and by which, according to Husserlian terminology, the assimilated object fills intentions. The "I-It" would designate the *subject* of idealist philosophy in relation with the world, referring to things and to humans treated as things. It would designate within discourse itself the reference of the Saying [*Dire*] to these realities and to the conjunctures that the Saying narrates or exhibits.

What is significant in this distinction is the original and irreducible character of the fundamental word, I-Thou: the I-It, as knowledge, does not found the I-Thou. The new philosophy of dialogue teaches that to invoke or to summon the other man as a *you* [*tu*], and to speak to him, does not depend upon a prior *experience* of the other; it does not derive, in any case, the meaning of the "you" from this experience. The sociality of dialogue is not a knowledge of sociality, dialogue is not the experience of the conjunction between men who speak to one another. Dialogue would be an event of spirit, at least as irreducible and as old as the *cogito*. In effect, for Buber, the Thou *par excellence* is invoked in the invisible Eternal Thou—nonobjectifiable, unthematizable—of God. For Gabriel Marcel, to name God in the third person would be to miss Him. There would be in dialogue, in the I-You, beyond the spirituality of knowledge that is *filled* by the *world* and in the world, the opening of transcendence.

Simultaneously, in dialogue is hollowed out an absolute distance between the I and the You, absolutely separated by the inexpressible secret of their intimacy, each being unique in its kind as *I* and as *you*, each one absolutely other in relation to the other, without common measure or domain available for some sort of coincidence (an inexpressible secret that is the other for me; a secret to which, for all time, I accede only by appresentation; a mode of existing of the other as other). On the other hand, it is also there that unfolds—or intervenes, disposing the *I* as I and the *you* as you—the extraordinary and immediate relation of dia-logue, which transcends this distance without suppressing it or recuperating it, as does the gaze that crosses the distance separating it from an object in the world, while comprehending and encompassing that distance. Here is a way of acceding to the other different from that of knowing him: to approach the neighbor.

Perhaps in thinking of the remarkable distinction Franz Rosenzweig makes in the human, between the *individual* belonging to the world and

always comparable to another individual, and *ipseity* (*die Selbstheit*);[7] in thinking of the solitude of the *Selbstheit* in which the I stands (and, to our mind, for which the secret of its psyche is the "how")—perhaps this is how we shall be able to measure, despite the relations among individuals, the ontological separation between human beings and appreciate the transcendence that gapes between them. We shall be able to measure, consequently, the extra-ordinary transitivity of dialogue or proximity, and the supra-ontological—or religious—signification of sociality or human proximity. The solitude of *Selbstheit*, according to Rosenzweig, must not be understood as Heidegger does, who makes it a *modus deficiens* of *Mitsein*.[8] In Rosenzweig, it would concern an *isolation* coming in no way from oneself and having no memory of community, yet an isolation foreign also to the separation of things that, as individuals, already belong "without knowing each other" to a common genus. It would concern a "nothing in common with anyone or anything" isolation, which has no need, we add incidentally, for a "transcendental reduction" of some kind to signify an "out of the world."

Absolute distance: one would be wrong to think of this as a logician would do, in the purely formal notion of a gap between terms of some sort, already distinct inasmuch as the one is not the other. The distance or absolute alterity of transcendence signifies *by itself* the difference and the relationship between the I and the You as interlocutors, in relation to which the notion of a "term of some sort" of the "something in general" (*etwas überhaupt*) is a formal abstraction. The concrete is the absolute distance and the relation of dialogue, older than any distinction of terms in any sort of conjunction. This absolute distance is refractory to the synthesis that the synoptic gaze of a third would like to establish between two human beings in dialogue. The I *and* the You are not embraceable objectively, there is no *and* possible between them, they form no totality. There is no unity that might be produced in the mind of a third party "over their heads" or "behind their backs," and which might here form an assemblage—just as there is not, from I to You, a thematization of the You or an experience of the You. The "You" is not an "objectification" where one would have merely steered clear of the reification of the other man. The Encounter, or proximity, or sociality, is not of the same order as experience.

But in the saying [*le dire*] of the dialogue, in the summons of a You by the I, an extra-ordinary and immediate passage is cleared, stronger than

any ideal tie and any synthesis that the *I think* would accomplish in aspiring to equal and comprehend. This is a passage where there is no further passage. It is precisely because the *You* is absolutely other than the I that there is, between the one and the other, dialogue. There perhaps lies the paradoxical message of all philosophy of dialogue, or a way of defining spirit by transcendence, that is, by sociality, by the immediate relation to the other. A relation different from all the ties that are established within a world where thought, as knowledge, thinks to its measure, where perception and conception grasp and appropriate the given and take satisfaction from it. This is a relation that, for Buber, is *the* Relation and which was "in the beginning." Language would not be there to *express* states of consciousness, it would be the incomparable spiritual event of transcendence and sociality to which any effort of expression—any wanting to communicate a thought content—already refers. Franz Rosenzweig understands it at the level of Revelation in the eminent and religious sense of the term, which signifies for him the setting in relation of the elements of the absolute, which are isolated and refractory to synthesis and to assembly in a totality; refractory to some sort of conjunction in which they lose—as in idealism—their very life.

One may legitimately ask oneself whether the internal discourse of the *cogito* is not already a derivative mode of the conversation with the other; whether the linguistic symbolism that the soul uses in "conversing with itself" does not suppose a dialogue with an interlocutor other than itself; whether the very interruption of the spontaneous impulse of thought reflecting upon itself, all the way to the dialectical alternations of reasoning where my thought separates from and rejoins itself as if it were other than itself—whether this interruption does not bear witness to an *original and foregoing* dialogue. We may wonder, consequently, whether knowledge itself and all consciousness does not begin in language. Even if dialogue itself ends by *knowing itself*—as is attested at least by the pages the philosophers devote to this—it is reflection that discovers it. But reflection, which supposes the suspension of the spontaneity of life, already supposes its being placed in question by the Other [*l'Autre*], which would not have been possible without a prior dialogue, without the encounter with another [*d'autrui*].

Posited before the unity of the *self-consciousness*, which is equal to itself and makes itself equal to the world, is thus the encounter in dialogue which would be a thought thinking beyond the world. There is in this

radical difference between the I and the You, placed in the relationship of dialogue wherein the encounter is formed, not a simple failure of recognition of the one by the other, or of the synthesis of their coincidence and their identification. There is, rather, the surplus or the *better* of a beyond oneself, the surplus and the better of the *proximity* of the neighbor; "better" than the coincidence with self, despite or because of the difference separating them. "More" or "better," signified in dialogue, not by some supernatural voice interfering in the conversation, nor by some prejudgment. "More" or "better than" would be the gratuitous gift or the grace of the other's coming to meet me, of which Buber speaks. Yet the surplus of fraternity can go beyond the *satisfactions* that one still expects from gifts received, even if gratuitous! This the philosophers of dialogue do not always say, although this would certainly be the essential idea they have made possible. Dialogue is the non-indifference of the *you* to the *I*, a dis-inter-ested sentiment certainly capable of degenerating into hatred, but a chance for what we must—perhaps with prudence—call love and resemblance in love. In saying this, one is not duped by morality or naively subject to the ideas and values of an environment. It is in the dialogue of transcendence that the idea of the good rises, merely by the fact itself that, in the encounter, the *other counts* above all else. The Relationship where the I encounters the You is the original place and circumstance of the ethical coming [*avènement*]. The ethical fact owes nothing to values; it is values that owe everything to the ethical fact. The concreteness of the Good is the worth [*le valoir*] of the other man. It is only to some formalization that the ambivalence of worth appears, as undecidable, at equal distance between Good and Evil. In the worth of the other man, the Good is more ancient than Evil.

Dialogue is thus not merely a way of speaking. Its significance has a general reach. It is transcendence. The saying involved in dialogue would not be one of the possible forms of transcendence but its original mode. Better again, transcendence has no meaning except by way of an I saying You. It is the *dia* of the dialogue. In the concrete context of the human, transcendence is thus a concept at least as valuable as that of immanence in the world, the ultimacy of which transcendence places in question. Contrary to the celebrated Heideggerian analyses, the fact of humanity approached from dialogue would reintroduce into philosophic reflection the *beyond* the world, without this signifying a simple recourse to what Nietzsche calls "the worlds behind the world" in the sense of traditional metaphysics. There lie new structures and conceptualization, having the resonance of a general philosophy beyond the anthropological and theological thematic. Buber shall insist upon the novel and primordial[9] pattern of the relation that one cannot close up within the psyche of the I or the You. It is the *between* (*Zwischen*), an origin that disposes the I as I and the You as You, and which evidently could not be understood anew as a third instance, a subject, or a substance that would here play a mediating role. This signifies a break not only with psychology but also with the ontological notions of both substance and subject, in order to assert a new modality of the between-the-two, itself signifying the ontology and the psyche of co-presence and of sociality. Above... rather than between-the-two.

Although the systematic significance of the new analysis of dialogue may be essential, its anthropological signification and its theological aspect must be underscored. One can not evoke here all the concrete descriptions to which the philosophical literature relative to dialogue gives rise. To the phenomenology of intentionality is juxtaposed something like a phenomenology of the Relation, often taking on a negative appearance. Thus, to the irreversible "polarity" of the intentional act—*ego-cogito-cogitatum*, where the *ego* pole can not be converted into the object pole—one opposes the reversibility or the reciprocity of the I-You: the I says "you" to a You who, as an I, says "you" to the I. The *activity* of the saying in the dialogue is *ipso facto* the passivity of the listening, the word in its very spontaneity is exposed to the response; the you is summoned as "exclusivity" and as not belonging to the world, even if the encounter itself is in the world; whereas intentionality approaches the object always against the horizon of the world. That a human spirituality might be possible which does not begin in knowledge, or in the psyche as experience, and that the relation to the you in its purity be the relation to the invisible God, is no doubt a new view on the human psyche, which was already emphasized above. Yet this is also very important for the orientation of theology: the God of prayer, of invocation, would be more ancient than the God deduced from the world or from some sort of *a priori* radiance and stated in an indicative proposition. The old biblical theme of man made in the image of God takes on a new meaning, but it is in the "you" and not in the "I" that this resemblance is announced. The very movement that leads to another leads to God.

It is in the extension of the I-Thou relationship and that of the social existence with man that, for Buber, the relation to God is produced. There also is the probable recovery of the biblical theme in which divine epiphany is always awaited starting from the encounter with the other man, who is approached as a you beginning from ethics. Need one recall texts such as Chapter 58 of Isaiah? Need one recall the perhaps less celebrated pages of the Pentateuch? In a significant way, the formula "fear of God" appears there in a series of verses that especially enjoin respect for man and concern for the neighbor; as if the order to fear God was not only added to enforce the orders "not to insult a deaf man"; "not to place an obstacle on the path of a blind man" (Leviticus 19:14); "not to wrong one another" (Leviticus 25:17); and "not to accept interest, nor profit from a fallen brother, though he be a stranger or a newcomer" (Leviticus 25:16, etc.). Yet it is as though the "fear of God" were defined by these ethical injunctions; as though the "fear of God" were this fear for another.

From Dialogue to Ethics

The descriptions of dialogue, and all this "phenomenology" of the I-Thou, have been reproached with proceeding negatively in relation to intentionality and to the structures of transcendental consciousness. They have been upbraided for practicing a negative psychology or negative ontology—the way others develop a negative theology—which would put into question the philosophical autonomy of the new thought. Yet dialogue, understood here as proximity throughout this conception, signifies the proper place and concrete circumstance of transcendence or the Relation, according to its double meaning of absolute distance and the crossing of this by language in the immediacy of the I-you. Would this dialogue not harbor an ethical dimension in which the rupture of dialogue with transcendental models of consciousness would appear more radically?

Let us note, first, that the philosophy of dialogue is oriented toward a concept of the ethical (*Begriff des Ethischen*) that is separated from the tradition that derives the ethical (*das Ethische*) from knowledge and from Reason as the faculty of the universal, and sees in the ethical a layer superposed upon being. Ethics would thus be subordinated either to prudence, or to the universalization of the maxim of action (where it was, to be sure, a question of the respect for the human person, but only as a secondary formulation, and deduced from the categorical imperative), or again to the contemplation of a hierarchy of values constructed like a Platonic world of ideas. Ethics begins in the I-You of dialogue insofar as the I-You signifies the worth of the other man or, still more precisely, insofar as within the immediacy of the relation to the other man alone (and without recourse to some general principle) a meaning such as worth [*valoir*][10] is sketched out. This is a worth attached to man coming out of the value of the You, or of the man who is other; a value attached to the other man. The descriptions of the "encounter" in Buber never avoid a certain axiological tonality. But does not even the immediacy itself of the Relation and its exclusivity, as opposed to the negation of the mediating or diverting terms, signify a certain *urgency* in the attitude to take with regard to the other man, a certain urgency about the intervention? Is not the very opening of the dialogue already a way for the I to uncover itself, to deliver itself, a way for the *I* to place itself at the disposition of the *You*? Why should there be saying? Would it be because the thinking being has *something* to say? But why should he have *to say* it? Why *would it not suffice* him to think about this thing which he thinks? Does he not say what he thinks precisely because it goes beyond that which *suffices him* and because *language* carries this deep movement? Beyond sufficiency, in the indiscretion of saying "you" [*tutoiement*] and of the vocative case, a demand for responsibility and an allegiance are signified simultaneously.

To be sure, in Buber, the I-Thou relationship is frequently also described as the pure face-to-face of the encounter, as a harmonious co-presence, as an eye to eye. Yet are the face-to-face, the encounter, and the "eye to eye" really reduced to a play of reflections in a mirror and to simple optical relations? In this extreme formalization, the Relation empties itself of its "heteronomy" and of its transcendence of as-sociation. From the outset, the I-you comprises an obligation in its immediacy, that is, as urgency and without recourse to any universal law. By its own meaning, it is inseparable from the valorization of the other as other in the You, and from a compulsion to service in the I. The worth of the You, the deaconship of the I—such are the semantic depths of the "primary word," the ethical depths.

There would be an inequality, a dissymmetry, in the Relation, contrary to the "reciprocity" upon which Buber insists, no doubt in error. Without a possible evasion, as though it were elected for this, as though it were thus irreplaceable and unique, the I as I is the servant of the You in Dialogue. An inequality that may appear arbitrary; unless it be—in the word addressed to the other man, in the ethics of the welcome—the first religious service, the first prayer, the first liturgy, the religion out of which God could first have come to mind and the word "God" have made its entry into language and into good philosophy. It is not, of course, that the other man must be taken for God or that God, the Eternal Thou, be found simply in some extension of the You. What counts here is that, from out of the relation to the other, from the depths of Dialogue, this immeasurable word signifies for thought, and not the reverse.

The way in which God takes on meaning in the I-You relation, to become a word of language, invites us to a new reflection. This reflection is not the subject of the present study. What was important here was to make it be felt that dialogue—contrary to *knowledge* and contrary to certain descriptions of the philosophers of dialogue—is a thinking of the *unequal*, a thought thinking *beyond* the given. It was to show the modality according to which, in dialogue or more precisely in the ethics of dialogue, in my deaconship with respect to the other, I think more than I can grasp. This is the modality according to which the ungraspable takes its meaning, or as one might also put it, the modality according to which I think more than I think. This is not a pure derision, nor a simple failure of knowledge. It is perhaps what is signified by the Cartesian paradox of the idea of the Infinite in me.

§ Notes on Meaning

The Dominant Theme

Does thought have meaning only through the knowledge of the world? That is, does it have meaning through the presence of the world and by its presence to the world; did this *presence* have to appear within the horizons of the past and the future, which are also dimensions of re-*presentation* in which presence is recovered? Or does the meaning in a meaningful thought exist, perhaps, in a way that is older than presence or re-presentable presence; that is, in a way more ancient and better than these? Is the meaning of meaningful thought a *certain* meaning, a signification already *determined*, under which the very notion of meaning comes to mind, before being defined by the formal structure of reference to a world unveiled, to a system, or to a finality? Is meaning *par excellence* the wisdom that should be able to justify being itself, or that which at least becomes anxious about this justification and this justice—the search for which still excites the talk, become quotidian, of men and women claiming to be preoccupied with the "meaning of life"? Is being its own reason for being; the alpha and omega of intelligibility, first philosophy and eschatology? Would not the "coming to pass" of being, which comes to pass, carry on, to the contrary, all the while demanding a justification, or posing a question preceding every question? In regard to the *for-the-other*—which, as humanity, manages to tear the "good conscience" from the *conatus*, from the being's animal perseverance in being, which is solely concerned with its space and its vital time—as devotion to the other and as dis-interestedness, doesn't it break the inherence in

152

being of the beings given over to themselves? Doesn't the *for-the-other* already attest to the question of wisdom *par excellence*? These problems constitute the dominant theme of the notes assembled here.

We will start from some of the positions of Husserlian phenomenology insofar as it is to this phenomenology that one of the traditions leads; a tradition characteristic of the philosophy in which the knowledge of beings—that of their presence—is the "natural site" of what is meaningful and amounts to the spirituality, or even the psyche, of thought itself.

Yet Husserlian philosophy is above all unimpeachable because it seems to provide an idea independent of this gnoseology. In effect, according to Husserl, it would be necessary, in order to rediscover the rationality of what is thought, to investigate the way in which what is *thought*—including being, notably—appears in *thought* itself. This recurrence of what is thought to the thought which is thinking would constitute, from a thought to thought, a new concreteness, the radical one relative to the concreteness of thought—and of being, notably—in its exhibition and in the ontological foundation of its quiddities or its essences, the ones by the others. This radical rise [*remontée*] of all that is *thought*, to its significance in the thought that is thinking—and, consequently, the reduction of all that is thought to its ultimate concreteness—would be unavoidable for the philosopher: it would loose thought from its adherence to the assemblage of beings and things and disengage it from the role that thought, already subject to influences, plays as the human soul among the beings and things and forces of the world. A reduction to an absolute thought. In its entanglement with actual, or potential, thoughts—always understood by Husserl as knowledge to some degree—the absolute thought, or absolute *consciousness*, is, according to the philosopher's expression, *donation* or *lending of meaning*. The *Reduction* would be one way to rejoin this thought in its pure psyche, uncovered (*unverhüllt*), *qua* pure element where, according to its own mode and in its first intentions, an originary semantics is intended and unfolded.

In the Reduction, the meaning of the meaningful would let itself be understood all the way to the meaning of that pure element where the originary semantics is deployed, where it stages itself in some fashion, unfolding, in this staging which the philosopher perceives as a concrete intrigue, according to connections already forgotten, deformed, or confounded within the objectivist rhetoric.

Yet in this ultimate concreteness—which no doubt shows itself to the philosopher, that is, is *known* to him—is significance exhausted in *manifesting* itself, in offering itself to knowledge? Even if everything ends by being known, we do not think that knowledge would be the meaning and the end of everything.

The Thought of Adequation

For Husserl—and the entire, venerable philosophic tradition he concludes or whose presuppositions he makes explicit—the "lending of meaning" is produced in a thought understood as a thought of... , as a thought of *this* or of *that*; a this or a that present to thoughts (*cogitationes*) *qua* thought (*cogitatum*), to the point that one could not determine or recognize any of them in reflection without naming *this* or *that* of which they are the thoughts. Thinking as "lender of meaning" is constructed like a thematization—explicit or implicit—of *this* or *that*; precisely as knowledge. The very breath of spirit in thought would be knowledge. This is what one expresses in saying that *consciousness*, as lender of meaning, is intentional, and articulated as a *noesis* of a *noema*, where the noema is *concrete* within the intention of the noesis. Through the *this* or the *that*, which can not be erased in the description of the *lending of meaning*, a notion such as the presence of *something* is sketched out from the moment of the birth of meaning. The presence of something: *Seinsinn*, the meaning of being according to Husserl, which will become in Heidegger—across all the harmonics of the history of philosophy— the being of the being [*l'être de l'étant*].

This "lending of meaning," constructed as knowledge, is understood in Husserl as "willing-to-come-in-this-way-or-another-to-this-or-to-that," and the reflection on this thought is understood as having to show *whereto* thought *wants to come* and *how it wants to arrive there*.[1] Intentionality is thus an intention of the soul, a spontaneity, a willing [*vouloir*], and the meaning lent [*prêté*], is itself, in some fashion, a willed [*voulu*]. The manner by which beings or their being are manifested to the thinking of knowledge corresponds to the manner by which consciousness "wills" this manifestation by the will or intention that animates this knowledge. The cognitive intention is thus a free act. The soul is "affected," but without passivity. It regains possession of itself in taking the given upon itself according to its intention. The soul awakes. Husserl will speak of a teleology of transcendental consciousness. In this way, the thought thinking the being from which it distinguishes itself is an internal process, a remaining-in-oneself: immanence. Therein lies a profound correspondence between the being and the thought. Nothing overflows the intention: the willed does not trifle with knowledge and does not surprise it. Nothing enters into thought "without declaring itself"; nothing enters "smuggled in." Everything is contained in the opening of the soul: presence is candor itself. The intentional distance—from being to thought—is also an extreme accessibility of being. The astonishment, as a disproportion between *cogitatio* and *cogitatum* wherein truth seeks itself, is reabsorbed in the truth that is rediscovered.

Presence, as the production of being, as manifestation, is *given* or a manner of being given (*Gegebenheit*). Husserl describes it as a filling of a void, as a satisfaction. He who insists upon the role of human incarnation in the perception of the given, upon the "body proper" (*Leib*) of consciousness—since it is necessary to circle around things in order to grasp them and to turn one's head and adapt one's eye and lend one's ear—will authorize us certainly to insist upon the primordial role of the hand: being is in *donation* and donation is to be understood in the literal sense of this word. It is concluded in the *hand that takes*. It is then in the taking hold of [*mainmise*], that presence is, "in its own way" (*eigentlich*), presence "in flesh and blood" and not only "in its image": presence is produced now.[2] It is in the taking in hand that "the thing itself" becomes equal to what the thought's intention "willed" and intended. The hand verifies the eye; it is in the hand that there comes about—irreducible to the tactile sensation—the taking hold of and the assuming. The taking hold of [*mainmise*] is not simply feeling, it is a "putting to the test." Before becoming a handling and use of implements, as Heidegger meant this, taking hold of is an appropriation. It is more thoroughly presence, one would be tempted to say, than presence in thematization. It is precisely through this manner of lending itself to the grasp, or of letting itself be appropriated—as a way by which presence makes itself given (*Gegebenheit*)—that presence is the presence of a content. And presence is the presence of a content of sensible qualities, arranging themselves, to be sure, under generic identities and, in any case, under the formal identity of the *something* (*etwas überhaupt*) which is a something that a forefinger can designate as a point within the presence of this assemblage and identify: a quiddity and identity of a thing, of a solid, a term, a being. The being is inseparable, certainly, from a world out of which designation and grasping tear it, but which every relation to the world presupposes. We would even dare wonder whether the distinction between *being* and the *being* is not an essential amphibology of presence, or of the *Gegebenheit*[3] which is outlined in manifestation. Hand and fingers! The incarnation of consciousness would not be a troublesome accident that happened to the thought thrown down from the height of the Empyrean into a body, but rather the essential circumstance of the truth.

To the truth itself, before its utilization and abuse in a technological world, belongs a primordial technical success, that of the forefinger designating the *something* and of the hand that seizes hold of it. Perception is a holding [*emprise*] and the concept, the *Begriff,* a com-prehending. The adequation of thought and being, at every level of reality, implies *concretely* all the infrastructure of sensible truth, as the inevitable foundation of all ideal truth. The reference of the categorial and the general to what is given straightforwardly (*schlicht gegeben*) is one of the fundamental intuitions of the *Logical Investigations* of Husserl, who, early on, indicated the thesis he upheld in the *Formal and Transcendental Logic,* according to which formal ontology refers to a material ontology and, consequently, to sense perception. It also refers to the thesis of his entire work, which points every notion, while respecting the differences of its level, back to the restitution of the elementary conditions of its transcendental genesis.[4] It is necessary that the idea of truth as a *hold* upon things have, somewhere, a nonmetaphorical sense. In the things that support and prefigure every superstructure, "to be" signifies *to be given and to be recoverable,* to be some *thing* and, thereby, a being.

In each of the themes always polarized around the "something," this "something," in its logical void as *etwas überhaupt,* does not fail to be referred, in its concreteness, to the thing, or to that which the hand grasps and holds—a content and a quiddity—and which the finger designates: this or that. A position and a positivity that are confirmed in the theses—or positional acts—of conceptual thought.

Presence—and being, which is thought starting from knowledge—is thus the opening and the given (*Gegebenheit*). Nothing comes to contradict the intention of thought and place it in check from out of some clandestinity, or out of an ambush plotted and carried out in the darkness or the mystery of a past or a future refractory to presence. The past is only a present that was. It remains commensurate with the presence of the present, of the manifestation that is perhaps only its emphatic perseverance.

It re-presents itself. That a past might have a signification without being the modification of a present in which it would have begun; that a past might signify an-archically, would doubtless indicate the rupture of immanence. Immanence connotes this assembling of the varieties of time [*du divers du temps*] in the presence of the representation. For the varieties of time, this way of not withholding themselves from synchrony, and thus—for the diversity itself of these varieties, made up of qualitative and spatial differences—their aptitude to enter into the unity of a genus or form are the logical conditions of synchronization, or synchronization's results. In the present—in the fulfilled present, in the present of ideality—everything can be thought together. Temporal alteration itself, examined in sense experience, which fills time and lasts in or through it, is interpreted starting with the metaphor of flux as its point of departure (a flux composed of drops that are distinct from each other yet, *par excellence*, "like two drops of water" that resemble each other). Temporal alterity is thought, consequently, as something inseparable from the qualitative difference of its contents, or as spatial intervals distinct but equal, discernible, and traversed in a uniform movement. This movement is a homogeneity that predisposes to synthesis. The past is presentable, retained or remembered, or reconstructed in a historic narrative; the future—protended, anticipated, and presupposed by hypo-thesis.

The temporalization of time—thought of as a flowing or temporal flux—would still be intentional. It is named from the "temporal object," synthesizable in the representation of the qualitative contents, "changing" and enduring in time. One ought to ask oneself, nevertheless, to what degree properly dia-chronic difference is not ignored or misjudged [*méconnue*] in what appears indissociable from its contents, and which causes one to imagine time as if it were composed of beings, of instants—atoms of presence or beings, designatable as terms that pass; a differentiation of the *Same*, yet lending itself to synthesis, that is, to the synchrony that would justify or give rise to the psyche as re-presentation: memory and anticipation. This is the priority of presence and re-presentation where dia-chrony passes as a privation of synchrony: the futurition of time is understood in Husserl in the form of pro-tention, that is, in that of anticipation, as though the temporalization of the future were a way of coming to presence. The retention of the impressional, impossible in the form of the punctual present—for it is already, for Husserl, almost ecstatically degraded into an immediate past—constitutes the *living present*.

In the cognitive psyche of presence, the subject or the I would be precisely the agent or the common site of representation, the possibility of the assemblage of the dispersed. Thus Brentano was able to maintain that the psyche is re-presentation, or based upon representation in all its forms—theoretical, affective, axiological, or active. And until the end Husserl affirmed a logical stratum of the objectifying act in all intentionality, even nontheoretical intentionality. *Spirit would be presence and relation to being.* Nothing of that which concerns it would be foreign to the truth, to the appearance of being.

In truth, thought thus goes out of itself toward being, without ceasing to remain, for all that, *at home with itself* [*chez elle*] and equal to itself; without losing its measure, without surpassing its measure. It *satis*fies itself in the being that, at first glance, it distinguishes from itself; thought satisfies itself in adequation. Adequation does not signify a mad, geometrical congruence between two incomparable orders, but rather suitability, accomplishment, *satis*faction. The knowledge in which thought shows itself is a thought thinking "to satiety," always according to its scale. Language, to be sure, suggests a relation *among* thinkers beyond the represented content, equal to itself and thus immanent. Yet the rationalism of knowledge interprets this alterity as the reunions of the interlocutors in the Same, of which they would be the unfortunate dispersion. In language, diverse subjects each enter into the thought of the other and coincide in reason. Reason would be the true inner life. The questions and answers of an "exchange of ideas" can hold just as well in a *single* consciousness. The relation between thinking beings would not have significance by itself and would count only as transmission of signs, thanks to which a multiplicity is united around a thought, the same. The multiplicity of consciousnesses in interaction would only have been the deficiency of a preliminary or final unity. Would the proximity of the one to the other not take on the meaning of a missed coincidence? Language would thus be subordinated to thought, even if in its immanent process, thought had to have recourse to verbal signs to comprehend—to encompass—and to combine ideas and preserve what was acquired.

The rigorous correlation between what manifests itself and the *modes* of consciousness allowed Husserl to assert both that consciousness lends meaning, and that being commands the modalities of the consciousness acceding to it, or that being commands the phenomenon. The end of this sentence receives from him an idealist interpretation: being is immanent to thought and thought, in knowledge, does not transcend itself. Whether knowledge be sensible, conceptual, or even purely symbolic, the transcendent or the absolute, in its would-be manner of being affected by no relation, cannot have a transcendent sense within knowledge without losing it at once. The very presence of transcendence to knowledge signifies a loss of transcendence and absoluteness. Presence excludes, ultimately, all transcendence. Consciousness as intentionality is precisely the fact that the meaning of the meaningful comes down to appearing [*l'apparaître*], that the very persistence of the being in its being is manifestation and that, in this way, being *qua* appearing is encompassed, equaled, and, in some manner, *carried* by thought. It is not because of some intensity or some firmness that would remain unequalable or unequal to the affirmation at work within the noetic identification—nor because of axiological modalities which the posited being would assume—that transcendence or absoluteness would be able to preserve a meaning upon which even its presence in manifestation could not inflict contradiction. There would be in the energy of manifestation—that is, in the noetic identification required for the *appearing*—all the intensity or all the firmness required by the *persistence in being*, whose manifestation would only be its emphasis. The notion of intentionality, when well understood, signifies at one and the same time that being commands the modes of access to being and that being *is* according to the intention of consciousness: intentionality signifies an exteriority in immanence and the immanence of all exteriority.

Yet does intentionality exhaust the modes according to which thought is meaningful?

Beyond Intentionality

Does thought only have meaning by way of the cognition of the world? Or is the eventual surplus in significance of the world itself over *presence* to be sought within an immemorial past, that is, in a past irreducible to a present gone by, in the trace of this past, which would be in the world its mark of a creature? We must not reduce this mark too quickly to the effect of a cause. The mark supposes, in any case, an alterity that could figure neither in the correlations of knowledge nor in the synchrony of representation. This is an alterity whose approach beyond representation our inquiry attempts precisely to describe, underscoring, in the being and the presence that re-presentation confers on it beyond its ontological contingency, its *moral challenge* [*mise en question morale*], its call to justification; that is, its belonging to the intrigue of alterity which is ethical from the first.

Would not thought be merely the thought of that which is equal to it and of that which places itself in correspondence with it—would thought be essentially atheism?

Is the meaningfulness of thought only thematization and, thus, re-presentation and, thus again, an assembling of temporal diversity and dispersion? Does thought reach toward the adequation of truth from the outset, toward the grasping of the given in its ideal identity as "something"? Would thought only have meaning before pure presence, a fulfilled presence that, consequently, in the eternal quality of the ideality, "no longer passes"? Is every alterity only qualitative, a diversity letting itself be collected into genera and forms, and susceptible to appear in the midst of the Same, as is permitted by a time that lends itself to synchronization through the re-presentations of knowledge?

The human suggests such questioning. Man identifies himself independently of some sort of characteristic quality which would distinguish one I from another and in which he would recognize himself. As "pure I's," the diverse I's are, from the point of view of logic, precisely indiscernible from each other. Yet the alterity of the indiscernible is not reduced to a simple difference in "content."

Thus the bringing together—of one I with another, of I with the other [*autrui*]—is not a synthesis among beings constituting a world, such as it shows itself either in representation or in the synchronization that knowledge imposes. Alterity, among the "indiscernible ones," does not appeal to a common genus, nor to a time synchronizable in re-presentation by memory or history. This is a gathering wholly other than that of synthesis: it is proximity, face to face, and society. *Face to face*: the notion of the face imposes itself here. It is not a qualitative datum added empirically to a foregoing plurality of I's or of psyches, or interiorities, like contents which can be, and are, added together into a totality. The face that here commands assembly founds a proximity different from that which regulates the synthesis uniting what is given "into" a world, or the parts "into" a whole. It commands a thinking that is older and more awakened than knowledge or experience. To be sure, I can have an experience of the other man, but precisely without discerning in him his difference as an indiscernible. Whereas the thought awakened to the face, or by the face, is the thought commanded by an irreducible difference: a thought that is not a thought *of...* , but from the outset a thought *for...* , which is not a thematization, which is rather a non-indifference for the other, disrupting the equilibrium of the equal and impassive soul of knowing [*connaître*]. This awakening must not be interpreted immediately as intentionality, or as a *noesis* equaling—as a full or an empty intention—its *noema* and simultaneous with it. The irreducible alterity of the other man, in his face, is strong enough to "resist" the synchronization of the noetico-noematic correlation and to signify the *immemorial* and the *infinite*, which do not "hold" in a presence or in re-presentation. An immemorial and an infinite that do not become immanence where alterity would again give itself up to representation, even when the latter is limited to a nostalgia of absence or a symbolism without images. I can, to be sure, have the experience of another and "observe" his face and the expression of his gestures as a set of signs that inform me of the states of soul of the other man, analogous to those that I experience. This is a knowledge by "appresentation" and by "intropathy" (*durch Einfühlung*), to remain with the terminology of Husserl, who is faithful in his philosophy of the other to the idea that *all meaning begins in knowledge.* But against this conception of the relation to another we make the reproach that it persists not only in imagining this relation to the other as an indirect knowledge—incomparable, certainly, to the perception wherein the known surrenders itself in the "original"—but also in still understanding it precisely as knowledge. In this knowledge, obtained from the analogy between the behavior of a foreign body objectively given and my own behavior, there is formed only a general idea of interiority and of the I. The indiscernible alterity of the other is precisely missed. As an alterity irreducible to the one that we attain by grafting a characteristic or a specific difference onto the idea of a common genus, this alterity is irreducible to a diversity assured of synthesis in a time—which is supposed and synchronizable—wherein it is dispersed as irreducible to the ultimate homogeneity necessary to all representation. In Husserl the other shall have thus lost his radical and indiscernible alterity only to return to the order of the world.

What we take as the secret of the other man in appresentation is precisely the flip side of a significance other than knowledge. It is the awakening to the other man in his identity, indiscernible for knowledge, a thought in which the proximity of the neighbor and the commerce with the other signifies, irreducible to experience, the approach of the first come.

This proximity of the other is the meaningfulness of the face—a meaningfulness to be specified—signifying directly from beyond the plastic forms that mask the face by their presence in perception. Prior to any particular expression, and beneath any particular expression that—already as a pose and a countenance given to oneself—covers over and protects, the face is nudity and destitution of expression as such, that is, extreme exposition, the defense-less itself. Extreme exposition—prior to any human intention—like a shot fired at point-blank range. An extradition of one beleaguered and tracked down, of one tracked down before any tracking and any round-up. This is a face in its uprightness of the *facing up to...* [*faire* face à...], a latent birth of the "shortest distance between two points": an uprightness of exposition to invisible death. An expression that tempts and guides the violence of the first crime; its murderous rectitude is already singularly adjusted in its sight to the exposition or the expression of the face. The first murderer is perhaps unaware of the result of the blow he will strike, but his intention of violence causes him to find the line according to which death affects the face of the neighbor with an unstoppable uprightness, traced as the trajectory of the blow that is struck and the arrow that kills. A murderous violence whose *concrete* signification is not reduced to negation—which is already a pure quality of judgment and whose intention one exhausts, doubtless prematurely, through the idea of annihilation; just as one too rapidly reduces to visibility, to phenomenality—and to the apparition of a form within the contents of a totality, beneath the sun and the shadows of the horizon— the nudity or the defenseless exposition of the face, its dereliction as a solitary victim and the rupture of forms in its mortality.

Yet this *facing me* [*en face*] of the face in its expression—in its mortality—summons me, asks for me, lays claim to me [*me réclame*]; as though the invisible death that the face of the other is facing—as a pure alterity, separated in some fashion from every whole—were my affair. As if, ignored by the other, whom it concerns already in the nudity of his face, death "regarded me" before its confrontation with me, before being the death that stares at me, myself.[5] The death of the other man implicates me and puts me in question as if, by this death that is invisible to the other who is thereby exposed, I became the accomplice by way of my indifference; and as if, even before being dedicated to him myself, I had to answer for this death of the other and not to leave the other in solitude. It is precisely in this calling to order of my responsibility by the face which summons me, questions me, and lays claim to me—it is in this putting into question—that the other is a neighbor.

And starting from this uprightness, held forth to the point of destitution, to the point of the nudity and the defenselessness of the face, we were able to say elsewhere that the face of the other man is, at once, my temptation to kill and the "thou shalt not kill" which already accuses me or suspects me and forbids me, but also questions me and lays claim to me.[6] As though there were something I could do and as though, already, I were indebted. It is out of the mortality of the other man—rather than out of some sort of nature or destiny, common from the first to "us other mortals"—that my non-indifference to the other has the irreducible signification of sociality. Non-indifference is not subordinated to the priority of my being-unto-death, which should measure all authenticity according to *Sein und Zeit,* wherein *Eigentlichkeit*—and nothing would be more peculiar to me, more *eigen* [my own], than death—discovers the signification of the human and of human identity.

This way of laying claim to me, of implicating me and appealing to me, this responsibility for the death of the other, is a significance irreducible to such a degree that it would be from this significance that the meaning of death must be understood. It must be understood beyond the abstract dialectic of being and its negation which, starting from violence reduced to negation and annihilation, one calls death. Death signifies within the concreteness of the impossible abandonment of the other to his solitude, or in the interdiction of this abandonment. Death's meaning begins in the interhuman. Death signifies primordially in the very proximity of the other man or in sociality.

It is starting from there that speculation, in the alternatives it raises without being able to decide among them, has a presentiment of death's *mystery.*

Responsibility for the other man, the impossibility of leaving him alone with the mystery of death, is concretely—across all the modalities of *giving*—the taking upon oneself [*susception*] of the ultimate gift of dying for another. Responsibility is not here a cold juridical exigency. It is all the gravity of the love of the neighbor—of love without lust—on which rests the congenital meaning of this used word and which all the literary forms of its sublimation or its profanation presuppose.

The Question

The point-blank exposition of the face of the other man and its demand that lays claim to me, breaking up the plastic forms of the appearing, measure concretely the passivity of his abandonment to the invisibility of death. Also, in its very quality of facing-me, the face measures concretely the violence that is perpetrated within this mortality. The invisible aspect of death or its mystery: here is an alternative forever unresolved between being and not being. But it is much more: an alternative between this alternative and another "term," an excluded and unthinkable third party; that by which precisely the unknown of death is unaware of itself otherwise than as the unknown of experience, excluding itself from the order in which knowing and not knowing play, excluding itself from ontology. Here is the latent birth of the problematic quality itself of the question arising from the demand that comes from the face of the other, as neither a simple failure of knowledge nor some modality of the certitude of the proposition of belief. This problematic quality signifies the shaking of the natural, of the naive ontological positing of the identity of a being; the inversion of the *conatus*, of the persistence and the problem-free perseverance of the being in being. This is a shaking and an inversion by which, as *myself*, I pierce beneath the identity of the being and may henceforth speak of *my* shaking, of *my* conatus, of *my* persistence in being, of *my* being put in question, just as I speak of my being put into the world; an entry into the concern-for-the-death-of-the-other-man—an awakening of a "first person" within the being. This is problematicity at its origin in the guise of my awaking to responsibility for the other, in the guise of a sobering up from my own existing.

A putting in question, in effect, in the demand of the face that lays claim to me. However, I cannot enter this by questioning myself, in the theoretical mode of a proposition within a statement. Rather this is a question where I enter strictly obliged to responsibility for the mortality of the other man and, concretely, as losing before the death of the other the innocence of my being. This is a putting in question before the death of the other which is like a remorse or, at least, like a hesitation to exist. Is not my existing, in its quietude and the good conscience of its *conatus*, equivalent to letting the other man die? The I as an I breaking, within a being that knows "what to believe," or the individual of a kind—even if this were the human-kind—its calm participation in the universality of

being, this I signifies as the very problematicity of the question. The I signifies this question across the ambiguity of the identical that calls itself *I*
at the apogee of its unconditional and autonomous identity, but where it
may acknowledge itself also as "a detestable I." The I is the very crisis of
the being of beings [*de l'être de l'étant*], not because the meaning of this
verb would have to be understood in its semantic tenor and would appeal to ontology, but because, as I, I already ask myself whether my being
is justified. This is a bad conscience that does not yet refer to a law. Concretely—that is, thought from its unavoidable "staging" in the phenomenon (or in the breaking of the phenomena)—this bad conscience, this
putting in question, comes to me from the face of the other who, in his
mortality, tears me from the solid ground on which, as a simple individual, I posit myself and persevere naively, and naturally, in my position.
This is a question that does not await a theoretical response in the guise
of "information." It is a question more ancient than that which tends toward the response, and thence perhaps toward new questions, themselves
older than the famous questions that, according to Wittgenstein, have no
meaning except where responses are possible (as if the death of the other
man posed no question). This is, rather, a question that appeals to responsibility. It is not a practical makeshift that would console a knowledge running aground in its adequation to being. Responsibility is not
the privation of knowledge, of comprehension, of grasping and holding,
but ethical proximity in its irreducibility to knowledge, in its sociality.

À-Dieu

The Same destined irrevocably to the Other:[7] this is an ethical
thought, a sociality that is proximity or fraternity, and not synthesis. This
is a responsibility for the other, for the first-come in the nudity of his
face. It is a responsibility beyond what I may or may not have committed in regard to an other [*autrui*], and for all that shall or shall not have
been my act. It is as though I were destined to the other [*l'autre*] before
being destined to myself. And this, in an authenticity that, precisely, is
not measured by what is proper to me, by *Eigentlichkeit*, or by what has
already touched me, but rather by pure gratuity toward alterity. A responsibility without culpability where I am nevertheless exposed to an
accusation that the alibi and non-contemporaneousness could not efface,
as though they established it instead. A responsibility coming from be-

fore my freedom, from before all beginnings in me, and from before every present. *Before*, but in what past? Not in the time preceding the present, wherein I might have contracted some engagement. In that case, my responsibility for the first-come would refer to a contact, a contemporaneousness. The other would no longer be now, where I respond for him, the first-come—he would be an old acquaintance. The responsibility for the neighbor is before my freedom in an immemorial past that is unrepresentable and was never present, more "ancient" than any consciousness of... I am committed, in responsibility for the other, according to the singular figure that a creature presents, responding to the *fiat* in Genesis, hearing the word before having been a world and in the world.

The radical diachrony of time, resistant to the synchronization of reminiscence and anticipation, and to the modes of re-presentation, is a surge of a thought which is not the embodiment of a content, but which is thought for... It is not reduced to thematization, to the knowledge adequate to the being of the consciousness of...

Yet the commitment of this "deep yore" of the immemorial comes back to me as an order and a demand. It comes back as a commandment, in the face of the other man, of a God who "loves the stranger," of an invisible, unthematizable God, who expresses himself in this face and for whom my responsibility for the other bears witness without referring to a previous perception. An invisible God that no relationship could rejoin, because He is a term in no relation, even intentionality, because He is precisely not a term but the Infinite. This is an Infinite to which I am destined by a non-intentional thought which no preposition in our language—not even the *à* [unto] to which we resort here—could translate the devotion. *À-Dieu*, for which diachronic time is its unique cipher, is at once devotion and transcendence. It is not certain that Hegel's notion of the "bad infinite" would admit no revision.

The Meaning of the Human

The proximity of the other man, in responsibility for him, thus signifies otherwise than that which "appresentation," *qua* knowledge, could ever derive from it. However, it also signifies otherwise than each one's internal re-presentation signified to each one. It is not certain that the ultimate and proper meaning of the human lies in its showing itself to the other or to itself. It is not certain that this meaning lies in what is manifested, or in manifestation, in the truth unveiled, or in the noesis of knowing. Is it certain that man might not have a meaning precisely beyond that which man can *be*, beyond that which he can *show himself*? Does this meaning not reside precisely in his face as the first-come, and in his foreignness (or, might we say, his alienness) as an other [*autrui*]? Does this meaning not reside in his face to the degree that it is precisely to this foreignness that his call to me, or his imposition on my responsibility, is attached? Is not this imposition on me, this devolving-upon-me of the stranger, the way by which there "arrives on the scene," or comes to mind, a god who loves the stranger who puts me in question by his demand, and to which my "here I am"[8] bears witness?

The significance of this diachronic foreignness of the other in my responsibility for him, or of this "difference among indiscernibles" without common genus, as I and the other [*l'autre*], coincides with a non-indifference in me for the other. Is this not the very significance of the face and of the original speaking that asks for me, holds me in question and awakes me or gives rise to my response or my responsibility? Before any knowledge that I might have of myself, before any reflective presence of me to myself, and beyond my perseverance in being and my resting in myself, do we not find here the *for-the-other* of the great sobering of the psyche into humanity and the *à-Dieu* breaking with the Heideggerian *Jemeinigkeit*?[9]

It is not a question of taking up the great thesis of psychoanalysis through these queries and conditionals. According to that thesis the analyst sees more rightly into the other man than the other man sees into his own spontaneous and reflected consciousness. In this case, it is not a question of seeing or knowing. We are asking whether the humanity of man is defined only by that which man *is*, or whether in the face that *asks for me* a meaning other, and older, than the ontological one is in the process of becoming meaningful and awaking us to another thought than that of knowledge, which is probably only the very pulsation of the I of good conscience. The meaning of the human is not measured by presence, not even by man's presence to himself. The signification of proximity overflows ontological boundaries, human *essence*, and the world. It signifies by way of transcendence and by way of the unto-God-in-me [*l'à-Dieu-en-moi*], which is the putting in question of me. The face signifies in destitution, in all the precariousness of questioning, and in the entire fortuity of mortality.

That Revelation be love of the other man, that the transcendence of the unto-God [*à-Dieu*] which is separated by a separation behind which no genus common to what is separated is recovered, nor even any empty form that would embrace them together; that the relationship to the Absolute or to the Infinite signifies ethically, that is, *in* the proximity of the other man who is a stranger and possibly naked, destitute, and undesirable, but that it signifies also *in* his face that asks for me, unexceptionably a face turned toward me and putting me in question—all this must not be taken as a "new proof of the existence of God." That is a problem that probably has no meaning save within the world. All this describes only the circumstance in which the meaning itself of the word "God" comes to mind. And it does so more imperiously than a presence could do. This is a circumstance in which this word signifies neither being, nor perseverance in being, nor any world behind the world—it signifies nothing less than a world!—without, in these precisely precise circumstances, these negations turning into negative theology.

The Right To Be

The face, beyond manifestation and intuitive disclosure. The face, as *à-Dieu*, is the latent birth of meaning. The apparently negative utterance of the *à-Dieu*[10] or of its signification is determined or concretized as responsibility for the neighbor, for the other man, for the stranger. Nothing obliges us to this responsibility in the rigorously ontological order of the thing, of something, of quality, number, and causality. This is the regime of the otherwise than being. The compassion and sympathy to which one might wish to reduce responsibility for the neighbor, as if to elements in the natural order of being, are already under the regime of the *à-Dieu*. Signification, the *à-Dieu*, and the for-the-other—concrete in the proximity of the neighbor—are not some sort of privation of vision, an empty intentionality, a pure aiming. They are the transcendence that perhaps makes possible all intuition, all intentionality, and all aiming.

What one continues to call the "identity of the I" is not originally a confirmation of the identity of the being in its "something." It is not some sort of exaltation of or higher bid by this identity of the "something" raising itself to the rank of a "someone." It is the "non-interchangeability," the uniqueness, the ethos of the irreplaceable that, indiscernible, is not individuated by some sort of attribute or by some "privation" playing the role of a specific difference. This is an ethos of the irreplaceable going back to this responsibility. This identity of the I or of the "oneself" signifies the character of the inalienable, attached to responsibility; it is tied to its ethic and thus to its election. It is an awaking to a truly human psyche and to an interrogation that, behind responsibility and as its ultimate motivation, is a question about the right to be. It is not disclosed in the brightness of its perseverance in being, however precarious or assured this perseverance might be through the mortality and the finitude of that being. Rather, it is assumed in hesitation and modesty, and perhaps in the shame of the unjustified one which no quality could cover, or invest, or fix firmly as a character discernible in its particularity. Naked in quest of an identification that can only come to it from an inalienable responsibility. A condition or noncondition to be distinguished from the structures that signify the ontological precariousness of presence, mortality, and anguish. We must remain attentive to an intrigue of meaning that is other than that of ontology, in which the very right to be is put into question. The "good conscience" going, in its reflection on the prereflective I, all the way to the famous self-consciousness, is already the return of the I awakened in responsibility. It is the return of the I as *for-the-other* or the I with a "bad conscience," to its ontological "integrity," to its perseverance in being, and to its health.

Subjection and Primogeniture

Yet, properly speaking, already in stating, here, the prereflective I, the I without a concept, the I anxious about its right to be before the face of the other, this I is elevated into a *notion of the I*: the I of the "bad conscience." It has shielded itself even in the thematization of these present remarks under the *notion of the I*. It has shielded itself, but has also forgotten, under the generality of the concept, the first person who is subject to others and incomparable to others, and who is precisely not an individual of a genus. In the first person it is an Ego [*un Moi*] and, in the equity of the concept, it is a pure individual of the genus in perfect symmetry and reciprocity with the other Egos. It is the equal, but it is no longer the brother of all the others. It is necessary to unsay the said on this point and to come back to our remarks and awaken anew to God. This is an awakening to the prereflective I who is the brother of the other and, in fraternity, who is responsible from the first for the other and not indifferent to his mortality. This I is accused of everything, but without a guilt that it might recall, and this before having taken any decision or having accomplished any free act, and consequently before having committed any offense from which this responsibility might have flowed. This is the responsibility of the hostage to the point of substitution for the other man. In Book 10 of his *Confessions*, Saint Augustine opposes to the *veritas lucens* [truth that shines] the *veritas redarguens*, or the truth that accuses or puts in question. These are remarkable expressions for the truth *qua* awakening to the spirit or to the human psyche. The prereflective I in the passivity of the *self*: it is only by the self, or by the I-in-question, that this passivity is conceived. This is the passivity more passive than any passivity, more passive than that which, in the world, remains the counterpart of an action of some sort and which, even as materiality, already offers a resistance: the famous passive resistance.

The responsibility of a hostage to the point of substitution for the other man—an infinite subjection. It is an infinite subjection unless this responsibility—always previous or anarchic, that is to say, without an origin in a present—might be the measure or the mode or the regime of an immemorial freedom, older than being, older than the decision and the acts. By way of this freedom the humanity in me, that is to say humanity as the I in its *à-Dieu*, signifies, despite its ontological contingency of finitude and the enigma of its mortality, a primogeniture and, in the inalienable responsibility, the uniqueness of the elected. There lies the uniqueness of the I. It is primogeniture[11] and election, the identity and priority of an identification and an excellence irreducible to those that can mark or constitute the beings within the order of the world, and the persons in their role, played as characters upon the social stage of history—that is, in the mirror of reflection or in self-consciousness. I have to respond for the death of the others before *having-to-be*. This is not an adventure happening to a consciousness that would be, firstly and from the outset, knowledge and representation. This I does not conserve its assurance in the heroism of the being-for-death in which consciousness asserts itself as lucidity and thought thinking *to the very end*. It is nonautochthony in being, which is not an adventure happening to a consciousness that is, even in its finitude, again or already, a good conscience without questions about its right to be and, consequently, anguished or heroic in the precariousness of its finitude. The bad conscience is an "instability" different from that threatened by the death and the suffering that pass for the source of all perils.

A question about my right to be, which is already my responsibility for the death of the other, interrupts the spontaneity, without circumspection, of my naive perseverance. The right to be and the legitimacy of this right do not refer, when all is said and done, to the abstraction of the universal rules of the law. However, in the last resort they refer—like this law itself and like justice—to the *for-the-other* of my non-indifference to death, to which is exposed the very uprightness of the other's face.[12] Whether he looks at me or not, he "concerns me."[13] The question of my right to be is inseparable from the for-the-other in me; it is as old as this for-the-other. This is a question against-nature, against the naturality of nature. But it is a question of meaning *par excellence*, prior to or beyond all the meaning games that we happen upon in the reference of words, the ones to the others, in our writing pastimes. It is a question of the meaning of being: not the ontological meaning of the comprehension of this extraordinary verb, but the ethical meaning of the justice of being. A pure question that asks for *me*, and in which thought awakens, against nature, to its untransferable responsibility, to its identity of the indiscernible, to itself. The question *par excellence*, or the first question, is not "why is there being rather than nothing?" but "have I the right to be?" This is a question of meaning that does not turn toward any natural finality, yet it is perpetuated in our strange human discourses on the meaning of life, wherein life awakens to humanity. A question that is repressed most of the time, it goes back to the extreme point of what one sometimes calls, too lightly, malady.[14]

§ The Bad Conscience and the Inexorable

> The I responsible for the other, an I without an I is fragility itself,
> to the point of being put in question through and through *qua* I,
> without identity, responsible for him to whom he cannot give a
> response, a responding that is not a question, a question that refers
> to the other without so much as waiting for a response from him.
> The Other does not respond.
> —Maurice Blanchot, *The Writing of the Disaster*

1. Starting from *intentionality*, consciousness[1] understands itself as a modality of the voluntary. The word "intention" suggests it, and in this way is justified the appellation of "acts," conferred upon the unities of intentional consciousness. On the other hand, the intentional structure of consciousness is characterized by representation. This structure would be at the base of all consciousness, theoretical and nontheoretical. This thesis of Brentano remains true for Husserl despite all the specifications the latter brought to it and all the precautions with which he surrounded it in his notion of objectifying acts. Consciousness implies presence or position-before-oneself, that is to say, worldliness, the fact of being-given. Presence is exposition to prehension [*la saisie*], to grasping, to comprehension, and to appropriation. Is intentional consciousness not, therefore, the detour according to which perseverance in being is practiced concretely; is it not the detour according to which is practiced an active hold upon the scene where the being of beings unfolds, is assembled and manifested? Consciousness is thus understood as the very scenario of the unceasing effort of *esse* in view of this *esse* itself. It is an almost tautological exercise of the *conatus*, to which the formal meaning of this privileged verb amounts—a verb we have called, too lightly, auxiliary.

Yet a consciousness *directed* upon the world and upon objects, structured as intentionality, is also *indirectly*, and as if by addition, consciousness of itself: consciousness of the active-I that represents to itself a world and objects, as well as the consciousness of its own acts of representation, the consciousness of mental activity. This is nevertheless an indirect, immediate consciousness, yet one without intentional aim, implicit, and of pure accompaniment. We say here non-intentional to distinguish it from internal perception to which it would be apt to convert itself. Internal perception, as reflected consciousness, *takes for its objects* the I, its states, and its mental acts. This is a reflected consciousness wherein the consciousness that is directed upon the world seeks assistance against the inevitable naïveté of its intentional rectitude, forgetful of the indirect experience [*du vécu indirect*] of the non-intentional and of its horizons, forgetful of what accompanies it. Consequently one is led—perhaps too rapidly—to consider, in philosophy, this non-intentional experience as a knowledge that is still non-explicit, or as a still confused representation that reflection shall bring to full light. It is considered to be an obscure context of the thematized world that reflection, or intentional consciousness, will convert into clear and distinct *data* like those that present the perceived world itself.

It is not forbidden, nevertheless, to wonder whether—beneath the gaze of reflected consciousness taken for self-consciousness—the non-intentional, experienced in counterpoint to the intentional, preserves and delivers its true meaning. The critique traditionally practiced with regard to introspection has always suspected here a modification that the so-called spontaneous consciousness would undergo under the scrutinizing and thematizing and objectivizing and indiscreet eye of reflection. This critique has here suspected something like a violation and a misreading of some secret. This is a critique always refuted, a critique always reappearing.

What happens, then, in this unreflective consciousness that one takes only for a prereflective one, and which, implicit, accompanies the intentional consciousness in focusing in reflection, intentionally, upon oneself, as if the thinking-I [*moi-pensant*] appeared to the world and belonged there? What might this alleged confusion, this implication, signify; what might it signify, in some sense, positively? Is there not reason to distinguish between the *envelopment* of the particular in a concept, the *implication* [*sous-entendement*] of what is presupposed in a notion, the *potentiality* of the possible in a horizon on the one hand, and the *intimacy* of the non-intentional in prereflective consciousness on the other hand?

2. Does the "knowledge" of the prereflective self-consciousness *know*, properly speaking? As a dim consciousness, an implicit consciousness preceding all intentions—or coming back from all intentions—it is not an act, but rather pure passivity. It is passivity not only by way of its being-

without-having-chosen-to-be, or by its fall into a pell-mell of possibles already realized before any assumption, as in the Heideggerian *Gewor-fenheit.*[2] It is a "consciousness" that, rather than signifying a self-knowledge, is effacement or discretion of presence. A bad conscience: without intentions, without aims, under the protective mask of the personage contemplating himself in the mirror of the world, assured and positing himself. This consciousness is without a name, without situation, without titles. A presence that dreads presence, naked of all attributes. Its nudity is not that of disclosure or exposure to view of the truth. In its non-intentionality, prior to all willing and before all fault, in its non-intentional identification, identity recoils before its affirmation. It recoils before that which identification's return to self may contain of insistence. A bad conscience or a timidity: it is without acknowledged culpability and responsible for its own presence. Like the reserve of what is not invested, of the unjustified, or of the "stranger on the earth," according to the expression of the psalmist. This bad conscience is a reserve of the one without a fatherland, or of the one without a home who dares not enter. The interiority of mental life is, perhaps, originally this. It is not in the world, but in question. By reference to which, and in "memory" of which, the I that already posits and affirms itself—or firms itself up—in the world and in being, remains rather ambiguous, or rather enigmatic, only to recognize itself as detestable, according to Pascal's expression, in the very manifestation of its emphatic identity of ipseity, in language and in the I-saying. The haughty priority of the A *is* A, this principle of intelligibility and significance, this sovereignty, this freedom in the human I is also, if we might say, the coming of humility. In the putting in question of affirmation and of the firming up of being, which is found even in the famous—and easily rhetorical—quest for the "meaning of life," it is as though the I in-the-world, which has already taken meaning from its vital psychic or social finalities, went back to its bad conscience.

The prereflective and non-intentional conscience could not be described as a becoming conscious [*prise de conscience*] of this passivity, as though within it were already distinguished the reflection of a subject positing itself as in the "indeclinable nominative," assured of its legitimate right to being and "dominating" the timidity of the non-intentional like some childhood of the spirit which it had to surpass, or like a bout of weakness which happened to an impassive psyche. The non-intentional is passivity from the first. The accusative is its first "case," in some manner. If the truth be told, this passivity which is the correlate of no action, does not describe the "bad conscience" of the non-intentional so much as it lets itself be described by it. A bad conscience that is not the finitude of existing, signified in anguish. My death, always premature, places in check the being that, *qua* being, perseveres in being, but this scandal does not shake the good conscience of being, nor the morality founded upon the inalienable right of the *conatus*. In the passivity of the non-intentional—in the very mode of its spontaneity and before any formulation of "metaphysical" ideas in this regard—is placed into question even the justice of the position in being that affirms itself with intentional thought, knowledge, and the sway of the now [*main-tenant*]: to be [*être*] *qua* bad conscience. This is to be in question but also unto the question; it is to have to respond—the birth of language. It is to have to speak, to have to say "I," to be in the first person or, precisely, to be me, but consequently, in the affirmation of its being as I, it has to respond for its right to be.

3. To have to respond for one's right to be, not by reference to the abstraction of some anonymous law, of some juridical entity, but in the fear for another. Was not my "in the world" or my "place in the sun," and my home a usurpation of places that belong to the other man, already oppressed by me or hungry? This is a fear for all that my existing—despite its intentional and conscious innocence—can accomplish of violence and murder. This is also a fear that goes back behind my "self-consciousness," whatever be—toward the good conscience—its reversions to pure perseverance in being. A fear that comes to me from the face of the other. It comes from the extreme uprightness of the face of the neighbor, tearing the plastic forms of the phenomenon. This is the uprightness of exposition to death, without defenses; and, before any language and any mimicry, a demand addressed to me from the depths of an absolute solitude; a demand addressed or an order signified, it is a putting in question of my presence and my responsibility. A fear and a responsibility for the death of the other man, even if the ultimate meaning of this responsibility for the death of the other were responsibility before the inexorable and in the ultimate extreme, the obligation not to leave the other man alone in the face of death. Even though, facing death, where the very rectitude of the face that calls for me finally reveals fully both in its defenseless exposure and its very facing-up; even though in the ultimate extreme the not-to-

leave-the-other-man-alone only consisted, in this confrontation and this powerless af-fronting [*affrontement*], in responding "here I am" to the demand that summons me. This is, doubtless, the secret of sociality and, in its ultimate gratuity and vanity, love of the neighbor, a love without lust.

The fear for another, as a fear for the death of the neighbor, is my fear, but it is in no wise fear *for* me. It thus contrasts with the admirable phenomenological analysis of affectivity that *Sein und Zeit* proposes: a reflected structure where emotion is always an emotion *about* [*émotion de*] something moving, but also emotion *for* [*émotion pour*] oneself, in which emotion consists in being moved, in being frightened, in being delighted, in becoming sad, etc.[3] Here we find a double "intentionality" of the *about* and the *for*, participating in the emotion *par excellence*—in anguish; being-for-death, where the finite being is moved *by* [*ému de*] its finitude *for* this same finitude. The fear for the other man does not turn back into anguish for *my* death. It overflows the ontology of the Heideggerian *Dasein*. An ethical troubling of being, beyond its good conscience of being "in view of this being itself," for which being-for-death marks the end and the scandal, but where it awakens no scruples.

In the "natural state" of the being-in-view-of-this-being-itself [*être-en-vue-de-cet-être-même*], relative to which all things, as *Zuhandenes*,[4] including the other man, seem to take on meaning, essential nature is put into question. This is a turning around that starts from the face of the other where, at the very heart of the phenomenon in its light, there signifies a *surplus* of meaning that one could designate as glory. Does what we call the word of God not come to me in the demand that summons and calls for me? Is it not this that, before any invitation to dialogue, tears the form under which the individual who resembles me appears to me, and only there shows himself to become the face of the other man? Relative to all the affectivity of the being-in-the-world, this is the novelty of a non-indifference, for me, of the absolutely different, the other, the unrepresentable, the ungraspable. That is to say, it is the Infinite that appoints me—tearing the representation beneath which the beings of the human race are manifested—in order to designate me the unique and the elected, in the face of the other, as if without possible evasion. As a call of God, this does not found a *relation* between me and Him who spoke to me. It does not found that which, by some sort of right, would be a conjunction—a co-existence or a synchrony, albeit ideal—between terms. The Infinite could not signify for a thought that goes to term and the unto-God [*l'à-Dieu*] is not a finality. This is perhaps what the word "glory" signifies beyond being: the irreducibility of the *à-Dieu*, or of the fear of God, to the eschatology by which, in the human, the consciousness is interrupted which went toward being in its ontological perseverance, or toward death which it takes for an ultimate thought. The alternative of being and nothingness is not ultimate. The *à-Dieu* is not a process in being. In the call to me, I am referred to the other man through whom this call signifies, to the neighbor for whom I have to fear.

The I thus called lies behind the affirmation of the being persisting analytically, or animally, in its being, and in which the ideal vigor of the identity, which identifies and affirms and firms itself up in the life of human individuals and in their struggle for existence. Vital, conscious, and rational, the marvel of the I [*moi*] claimed by God in the face of the neighbor, or disencumbered of itself and fearing God, is thus like the suspension of the eternal and irreversible return of the identical to itself, and that of the intangibility of its logical and ontological privilege. A suspension of its ideal priority, which negates all alterity, and excludes the third party. A suspension of war and politics, which passes for the relationship of the Same to the Other. In the deposition by the I of its sovereignty as an I, and in its modality as detestable, signifies the ethical, but probably also the very spirituality of the soul. The human, or human interiority, is the return to the interiority of the non-intentional consciousness; it is the return to the bad conscience, to its possibility of dreading injustice more than death, of preferring the injustice undergone to the injustice committed and which justifies being by that which assures it. To be or not to be: the question *par excellence* probably does not lie therein.

"Everything is in the hands of God, save the fear of God," states Rav Hanina, cited in an antique page of the Talmud (Tractate Berakhot 33B). The fear of God would be man's affair. The fear that, in his omnipotence, the all-powerful God of theology cannot fail to inspire in the creature, is thus not the fear of God who, according to what follows of the remark of Rav Hanina, is "the unique treasure of the treasury of the Heavens."

§ Manner of Speaking

We would like, in a few pages, to grapple with the contradiction of principle that would exist in asserting the independence of ethical intelligibility relative to theoretical thought and to being; and this, in a discourse that is itself theoretical, and for which the aspiration to *full consciousness* would persist nevertheless in affirming the *de jure* priority of the "bad conscience" in the order of the meaningful.

Philosophy, like science, like perception, lays claim to a knowledge [*savoir*]: philosophy says "how it is"; its theoretical essence would be undeniable. That is true for all our discourse, from its first to its last proposition. The meaning of what is said in philosophy is a knowledge, true or erroneous, and is referred to the *being* [*l'être*] correlative with this knowledge: it is ontology. The privilege of these correlative referents, knowledge and being—that is to say, the privilege of theoretical intelligibility or of ontology among the modes or regimes of intelligibility or meanings other than what one could imagine or find—shall be attested by the inevitable recourse to knowledge and being that comes to pass even in a philosophical utterance which, eventually, dares to contest this privilege. The *One* of the first hypothesis of Plato's *Parmenides*, which should "neither be named, nor designated, nor opined, nor known" (142 a), does not separate itself from being, since it is named, designated, and known in the remark that utters, and aims at demonstrating, this separation of the One and of being.

The model of such a demonstration is evidently the same as that of the classical refutation of skepticism, which furthermore has never prevented the return and the renewal of skeptical discourse, nor its pretension to a philosophical dignity. The intellectual vigor of this model comes from the fact that the negation of the truth is not able to prevent the reflexive return of thought upon this negation. This reflexive return then grasps in the negation the utterance of a truth that sets itself in the place of the negation of the truth: an affirmation promised and permitted to every reflexive return that recognizes being even in the significance of nothingness.

One ought to ask oneself, nevertheless, whether all negation admits reflection such as this, whether poetic thinking, for example, operating directly with the matter of words, and finding them, as Picasso would say, without searching for them, has the time to listen to the reflection. One ought to ask oneself whether poetic thinking and speaking, notably, are not precisely strong enough or devoted enough to their kerygma, and sufficiently unimpeachable to prevent this turning back of reflection or to refuse to listen to its contradiction; whether poetry is not defined precisely by this perfect uprightness and by this urgency. One ought to ask oneself especially whether in another manner—whether in its manner—despite its theoretical essence, philosophy, in a sort of alternation or ambiguity which is the enigma of its vocation, is not free sometimes to take as ultimate the ontological suggestions and style of the reflection to which philosophy listens, and sometimes—and immediately—to take these for simple forms, necessary to the *visibility* of the meaning that is thought. Although, for example, as an indirect question, the indicative proposition under its categorical form might carry and embody the *question* as a derived modality of the assertion, of *apophansis*, of the position of belief understood as an original modality, the philosopher, while thematizing the problematic quality of the *question* as if it were being, can search for its proper, original meaning, even if it had to go back, as we have suggested, to the bad conscience of being. The refutation of skepticism, which we have evoked as a model, also operates at the heart of a rationality proper to the knowledge of being, proper to ontology whose regime is already established. But the philosopher can also ask himself whether the establishment of ontological intelligibility does not already proceed from an ontological thought, and this even when this establishment exposes itself—lets itself be seen—in submitting already, in the propositions in which it exposes itself, to the regime whose legitimacy it is only in the course of establishing.

No one will doubt that this submission to the forms of the exposition might not be accidental.[1] No one in effect could fail to recognize that the theoretical rationality of ontology is in no way some sort of adventure of the significance of meaning, even if there is reason to contest that it signifies by an ultimate or an original significance. Ontology is precisely truth of being, a dis-covering, an un-veiling, a causing to see. Yet is it the *seeing* and the *causing to see* that justify the *seeing*? Is it certain that the truth justifies, finally, the search for the truth, or that the search for the truth is justified by itself, as though the truth coincided with the Idea of the Good? "It is knowledge . . . as an original, meaning-giving consciousness in all its forms which is the ultimate source *de jure* for every rational assertion." This Husserlian proposition has value, doubtless, for the science already set up before being. Does it apply unequivocally to the philosophical knowledge that claims to think behind science? It is not a simple play of metaphors that rationality might call itself *justification* and not always demonstration, or that intelligibility refer to justice. Do the reasons that a certain reason ignores cease for all that to signify in a meaningful way? Without attributing these "reasons which Reason does not know" to the heart, or in questioning oneself about the sense that would be fitting to confer upon this vocable, philosophy can hear these reasons behind the ontological forms that reflection reveals to it. The meaning that philosophy lets us see with the aid of these forms frees itself from the theoretical forms which help it to see and expresses itself as if these forms were not precisely encrusted in that which they allow to be seen and said. In an inevitable alternation, thinking comes and goes between these two possibilities.

It is in this alternation that the enigma of philosophy resides, relative to ontological dogmatism and to its unilateral lucidity. But it is there also that the permanence of philosophy's crisis resides. This signifies, concretely, that for philosophy the ontological proposition remains open to a certain reduction, disposed to unsaying itself and to wanting itself wholly otherwise said.

Notes

Notes

The following abbreviations are used for frequently cited editions:

AEAE   Emmanuel Levinas, *Autrement qu'être ou au-delà de l'essence* (The Hague: Martinus Nijhoff, 1974). Pocket edition of the French text was published by Livre de Poche, Paris, 1990.

OBBE   Emmanuel Levinas, *Otherwise than Being or Beyond Essence*, trans. Alphonso Lingis (Dordrecht: Kluwer, 1991).

PH   Ernst Bloch, *Das Prinzip Hoffnung* (Frankfurt am Main: Suhrkamp Verlag, 1959); trans. Neville Plaice, Stephen Plaice, and Paul Knight as *The Principle of Hope* (Cambridge, Mass.: The M.I.T. Press, 1986).

TaI   Emmanuel Levinas, *Totality and Infinity: An Essay on Exteriority*, trans. Alphonso Lingis (Pittsburgh, Pa.: Duquesne University Press, 1969).

TeI   Emmanuel Levinas, *Totalité et infini. Essai sur l'extériorité* (The Hague: Martinus Nijhoff, 1961). Pocket edition of the French text was published by Livre de Poche, Paris, 1994.

In citations of *AEAE*, page numbers for the first edition will be given first, followed by those for the pocket French edition in brackets. In citations of *PH*, page numbers for the German edition will be given first, followed by those for the English edition in brackets.

Foreword

1. [Levinas is playing here with the transitive and intransitive sense of the verb *trancher*. As a transitive verb it means to divide, to separate, to cut short or in-

terrupt, among other senses. In the present context, however, the verb is intransitive and used with the preposition "sur," which means to be distinguished with clarity, to form a contrast or an opposition, or to stand out from something. Notwithstanding the intransitive here, that which contrasts with phenomenality does also interrupt it and put it to an end, temporarily at least.—Trans.]

2. The ideas of our argument were presented in a Study Circle of Jewish Students in Paris, and have also served as the conclusion to a series of lectures on "The Old and the New," given in a seminar directed by Father Joseph Doré at the Institut Catholique de Paris, in May 1980.

3. [Levinas writes "le penser à Dieu," using a nominalized infinitive rather than the noun "la pensée," thereby preserving the activity of thinking. More important, however, the preposition *à* here can be read either as a thinking whose object is God, or as the thinking of God. The expression parallels his designation of the non-ontological relationship of responsibility for the other as an *à-Dieu.*—Trans.]

4. The paradoxical, formal feature of this idea, containing more than its capacity and the breaking of the noetico-neomatic correlation in it, is, to be sure, subordinate in the Cartesian system to the search for a knowledge. It becomes a linkage in a proof of the existence of God which thus finds itself exposed, like every knowledge that is correlative to being, to the trial of the critique that suspects, in the surpassing of the given, a transcendental illusion. Husserl reproaches Descartes for having precipitously recognized the soul in the *cogito*, that is, a part of the world, whereas the *cogito* conditions the world. Likewise we could contest this reduction of the problem of God to ontology, as if ontology and knowledge were the ultimate region of meaning. In the extraordinary structure of the idea of the Infinite, does not the unto-God [*l'à-Dieu*] signify through a spiritual intrigue which coincides neither with movement marked by finality nor with the self-identification of identity such as it is deformalized in the consciousness of self?

5. The unto-God [*l'à-Dieu*] or the idea of the Infinite is not a species for which intentionality or aspiration would designate the genus. The dynamism of desire, on the contrary, refers back to the unto-God, which is a thought deeper and more archaic than the *cogito*. [The expression *à Dieu* is rendered as "unto God" because the preposition "unto" combines two senses of the original *à*: the sense of movement toward something or somewhere, and the connotation of a relationship with something.—Trans.]

Ideology and Idealism

NOTE: The ideas presented in this study were given in a succinct form at the June 1972 meeting of the Société de Philosophie de Fribourg en Suisse. Under the title "Ethics as Transcendence and Contemporary Thought," they were presented in Israel, in July 1972, at the Summer Institute on Judaism and Contemporary Thought, in Hebrew. They were also given at a public lecture under the aegis of the Katholieke Theologische Hogeschool in Amsterdam on November 30, 1972. On a number of points these ideas intersect some of the themes presented by Jean LaCroix forcefully and concisely in his *Le Personnalisme comme auti-idéologie* (Paris: P.U.F., 1972).

The present essay first appeared in Enrico Castelli, ed., *Démythisation et idéologie*, Proceedings of the Colloquium organized by the International Center for Humanist Studies and by the Institute of Philosophical Studies of Rome (Paris: Editions Aubier, 1973).

1. The following lines attempt to respond to the solid critique of the idea of suspicion made by Claude Bruaire.

2. Just as Plato's denunciation of rhetoric supposes the moral scandal of the condemnation of Socrates.

3. We owe this comparison of Husserl's procedure of the transcendental reduction, evoked by the term *ēpochē*, to a remark made by Filiasi Carcano. The ex-ception to being that we call "disinterestedness" shall have—as we will see further on—an ethical sense. Ethics would thus be the possibility of a movement as radical as the transcendental reduction.

4. Hegel, *Encyclopédie*, edition of 1827 and 1830, ed. Lasson, trans. B. Bourgeois, 93–94, p. 357. [See William Wallace, trans., *Hegel's Logic. Being Part One of the 'Encyclopedia of the Philosophical Sciences' (1830)* (Oxford: Clarendon Press, 1975).—Trans.]

5. This revolt expresses this spirit or, perhaps, already alters it into a caricature. Certainly. And this strange destiny of a revelation within a caricature merits separate reflection. But the caricature is a revelation from which one must sift out or disengage meaning; a meaning that demands correction, but which one may neither ignore nor neglect with impunity.

6. [This term is formed with attention to the Latin etymology, emphasizing the sense of the preposition *inter* (among) and infinitive *esse* (being). See *OBBE*, chapter 1, "Essence and Disinterestedness," pp. 3–20.

In that work, Levinas explains, "*Esse* is *interesse*; essence is interest. This being interested does not appear only to the mind surprised by the relativity of its negation, and to the man resigned to the meaninglessness of his death; it is not reducible to just this refutation of negativity. It is confirmed positively to be the *conatus* of beings. And what else can positivity mean but this *conatus*? Being's interest takes dramatic form in egoisms struggling with one another, each against all, in the multiplicity of allergic egoisms which are at war with one another and are thus together. War is the deed or the drama of the essence's interest" (see *OBBE*, p. 4; *AEAE*, pp. 4–5 [15]).

On the other hand, dis-interestedness, the ego's stepping out of the order of being, or transcendence without return, is the "proximity of the one to the other, the commitment of an approach, the one for the other. . . . Here, the perpetual conflict amongst competing beings is interrupted and 'inverted.'" Dis-interestedness "sets forth an order more grave than being and antecedent to being . . . without compensation, without eternal life, without the pleasingness of happiness" (see *OBBE*, pp. 5–6, 16, 55; *AEAE*, pp. 6 [17]; 20 [33]; 70 [92]). Also called the "Saying," dis-interestedness refers to Levinas's "pre-original language" or substitution of the one for the other.—Trans.]

7. [The indefinite pronoun *autrui* means "another" or "the others," according to context. As the object case of *autre*, *autrui* is used principally as an indirect object or the complement of the direct object. When it is the subject of a statement, it is marked by a certain abstractness, and frequently replaces "the others." English cognates are thus "another" or "others." I therefore use these, and "the other," for *autrui* according to context. The French term *l'autre* will be translated principally as "the other." Capitalization follows Levinas's text.—Trans.]

8. [Although the French term for a literal neighbor, one who lives close by, is *voisin*, I translate *prochain* as "neighbor" in the sense of one who is or comes near; not, however, in a specifically spatial sense.—Trans.]

9. In Talmudic literature, the burial of a human corpse which has no one who wants to or who can take care of it, is called the "mercifulness of truth." Should the high priest encounter it, while on his way to the Temple to celebrate Yom Kippur, he must not hesitate to "make himself impure" by contact with the corpse. The "mercifulness of truth" takes priority over the liturgy on the Day of the Pardon. A symbol of an absolutely gratuitous mercy. It is the mercy that one renders to the other "as if he were dead" and not a law for the dead, for which the Gospel had a severe expression.

10. [Enrico Castelli Gattinara (University of Rome) was the director of the Istituto di studi filosofici di Roma and the Centro internazionale di studi umanistici. The Institute and the Center sponsored yearly an international colloquium devoted to the question of demythification (*démythisation*), hermeneutics, and theology. The colloquium met yearly for almost two decades, beginning in 1961. It brought together philosophers and theologians including Levinas, Hans-Georg Gadamer, Paul Ricoeur, Alphonse de Waelhens, Gershom Scholem, Karl Rahner, Rudolf Bultmann, and Henri de Lubac, among others. The *Actes* of the colloquium were published simultaneously in Italian and French (Editions Aubier-Montaigne), under the general title *Études sur la Démythisation*. Castelli Gattinara was also the author of a number of works in theology, including *Les Présupposées d'une théologie de l'histoire* (Paris: Librairie J. Vrin, 1954).

Here Levinas may be referring to Castelli, "Introduction à l'analyse du langage théologique: 'Le Nom de Dieu,'" in Castelli, ed., *L'Analyse du langage théologique: Le Nom de Dieu* (Paris: Editions Aubier, 1969), pp. 15–22.—Trans.]

11. It is thus that we read the Talmudic remark, accentuating it vigorously: "Judge not your fellow man [*ḥaver*] until you have come to stand in his place." *Treatise of Pirke Avot* 2:5. [The sense of the Hebrew *ḥaver* runs from that of "fellow man" to that of "friend" or "companion."—Trans.]

12. See, for example, *AEAE*, chapter 3, "Sensibilité et proximité," §6, "Proximité," pp. 129–55 [100–155]. [*OBBE*, chapter 3, "Sensibility and Proximity," §6, "Proximity," pp. 81–97.—Trans.]

13. [Levinas is playing on the notion of place and giving place with an untranslatable idiom. *Donner lieu* means to furnish the space in which an event occurs or a quality is perceivable. The English equivalent "to give rise to" an event does not preserve this notion of space or site.—Trans.]

14. Tractate *Berakoth* 32B, Tractate *Baba Metzia* 59B. The two texts must be read together.

From Consciousness to Wakefulness

NOTE: First published in French in the Dutch journal *Bijdragen* 35 (1974).

1. Is not speaking of an *insecurity of reason* to accept implicitly a reason in the guise of lucidity, exercised in the light of being, but threatened by the possible inconsistency of manifested being, threatened by illusions? And yet in the present essay we contest precisely this ontological interpretation of reason in order to make our way toward a reason understood as *watchfulness* or *vigil*, where objectivity and objectification are only lifted at a certain depth, there where sleep is not yet dissipated. The language of contestation used here remains, itself, ontological in its structure. But that signifies that the level of lucidity that awakening attains is not indeterminate or arbitrary, and that this level is indispensable to awakening. It shall be necessary to show this further on.

2. [The "Prolegomena" refers to the first volume of Husserl's *Logical Investigations*, subtitled "Prolegomena to Pure Logic" and first published in 1900. See Edmund Husserl, *Logical Investigations*, vol. 1, trans. John N. Findlay (New York: Humanities Press, 1970). See Husserl, *Logische Untersuchungen*, vol. 1, in *Gesammelte Werke* (*Husserliana*), vol. 18, ed. Elmar Holenstein (The Hague: Martinus Nijhoff, 1975).—Trans.]

3. *Phänomenologische Psychologie*, §27, pp. 147 ff., in *Husserliana*, vol. 9, ed. Walter Biemel (The Hague: Martinus Nijhoff, 1959). [For the English translation, see Edmund Husserl, *Phenomenological Psychology: Lectures Summer Semester 1925*, trans. John Scanlon (The Hague: Martinus Nijhoff, 1977).—Trans.]

4. This is so, to the point of being extended into the research institutions, the laboratories and amphitheaters of the universities that orient these "orientations." These "conditions" of the appearing of "being in its truth" form, evidently, a part of being and the world and justify the recovery of the psyche by objectivity, and the extension of science to psychology.

5. [Edmund Husserl, *Phenomenological Psychology.*—Trans.]

6. In virtue of a penchant "in no wise fortuitous," we cite the *Recherches logiques* following Hubert Elie's translation, in collaboration with Arion L. Kelkel and René Scherer, vol. 2, part 1 (Paris: P.U.F. Collection Epiméthée, 1961 and 1969), p. 10. In the appendix of this volume one finds the variants that distinguish the first edition, in the German text of 1901, from the second.

7. [For the first edition, see Husserl, *Logische Untersuchungen: Untersuchungen zur Phänomenologie und Theorie der Erkenntnis*, vol. 2 (Halle: Max Niemeyer, 1901). The English translation by J. N. Findlay was made from the second edition, 1913 and 1921: *Logical Investigations* (New York: Humanities Press, 1970).—Trans.]

8. *Recherches logiques* (French ed. of ibid.), trans. Hubert Elie, with Arion Kelkel and René Scherer, 2d ed. rev. (Paris: P.U.F., Collection Epiméthée, 1961; 1969), vol. 2. "Notes Annexes," p. 264.

9. Ibid., pp. 7–8. The beginning of this citation is given according to the first edition of the *Logical Investigations*. See also the remarks in the appendix of the French translation of Elie et al., p. 263; English trans., p. 251.

10. Husserl, *Logische Untersuchungen*, p. 10; English trans., p. 253.

11. Ibid., pp. 11, 264; English trans., p. 254.

12. [A "signitive" act may be understood as any act in which something performs or serves to create a sign or meaning. See *OBBE*, p. 96; *AEAE*, p. 122 [153].—Trans.]

13. Edmund Husserl, *Méditations Cartésiennes*, trans. Emmanuel Levinas and Gabrielle Peiffer (Paris: Armand Colin, 1931), p. 19. [The English translation by Dorion Cairns (Dordrecht: Martinus Nijhoff, 1960), p. 23, states, "only an indeterminately general presumptive horizon extends, comprising what is strictly non-experienced but necessarily also-meant. To it belongs not only the ego's past, most of which is completely obscure . . . ."—Trans.]

14. Husserl, *Méditations Cartésiennes*, p. 13. [In the English translation, see p. 16. This is but one of the places in which the two translations diverge considerably. The reason for this is that the Peiffer and Levinas translation (1931) proceeded from the 1929 edition of Husserl's *Cartesian Meditations*, which was later edited by Stephan Strasser for publication as the first volume of the *Gesammelte Werke* in 1950. Cairns, on the other hand, follows Strasser above all, with attention to a typescript dating from 1933. Here I follow Peiffer's and Levinas's translation.—Trans.]

15. Husserl, *Méditations Cartésiennes,* p. 20 in the Peiffer and Levinas translation. [In the Cairns translation, p. 23.—Trans.]

16. Ibid., p. 19; English translation, p. 22.

17. Ibid., pp. 25, 129; English translation, pp. 29, 151–52.

18. Ibid., p. 130; English translation, p. 152.

19. See *TeI,* p. 65 ff.; *TaI,* p. 85 ff. [Also see Husserl, *Méditations Cartésiennes,* p. 130; English translation, p. 152.—Trans.]

20. Husserl, *Méditations Cartésiennes,* p. 19; English translation, p. 22.

21. Husserl, *Phänomenologische Psychologie,* p. 166 ff.

22. Such, at least, that this immanence is thought by Husserl, even in 1925, where the immanent remained apodictic and adequately perceived. Cf. *Phänomenologische Psychologie,* §34, p. 171 ff. The lived is always different, but, perceived adequately, is real, without any element of an "unreal" presence, without any ideality. The objective Same is ideality, perceived through the lived and always inadequately. But what is diverse in the lived constitutes a coherence—a whole. It is not chaotic.

23. And doubtless the attachment to the Same is impenitent. And one may justify this impenitence by the waking itself, which, [as] responsibility for Another [*Autrui*], has need of justice, of comparison, of lucidity, of knowledge, of presence, of being, of ontology. Cf. our *AEAE,* p. 201 ff. [246 ff.]; *OBBE,* p. 158 ff. Without cease the Infinite shall be brought back to the Same, awakened by this *without cease.*

24. Unless they suggest it, both in the Daimon of Socrates and in the entry, *by the door,* of the agent intellect in Aristotle.

25. In *Experience and Judgment* Husserl shows in the *I asleep*—indifferent with regard to that which detaches itself or stands out (*sich abhebt*) in consciousness but does not yet "affect" it with the intensity necessary to awake it— the distinction of the "proximity" and of the "remoteness" of objects. [See Husserl, *Experience and Judgment: Investigations in a Genealogy of Logic,* rev. and ed. Ludwig Landgrebe, trans. James S. Churchill and Karl Ameriks (Evanston, Ill.: Northwestern University Press, 1973). See §17, "Affection and Turning-toward of the Ego. Receptivity as the Lowest Level of the Activity of the Ego," pp. 76–79.—Trans.]

Likewise in appendix 24 of the *Phenomenological Psychology* of 1925 (*Husserliana,* vol. 9, pp. 479–80): "The directing-oneself-toward . . . is an intentional modification of the not-yet-directing-oneself-toward. . . . The [fact of] not carrying out the (intentional) act" has still different modes: to affect the I (to arouse an interest, to furnish the I with motives for taking positions, to excite and eventually to furnish a stimulus entering into competition with other stimuli—from all this result the modal differences), not to affect it [the I] and yet to remain conscious in the living present with an "absence of interest" which is a modality in the I that relates to it; the I *sleeps with regard* to that and that is, in this sense, unconscious . . . . "Throughout all the lived [experience] of the consciousness and throughout all the modifications of the lived, through the unconscious, passes the synthesis of the identity of the I. Properly speaking everything belongs to the awakened I *qua* continually thematizing, accomplishing acts, functioning as a living I of presence, but also functioning in passive works, in the associations and the syntheses of passive constitution" (p. 481). See also in the same volume 9 of the *Husserliana*, p. 313, *Amsterdamer Vorträge*.

26. See the preceding note.

27. *Husserliana* 9, p. 209.

28. Ibid., p. 208.

29. [See *OBBE*, pp. 49–51; *AEAE*, pp. 62–64 [82–86].—Trans.]

30. "As if"—not the uncertainty or simple verisimilitude of the philosophies of the "*als ob.*" The latter, despite their empirical prudence, remain attached to the truth-result, to the ideal identity of the objective, and, more generally, to the univocity of presence and of being. We hear in the "as if" the equivocation or the enigma of the nonphenomenon, the nonrepresentable: a witnessing, from before thematization, that attests *a-"more"-awaking-a-"less"-which-it-disturbs-or-inspires*, [which attests] the "idea of the Infinite," the "God in me"; and *then*, the non-sense of an indecipherable trace, the *tohu vavohu* [chaos, confusion] of the *il y a*. Nonsynchronizable diachrony, enigmatic significance and, only thus, signifying beyond being or God. The notion of insomnia, in its distinction with that of consciousness, appeared to us in our little book of 1947, entitled *Existence and Existents* precisely in its moments of non-sense. We then wrote, "We are, thus, introducing into the impersonal event of the *there is* not the notion of consciousness, but of wakefulness, in which consciousness participates, affirming itself as a consciousness precisely because it only participates in it. Consciousness is a part of wakefulness, which means that it has already torn it open. It contains, precisely, a shelter from that being with which, depersonalized, we make contact in insomnia; that being which is not to be lost, nor duped, nor forgotten, which is, if one may attempt the expression, completely sobered up." See Levinas, *De l'existence à l'existant* (2d ed., Paris: J. Vrin, 1986), p. 111. [For the English translation, see *Existence and Existents*, trans. Alphonso Lingis (Dordrecht: Kluwer Academic Publishers, 1988), p. 66, translation modified.—Trans.]

31. [See *OBBE*, p. 122; *AEAE*, p. 157 [195].—Trans.]

32. In order to name the religious awakening of Samson, the Hebrew Bible says, "the spirit of the Eternal began to move him at Mahanehdan . . . ." (Judges 13:25). For "move" [*agiter* in French] it uses the term *lepaamo*, a word with the same root as the word *paamon*—bell. The spirit is moving like the beating or the percussion with which resound or vibrate the sounds of a bell.

33. Has the presence unto self in the *Cogito* ever been convincing because of the *type* of evidence put forward? Has Descartes ever convinced us, in the *Discourse on Method*, that the certitude of the *Cogito* taught us "that the things which we conceive very clearly and distinctly are all true"?

34. [See Husserl, *Die Krisis der europäischen Wissenschaften und die transzendentale Phänomenologie: Eine Einleitung in die phänomenologische Philosophie*, ed. Walter Biemel (The Hague: Martinus Nijhoff, 1954, 1962). Translated by David Carr as *The Crisis of European Sciences and Transcendental Phenomenology* (Evanston, Ill.: Northwestern University Press, 1970). See also Husserl, *Ideen zu einer reinen Phänomenologie und phänomenologischen Philosophie: Erstes Buch. Allgemeine Einführung in die reine Phänomenologie* (1913), in *Gesammelte Werke* (*Husserliana*), vol. 3, ed. Walter Biemel (The Hague: Martinus Nijhoff, 1950). Translated by W. R. Boyce Gibson as *Ideas* (New York: Humanities Press, 1967). And finally, see Husserl, *Cartesianische Meditationen und Pariser Vorträge* (1929), in *Gesammelte Werke* (*Husserliana*), vol. 1, ed. Stephan Strasser (The Hague: Martinus Nijhoff, 1950) Translated by Dorion Cairns as *Cartesian Meditations* (The Hague: Martinus Nijhoff, 1969, 1973).—Trans.]

35. [The French verb *embourgeoiser* refers to the process by which someone or something takes on characteristics typical of the *bourgeois*.—Trans.]

36. [The first person singular pronoun, *moi*, here used as a substantive taken from the dative case, translates the German *das ich*, so I translate it as "the I" and include in brackets those instances where *moi* is capitalized.—Trans.]

37. Paradoxically, human corporeality here offers not an obstacle but a path.

38. ["Excession" is defined as a "going forth" or "going out." In the present context Levinas is attentive to a sense closer to that which "exceeds" in some fashion what any form can hold.—Trans.]

39. See *AEAE, passim*, and notably chapter 4, p. 125 [156]; *OBBE*, p. 99.

40. If the awakening takes its concrete figure in responsibility for another, representation, identity, and equality are justified out of justice. Equality depends on equity, for which knowledge is necessary; as a civilization of knowledge is necessary to the spirituality of wakefulness—as some *presence* is necessary to consciousness and the philosophical text. But as extreme lucidity, philosophy, ever correlative with being and expressing itself in a language that Derrida calls logocentric, already unsays itself. In statement or its "said" [*dit*] are distinguished the paths that lead to knowledge and to presentation on the one hand, and to life, which—otherwise than being or before the *essence of being*—signifies the Infinity of the Other. This is a distinction that remains an enigma and a dia-chrony. See *OBBE*, pp. 153–71; *AEAE*, pp. 195–218 ff. [239–66].

41. "Jeshurun [Israel] waxed fat, and kicked" (Deuteronomy 32:15). This is a desensitization that is not equivalent to ideology; for it is in the full rest of the

Same, which reason "has purchased for itself" legitimately; a rest without the influence of any impulse or any desire. Yet this is a numbness that certainly opens reason to ideologies.

On Death in the Thought of Ernst Bloch

NOTE: First published in Gérard Raulet, ed., *Utopie, Marxisme selon Ernst Bloch: Un système de l'inconstructible. Hommages Ernst Bloch pour son 90e anniversaire* (Paris: Payot, 1976).

1. Ernst Bloch, *Das Prinzip Hoffnung* (*PH*) (Frankfurt am Main: Suhrkamp Verlag, 1959), vol. 2, p. 1608; translated by Neville Plaice, Stephen Plaice, and Paul Knight as *The Principle of Hope* (Cambridge, Mass.: M.I.T. Press, 1986), vol. 3, p. 1359.

2. Bloch, *PH*, p. 1605 [1357].

3. *PH*, p. 1606 [1357].

4. *PH*, p. 1615 [1363].

5. *PH*, p. 1604 [1355].

6. It is not a question of contesting the Greek sources of Ernst Bloch's thought, nor of questioning the crushing predominance, in his mind, of Western culture over his properly Jewish culture. The latter probably amounts to the reading of the Old Testament (in translation) and to elements of folklore imported from the Jewish ways [*juiveries*] of the European East with the Hasidic stories much appreciated in the West. The rabbinical context, that is to say the Talmudic context, of these texts—without which there exists no postbiblical Judaism—seems to be little known to the eminent philosopher. And yet numerous, clearly Jewish—or Judaically accentuated—motifs are present in his work. Here then is a (certainly incomplete) inventory of these, sketched a bit meagerly. (1) Utopia to be compared with what the Talmudic texts call—beyond messianism—the *world to come*, which "no eye has seen." (2) A world to come to which each one brings his part. *To have one's part in the world to come* is expressed in the Talmud as, *to bring one's part to the world to come.* (3) The world as incomplete: compare the literal expression of the end of verse three of chapter 2 of Genesis: "the work that God created to be done." (4) The radical *rapprochement* of ontology and of ethics [wherein] the latter is not only *the sign* of the perfection of being, but the *completion* [of it] as well. [This is to be] compared with the very numerous Talmudic texts in which the Torah—[as] doctrine of justice—is the instrument, the model, as well as the ground and foundation of the world. Its perturbation threatens the cosmos with the return to nothingness. (5) The freedom of man in-view-of-the-Work [*en vue de l'oeuvre*] is to be compared with [the words], "I brought you out of slavery in Egypt in order that you be

my servants." (6) The world conceived as *Heimat* [homeland] is to be brought together with the notion of the *promised land,* expelling [*vomissant*] unjust societies, but which is neither a living space nor a native land above all. (7) The anticipation of the utopian world in astonishment before the most simple realities which become "my affair": *Tua res agitur* [your own cause is at stake] is to be compared with the wonder expressed by the blessings that punctuate the day of the religious Jew. [The theme of] the possibility of understanding the pages of Buber wherein the relation with things is presented on the model of the I-Thou. (8) Death which only bites the skin of humanity is to be brought together with the biblical notion of life "feasted with days" (without this satiety having a sort of aftertaste of disgust).

[For Levinas's concept of ethics, see *TaI*, p. 43; *TeI*, p. 13. There, Levinas writes, "We name this calling into question of my spontaneity by the presence of the Other, ethics."—Trans.]

7. On the notion of disaster [*désastre*], see the notes of Maurice Blanchot in his essay in *Nouveau Commerce* 30–31 (spring 1975), pp. 21 ff. Republished as *Ecriture du Désastre* (Paris: Gallimard, 1981). [Translated by Ann Smock as *The Writing of the Disaster* (Lincoln: University of Nebraska Press, 1986).—Trans.]

8. It is not onto the Spinozist path (where, meanwhile, the philosopher thinks "of nothing less than death" because he thinks of the immortal life in the divine totality when he truly thinks) that Ernst Bloch will enter. While admiring Spinoza's immanentism to the degree to which it excludes finalist aims and the violence of a God outside of being from the real, Bloch refuses from the outset this ready-made world "like a crystal, with the sun in the zenith, so that nothing casts a shadow" (*PH*, p. 999 [852]). This is a world with neither history nor development, this "complex of becoming," this "astralo-mythical, then pantheist, then mechanist" substitute for the totality which "is situated in its place as the unity of the *given* world." "It [this world] shall be against contentment experienced in its sufficiency" (*PH*, p. 362 [p. 311]). For Ernst Bloch, the world is yet to be made and to be transformed, and it is in *praxis* that it is true.

[For Levinas's own remarks on Spinoza's ontology see *Totality and Infinity*, p. 301; *TeI*, p. 278.—Trans.]

9. [For Levinas's remarks on a modality of being in which the absolute significance of death may be overcome, see *TaI*, pp. 56–58, 232–36; *TeI*, pp. 27–29, 208–13.—Trans.]

10. [The expression "*la geste d'être,*" here translated as "gesture" or "move of being," must be understood as the movement by which being shows itself, or the way in which being signifies actively as meaningful. I am indebted to Robert Bernasconi for suggesting "being's move." Also, in this regard see Adriaan Peperzak's remarks in his "Philosophy and the Idea of the Infinite," in *To the Other: An Introduction to the Philosophy of Emmanuel Levinas* (West Lafayette, Ind.:

Purdue University Press, 1993), p. 100n34. In *Totality and Infinity*, Levinas refers to the process-like quality of being as manifestation, movement, and events, using the reflexive verb *se produire*. In this work, being is "produced," it comes to pass; it is inseparable from signification. See *TaI*, pp. 26, 305; *TeI*, pp. xiv, 281. For a discussion of the *"geste d'être,"* see *OBBE*, pp. 23–26, 99, 131; *AEAE*, pp. 29–33 [43–48]; 126 [157]; 167 [206].—Trans.]

11. [Henri Bergson, *The Two Sources of Morality and Religion*, trans. R. Ashley Audra and C. Breton (New York: Henry Holt, 1974).—Trans.]

12. [For a discussion of this "path of spirituality," in which the future takes place invisibly, see also Levinas, *OBBE*, pp. 29–31, 162–65; *AEAE*, pp. 36–39 [51–54]; 207–10 [253–56]. For his remarks on the "holy" as that which remains separate from the order of being and subjectivity, see *OBBE*, pp. 57–59; *AEAE*, pp. 74–76 [96–99].—Trans.]

13. [Levinas translates Heidegger's *Sein zum Tode* not as "Being-towards-death," but as "being-for-death."—Trans.]

14. [See Bloch, *PH*, p. 1385 [1178]—Trans.]

15. [For a discussion of Levinas's notion of ipseity, see the sections entitled "Recurrence" and "The Self" in *OBBE*, pp. 102–9, 109–13; *AEAE*, pp. 130–39 [162–73]; 139–44 [173–79]. Ipseity refers to the unchosen, ethical election of the "self" by an other. Election occurs prior to a subject's reflection upon the "event" thereof.

Also see Lingis's discussion of ipseity in his "Translator's Introduction," in Levinas, *Collected Philosophical Papers*, trans. Alphonso Lingis (Dordrecht: Kluwer Academic Publishers, Phaenomenologica 100, 1986 and 1993), pp. xxi–xxiv.

For the thematic antecedents of *OBBE*'s discussion of the passive self underlying the cognitive and conative "identity" of the ego, or subject, see "The Ego and the Totality" in *Collected Philosophical Papers*, pp. 25–45. First published in French in the *Revue de Métaphysique et Morale* 59 (1954), pp. 353–73. See also "Language and Proximity," in *Collected Philosophical Papers*, trans. Lingis, pp. 109–26. First published in *En Découvrant l'Existence avec Husserl et Heidegger*, 3d ed. (Paris: J. Vrin, 1982), pp. 218–36. And finally, see "Separation as Life," in *TaI*, esp. pp. 117–20; *TeI*, pp. 90–92.—Trans.]

16. This is in the sense of a very remarkable fragment of Bloch's *Spuren* (Berlin: Paul Cassirer Verlag, 1930) entitled "Der Schwarze" ("The Black"). For the French translation, see *Traces* (Paris: Gallimard, 1968), p. 30.

17. *PH*, p. 1388; English translation, p. 1180.

18. Bloch, *Spuren*, p. 275 (p. 235 in the French translation). See under the heading "Astonishment."

19. [The full sentence is *"Nam tua res agitur, paries cum proximus ardet."* See Horace, *Epistles* I, 18, 84. It is translated as "Tis your own safety that's at stake

when your neighbor's wall is in flames." See Horace, *Satires, Epistles and Ars Poetica*, trans. H. Rushton Fairclough (New York: Putnam, 1929; Loeb Classics), p. 375.—Trans.]

20. *PH*, p. 1388.

21. *Spuren*, p. 275 (p. 235 in the French translation).

22. Ibid., p. 276 (p. 237 in the French translation).

23. [In English in the text.—Trans.]

24. *PH*, p. 1608; English translation, p. 1359.

25. [*Ereignis* is generally translated as event, incident, action; here, by placing a hyphen after the inseparable prefix "er," Heidegger is emphasizing the active appropriation of something, or the act of making something one's own (the transitive verb, *eignen*, can be translated "to own").—Trans.]

26. [For Levinas's understanding of the notion of "creature," see *TaI*, pp. 84–90, 102–5, 278–80; *TeI*, pp. 57–62, 75–78, 255–57.—Trans.]

From the Carefree Deficiency to the New Meaning

1. We write ess*a*nce with *a* to designate by this word the verbal sense of the word *to be*: the effectuation of being, the *Sein* distinct from the *Seiendes*.

2. [John Macquarrie and Edward Robinson have translated *Jemeinigkeit* with the neologism "mineness"; see *Being and Time*, §9, p. 68.—Trans.]

3. ["L'être s'agrée agréable."—Trans.]

4. [See *OBBE*, pp. 182; *AEAE*, p. 230 [280].—Trans.]

5. Maurice Blanchot, "Discours sur la patience," in *Le Nouveau Commerce* 30–31 (spring 1975); rpt. in *Ecriture du Désastre* [*The Writing of the Disaster*]. I am breaking the word into "dis-aster" and underscoring in the text cited the word "disaster." [Levinas breaks the word "disaster" into its hyphenated form to emphasize that contemporary disaster is tantamount to the loss of a fixed point of reference for human beings. It points also to the absence of cosmic or cosmological models to the imitation of which one could legitimately devote one's life. See the essay on Blanchot.—Trans.]

6. [On the neologism "dis-interested-ness" see "Idealism and Ideology" in this volume, n3.—Trans.]

7. [On the notion of a passivity prior to consciousness and reflection see *OBBE*, pp. 48–56, 109–13; *AEAE*, pp. 61–72 [81–94]; 139–44 [173–79].—Trans.]

8. [On the hypostasis, see *OBBE*, pp. 105–6; *AEAE*, pp. 134–36 [167–68]. Also see chapter 5, "L'Hypostase," in Levinas's early work *De l'existence à l'existant* (2d ed., Paris: J. Vrin, 1986), pp. 107–74, esp. p. 121. Translated by Alphonso Lingis as *Existence and Existents* (Dordrecht: Kluwer Academic Publishers, 1988), pp. 65–96, esp. p. 71. In this work the hypostasis is contrasted with the "Da" of Heidegger's *Da-sein* and compared with the present.—Trans.]

9. [For a discussion of the interruption of finite thought by the unthinkable Infinite and its ethical significance, see chapter 5, §2, "The Glory of the Infinite," in *OBBE*, pp. 140–52; *AEAE*, pp. 179–94, [220–38].—Trans.]

10. Cf. §3 of "The Bad Conscience and the Inexorable" in this volume.

11. Cf. §4, "Divine Comedy," in "God and Philosophy" in this volume.

12. [Also see chapter 5, §1.e., "The-One-for-the-Other Is Not a Commitment," in *OBBE*, pp. 136–40; *AEAE*, pp. 174–78 [214–19]; also *OBBE*, pp. 149–52; *AEAE*, pp. 190–94 [233–38]. For Levinas's discussion of the notion of the "sacred" and his distinction between "sacredness" and "holiness," see §4, "Divine Comedy," in the essay "God and Philosophy" in this volume. Also see Levinas's collection of Talmudic interpretations, *Du Sacré au Saint: Cinq Nouvelles Lectures Talmudiques* (Paris: Éditions du Minuit, 1977), chapter 3, "Désacralisation et désensorcellement. Traité Sanhedrin," pp. 82–121. Translated by Annette Aronowicz as "Desacralization and Disenchantment," in *Nine Talmudic Readings* (Bloomington and Indianapolis: Indiana University Press, 1990), pp. 136–60.—Trans.]

God and Philosophy

NOTE: The ideas set forth here have already been presented in diverse forms in the following lectures: at the University of Lille, March 13, 1973; at the annual congress of the Association des Professeurs de Philosophie of the Facultés Catholiques de France, May 1, 1973; at the symposium organized by the Académie des Sciences et des Humanités d'Israël and the Département de Philosophie of the University of Jerusalem in honor of the ninetieth birthday of Professor Hugo Bergman on December 23, 1973 (in Hebrew); at the Facultés Universitaires Saint-Louis in Brussels on February 21 and 22, 1974; at meetings organized by the Centre Protestant d'Etudes on March 3, 1974; and by the Faculté de Théologie Protestante on March 4, 1974 in Geneva.

This text is based on the essential contents of each of these papers. Its itinerary of conferences has taken on an ecumenical character. This is recalled here especially to give homage to the life and the work of Professor Hugo Bergman who, taking up residence very early in Jerusalem, always remained faithful to the universal vocation of Israel, which the Zionist State was only to serve, making possible a discourse addressed to all men in human dignity in order to be able to respond, consequently, for all men, all our neighbors.

This work first appeared in *Le Nouveau Commerce* 30–31 (spring 1975), pp. 97–128. [First translated by Alphonso Lingis in *Collected Philosophical Papers*, pp. 153–73. The essay also appears in Seán Hand, ed., *The Levinas Reader* (Cambridge, Mass.: Basil Blackwell, 1989), pp. 166–89.—Trans.]

1. [See Jeanne Delhomme, *La Pensée et le réel: Critique de l'ontologie* (Paris: P.U.F., 1967); also see *L'Impossible Interrogation* (Paris: Desclée, 1971).—Trans.]

2. Cf. *OBBE*, pp. 153–62; *AEAE*, pp. 195–207 [239–53].

3. [In the French text, "L'insomnie—la veillée de l'éveil—est inquiétée du cœur de son *égalité* formelle ou catégoriale par l'*Autre* qui dénoyaute tout ce qui, en elle, se noyaute en substance du Même, en identité, en repos, en présence, en sommeil" (pp. 98–99).—Trans.]

4. [See note 6, "Ideology and Idealism."—Trans.]

5. A necessity required by justice, which nevertheless is required by vigilance, and thus by the Infinite in me, by the idea of infinity.

6. [Levinas borrows the term *"synopsie"* from a medical lexicon in which it refers to the sort of synesthesia in which a subject perceives, for example, a sound as if it had a determinate color. I avoid translating *synopsie* with "synopsis," which carries connotations of brevity rather than a seeing-together or confusion of sensations.—Trans.]

7. [Levinas is here playing on the movement of being and of consciousness, using forms of the verb *aller*, "to go." He writes, "tout ce qui s'en va dans le passé se sou-vient ou se retrouve par l'histoire" (p. 101).—Trans.]

8. The notion of experience is inseparable from the unity of presence, from simultaneity, and consequently, it refers to the unity of apperception which does not come from outside "to become conscious" [*prendre conscience*] of the simultaneity. This notion belongs to the very "mode" of presence: presence—being—can only be as a thematization or an assembly of the transitory and, from then on, as a phenomenon that is thematic exhibition itself. Not all signification returns to experience. Not all signification is resolved into manifestation. The formal structure of meaningfulness—the one-for-the-other—does not come back directly to the "to show itself." To suffer-for-an-other, for example, has a meaning in which knowledge is adventitious. The adventure of the knowledge characteristic of being, which is ontological from the outset, is not the sole mode, nor the preliminary mode, of intelligibility or of meaning. It is necessary to put experience into question as the source of meaning. One cannot show that meaning, as knowledge [*savoir*], has its motivation in a meaning that, at the outset, has nothing of knowledge. That philosophy itself be knowledge or cognition [*connaissance*] is not thereby contested. But the possibility for knowledge [*savoir*] to encompass all meaning is not the reduction of all meaning to the structures imposed by its exhibition. From here comes the idea of a dia-chrony of truth in which what is said must be unsaid and the unsaid again unsaid [*où le dit doit être dédit et le dédit encore dédit*]. In this sense, the skeptical essence of philosophy can be considered seriously. Skepticism is not an arbitrary contesta-

tion, it is a doctrine of trial and examination, although irreducible to the scientific type of examination.

[For a discussion of the notions of "dia-chrony," the "Saying," and the "Said," see chapter 2, §§3 and 4, "Time and Discourse" and "Saying and Subjectivity," in *OBBE*, pp. 31–59; in *AEAE*, pp. 39–58 [58–76]; 55–77 [78–99]. For Levinas's description of skepticism and its inexorable return, see chapter 5, §5, "Skepticism and Reason," in *OBBE*, pp. 165–71; in *AEAE*, pp. 210–18 [256–66].—Trans.]

9. This possibility of conjuring away or of missing the division of truth into two times, that of the *immediate* and that of *reflected time*, merits consideration and prudence. It does not lead necessarily to the subordination of the latter to the former, or the former to the latter. The truth as *dia-chrony*, as refusing the synchronization of the synthesis, is perhaps what is proper to transcendence.

10. The latent birth of the negation resides not in subjectivity, but in the idea of the Infinite. Or, if you will, in subjectivity *qua* idea of the Infinite. It is in this sense that the idea of the Infinite, as Descartes would have it, is a "genuine idea" and not only that which I conceive "by the negation of what is finite."

11. Descartes, questioning himself on "the manner by which I acquired this idea," on the meaning of this receptivity, states in the third Meditation, "For I did not acquire it from the senses; it has never come to me unexpectedly, as usually happens with the ideas of things that are perceivable by the senses, when these things present themselves to the external sense organs—or seem to do so." In the ideas of sensible things the surprise of experience is assumed by the understanding that extracts from the senses the clear and distinct intelligible; this permits us to say that the things of the senses "seem to present themselves to the external sense organs." A process of receptivity! "And it"—the idea of infinity, continues Descartes—"was not invented by me either; for I am plainly unable either to take away anything from it or to add anything to it. The only remaining alternative is that it is innate in me, just as the idea of myself is innate in me, it was born and produced with me from the time when I was created." Cf. *Meditationes de prima philosophia*, in Charles Adam and Paul Tannery, eds., *Œuvres de Descartes* (Paris: J. Vrin, 1964–1974), p. 51. [English translation from J. Cottingham, R. Stroothoff, and D. Murdoch, trans., *Descartes: Selected Philosophical Writings* (Cambridge, Eng.: Cambridge University Press, 1988), p. 97. The last clause, beginning with the words "it was born," is not in the English translation. I have added it following the passage as Levinas cites it here.—Trans.]

12. [For a discussion of the an-archic origin of this Idea, and of the trace of the Infinite, see chapter 3, subsection e, "Proximity and Infinity," and chapter 4, §1, "Principle and Anarchy," in *OBBE*, pp. 93–94 and 99–102; in *AEAE*, pp. 118–20 [148–50], and 125–30 [156–62].—Trans.]

13. Or, as Descartes puts it, "which is *created.*"

14. [For a discussion of vulnerability *vis-à-vis* the other, which Levinas calls the "Saying," and language as thematized and thematizing (the "Said"), see *OBBE*, chapter 2, pp. 37–38, 45–51, and chapter 5, pp. 153–62; in *AEAE*, chapter 2, pp. 47–49 [64–67]; 58–65 [78–86]; and chapter 5, pp. 195–207 [239–53].—Trans.]

15. "This is the Eternal who comes from his place, who descends and tramples the heights of the earth. Under his feet the mountains melt, the valleys crack: as wax melts under the action of fire and the waters rush over a fall" (Micah 1:3–4). "That which supports cedes to what is supported," it is overturned or crumbles; it is this "structure" (which is, if we may say so, dis-structure itself) which this text states and expresses, independently of its authority—and of its "rhetoric"—from the Holy Scriptures.

16. See *TaI*, §1, pp. 33–105 and *passim*; in *TeI*, pp. 3–78 and *passim*.

17. [With this term, Levinas underscores the etymological sense of "inter," or among, and "esse," or being. Dis-inter*estedness* [dés-intér*essement*] or away from, out of, our engagement with beings.—Trans.]

18. Plato, *The Symposium*, 192c.

19. Ibid., 192e.

20. [For a similar if more elaborate discussion of love and erotic life, see §4, parts A and B, "The Ambiguity of Love" and "Phenomenology of Eros," in *TaI*, pp. 254–66; in *TeI*, pp. 232–44. In the 1961 work, however, Levinas remarked that although love is a sort of intentionality, it does not "shed light." Moreover, "nothing is further from *Eros* than possession," pp. 260, 265; *TeI*, pp. 237, 243.—Trans.]

21. Cf. *OBBE*, chapter 4, "Substitution," pp. 99–129; in *AEAE*, pp. 125–66 [156–205].

22. Franz Rosenzweig interprets the *response* given by Man to the Love with which God loves him as the movement toward the neighbor. See *Stern der Erlösung*, part 3, book 2. [Translated from the 2d ed. (1930) by William W. Hallo as *The Star of Redemption* (New York: Holt, Rinehart and Winston, 1971), part 3, book 2, pp. 336–79.—Trans.]

This is the recovery of the structure that commands a homiletic theme of Jewish thought: "the fringes at the corners of the clothes," the view of which must recall to the faithful "all the commandments of the Eternal" (Numbers 15:38–40), are expressed in Hebrew as *tsitsit*. This word is placed together, in the ancient rabbinical commentary called *Sifrei*, with the very *tsuts*, a form of which, in the Song of Songs 2:9, signifies "to watch" or "regard": "My beloved . . . watches by the trellis-work." The faithful one, looking at the "fringes" that remind him of his obligations, thus returns his gaze to the Beloved who watches him. This would be it: the *vis-à-vis* or the face to face with God!

23. It is the meaning of the beyond, of transcendence, and not of ethics that our study seeks. It finds this meaning in ethics. We write *signification*, because ethics is structured as one-for-the-other; a signification of the beyond being, because outside of all finality in a responsibility that always increases: dis-interestedness where being rids itself of its being.

24. A trace of a past that was never present, but an absence that still troubles. [Also see *OBBE*, pp. 93–97; *AEAE*, pp. 118–24 [148–55].

For a discussion of the *There is*, see *OBBE*, pp. 3–4, 162–65, 175–78; *AEAE*, pp. 3–4 [13–15]; 207–10 [253–56]; 219–22 [269–73].—Trans.]

25. A diachronous truth, or dia-chrony of the truth without a possible synthesis. Contrary to what Bergson teaches us, there would be a "disorder" that is not an other order, there where the elements cannot make themselves contemporary, in the manner, for example (but is this an example or the ex-ception?), by which God contrasts with the presence of re-presentation.

26. [Levinas frequently speculates on two senses of the "in" of "infinite": the privative, and what might be called an immanent sense, that of a placing *in*, or an *in*-spiration. See §4 in "From the Carefree Deficiency to the New Meaning," and §§3 and 4 in "God and Philosophy," this volume. Also see *OBBE*, pp. 123–29; 145–49; *AEAE*, pp. 158–66 [196–205]; 185–89 [228–33]. Here, he refers to the "in" of the French term *inassumable*, the sense of which is lost when translated into English as "unassumable."—Trans.]

27. [See also chapter 4, §4, "Substitution," in *OBBE*, pp. 113–18; *AEAE*, pp. 144–51 [179–88].—Trans.]

28. [In French (and Scottish) law, "to compear" is to appear in court personally or represented by an attorney. I thus retain the play of pronouns and *parere*, although the English term is more obscure than the French one. It is the notion of appearing in court, or before a judge, that Levinas intends here.—Trans.]

29. This is a devotion as strong as death and, in a sense, stronger than death. Within *finitude*, death outlines a destiny which it interrupts, whereas nothing could dispense me from the response to which I am held *passively*. The tomb is not a refuge; it is not a pardon. The debt remains.

30. [Levinas here employs an expression dear to Heidegger. Cf. the end of Heidegger's lecture *Das Wesen der Sprache* (1957–58): "For the phonetic-acoustic physiological explanation of the sounds of language does not know the experience of their origin in ringing stillness, and knows even less how sound . . . is defined by that stillness." In *On the Way to Language*, trans. Peter D. Hertz (New York: Harper and Row, 1971), see, for example, pp. 122 ff. Also see *OBBE*, p. 135; *AEAE*, pp. 172 [211].—Trans.]

31. Genesis 18:27.

32. Exodus 16:7.

33. The one-for-the-other, as a formal structure of signification, is the significance or the rationality of signification which, here, does not begin by exposing oneself in a theme, but which is my opening to the other, my sincerity or my *veracity.*

34. [The French text, which reads, "Accusatif merveilleux: me voici sous votre regard . . . ," could also be translated to highlight an accusative indiscernible in English: "you see me here beneath your gaze . . . ." The French idiom, *"me voici,"* has preserved the accusative form *me*, which English translates as "here I am." The preposition *voici* amalgamates "to see" or *voir* in the form *vois* and the preposition *ci*, or here. *Voici* is thus "you see me here."—Trans.]

35. Isaiah 57:19. [I follow Levinas's French citation here.—Trans.]

36. [The French text reads, "Elle constitue, en-deçà de l'unité de l'aperception . . . ." I translate the French locative preposition *en-deçà* according to the context as "within," "prior." In those cases where Levinas explicitly refers to the temporality of responsibility or the nonthematizable and ethical "otherwise than being," I follow Lingis's choice of "hither" side. This *"in*-side" or hither side must be understood as an imperceptible accompaniment in experience, whose meaning is lost when we attempt to bring it into discourse as if it were, indeed, experience. See *OBBE*, pp. 9–11; *AEAE*, pp. 10–13 [22–25]. For discussion of "Inspiration" and the "hither side," see *OBBE*, pp. 14–15, 109–18, 124; *AEAE*, pp. 17–19 [30–32]; 139–51 [173–88]; 160 [198].—Trans.]

37. Amos 3:8; the verse begins, "The lion hath roared, who will not fear?"

38. [The French text reads, "La clarté du visible—signifiait." This remark must be understood to mean that, for the Western tradition, identification and predication—which Levinas calls more strictly "apophansis"—are the exclusive modes by which something is brought to light. But the metaphor of clarity must not be separated from meaning itself.—Trans.]

39. It is quite remarkable that the word "significance" [*signifiance*] could have the meaning, empirically, of a mark of attention given to someone.

40. [The French text reads, "Se *dessine*-t-elle d'ailleurs cette signifiance plus antique que tout dessin?" The adverbial phrase *d'ailleurs* is generally translated as "besides" or "moreover"; it can also mean "from another place." In the present discussion, this second sense should not be overlooked in light of the discussion of "otherwise than being."—Trans.]

41. See *OBBE*, pp. 46–47, 153; *AEAE*, pp. 59 [78–79] and 195 [239–40].

42. [In English in the text. Cf. 1 in "Ideology and Idealism" in this volume.—Trans.]

43. [The encompassment or *englobement* of which Levinas speaks is that of idealist systems, particularly that of Hegel.—Trans.]

44. [In English in the text.—Trans.]

Questions and Answers

NOTE: Published for the first time in *Le Nouveau Commerce* 36–37 (spring 1977), pp. 61–86.

1. Cf. above, "Ideology and Idealism," §5, "The Other in the Form of the Other Man"; and "On Death in the Thought of Ernst Bloch," §3, "Death, Where Is Your Victory?"

2. [In *TaI*, justice is not so clearly tied to the third party as it will be in *OBBE* and here. For the discussion of justice and the third party in *OBBE*, see pp. 157–65; in *AEAE*, pp. 199–210 [244–56]. Trans.]

3. [On the un-saying, or *dé-dire*, see *OBBE*, pp. 43–48, 153, 170; *AEAE*, pp. 56–61 [75–81]; 195–96 [239–41]; 215–16 [263–64].—Trans.]

4. [*OBBE*, pp. 143, 181; *AEAE*, p. 182 [223]; 228 [278].—Trans.]

5. [*OBBE*, pp. 115, 121, 193 n. 35; *AEAE*, p. 146 [181]; 155 [192]; 120 n. 35 [150 n. 1].—Trans.]

6. [The French text reads, "Vous dîtes que le langage traduit aussi bien qu'il trahit" (p. 139). The expression is taken directly from Levinas, who plays frequently upon the near-homonymy of *traduire* and *trahir*. See, for example, *OBBE*, pp. 6–7; *AEAE*, pp. 7–8 [17–19].—Trans.]

7. [The French expression *me voici* has preserved the accusative form, *me*, which English cannot translate in so concise a formula. The preposition *voici* is the contemporary amalgamation of the verb "to see" or *voir* in the second person singular, imperative form *vois*, and the preposition *ci* or here. *Voici* could thus be expressed as "you see me here," or "vois moi ici," "tu me vois ici." In these formulations, the subject is not "I," but "you" or *tu.*—Trans.]

8. [See "From the Carefree Deficiency to the New Meaning," §1, note 3.—Trans.]

9. [*Eigentum* may be translated, literally, as "property" or "possession."—Trans.]

10. [The French text reads, "Cette lecture de Heidegger m'a été certainement dictée par l'idée que le moi humain, le soi-même, l'unicité du moi, c'est l'impossibilité de se dérober à l'autre." I reproduce it here to avoid confusion with Levinas's previous use of *Moi*, which refers to the concept of the I, and to note that, here, what is important is not the notion of the I but what he calls the uniqueness of the I, which is "ipseity." Cf. *OBBE*, pp. 109–13, 125; *AEAE*, pp. 139–44 [173–79]; 160 [198].—Trans.]

11. [For a discussion of the concepts of "inspiration" and "witness," see chapter 5, §2, "The Glory of the Infinite" (esp. subsections a–d) in *OBBE*, pp. 140–52; in *AEAE*, pp. 179–89 [220–38].—Trans.]

12. [See §4, part G, "The Infinity of Time," *TaI*, pp. 281–85, esp. 284–85; *TeI*, pp. 257–61, esp. 261.—Trans.]

13. [See §4, "Beyond the Face," in *TaI*, pp. 251–85; in *TeI*, pp. 229–61. As Levinas writes in *TaI*, "*Eros* . . . goes beyond the face" (p. 264; *TeI*, p. 242) when it issues in fecundity. Levinas writes, "This triumph of the time of fecundity over the becoming of the mortal and aging being, is a pardon, the very work of time." *TaI*, p. 282; *TeI*, p. 259.—Trans.]

14. [Levinas, *Time and the Other*, trans. Richard A. Cohen (Pittsburgh: Duquesne University Press, 1987). Originally published as "Le temps et l'autre," in Jean Wahl et al., eds., *Le choix—le monde—l'existence*, Cahiers du Collège philosophique (Grenoble and Paris: Arthaud, 1947), pp. 125–96. Published in book form with a preface by Levinas as *Le Temps et l'Autre* (Montpellier, France: Fata Morgana, 1979).—Trans.]

15. [From *deferre* or "to carry," or in later Latin, "to do honor to."—Trans.]

16. [Vladimir Jankélévitch, *La Mort* (2d ed., Paris: Flammarion, 1977).—Trans.]

17. [Horace's remark "Nam tua res agitur, paries cum proximus ardet" may be translated as "'Tis your own safety that's at stake when your neighbor's wall is in flames." See Horace, *Satires, Epistles and Ars Poetica*, trans. H. Rushton Fairclough (New York: Putnam, Loeb Classics, 1929), p. 375. Also see "On Death in the Thought of Ernst Bloch," §3, "Death, Where Is Your Victory," in this volume.

18. [See also *OBBE*, p. 126; *AEAE*, pp. 162 [201].—Trans.]

Hermeneutics and Beyond

NOTE: This essay first appeared in "Herméneutique et philosophie de la religion," *Actes du Colloque Organisé par le Centre International des Etudes Humanistes* and by the Institut d'Etudes Philosophiques de Rome (Paris: Aubier, 1977).

1. This difference has, perhaps, no sense in the ontological version that we give it, whereas it should be a question of a *beyond-being*.

2. We write ess*a*nce with an *a* in order to express thereby the act or the event or the process of *esse*, the act of the verb "to be" (*être*).

3. See G. W. F. Hegel, *Wissenschaft der Logik. Zweiter Teil*, ed. Georg Lasson (Leipzig: Felix Meiner, 1923), p. 2. Translated by A. V. Miller as *Hegel's Science of Logic* (New York: Humanities Press, 1969).

4. Husserl, *Phenomenological Psychology*, p. 112 (p. 384 in the French ed.). [Translation modified to follow Levinas's French text; Levinas's emphasis.—Trans.]

5. [Levinas is underscoring the parts of the words "perception" and *Begriff* which contain the term for grasping or seizing. In the first, the italicized "ception" refers to the Latin *cipere* from *capere*, to seize, take. In the second, the German term for concept, *Begriff*, is related to the verb *greifen*, meaning to seize or to grasp.—Trans.]

6. Husserl, *Cartesian Meditations,* p. 12 (p. 10 in the French ed.).

7. [See Husserl, "Second Meditation. The Field of Transcendental Experience Laid Open in Respect of its Universal Structures," in *Cartesian Meditations,* pp. 27–55.—Trans.]

8. [Levinas hyphenates "enormous" to underscore its etymological sense of what is "*ex-norma*" or outside the rule.—Trans.]

9. [For Levinas's discussion of the Saying and the Said, see *OBBE,* chapter 2, §3b–c; §4; and chapter 5, §3, respectively pp. 34–38, 45–59, and 153–62; in *AEAE,* pp. 43–49 [60–67]; 58–76 [78–99]; and 195–207 [239–53].—Trans.]

10. [The French text reads, "malheur de la conscience malheureuse."—Trans.]

11. We shall not once again reproduce our analysis of the ethical relation wherein language is born. We have described the *fission* of the I before another to whom he responds beyond all engagement, infinitely, as a hostage, [and] bearing witness, by way of this responsibility, to the Immemorial within time; bearing witness of the Infinite which, [as] witnessed, does not arise as objectivity. A witness from out of the ethical relation that, as unique in its kind, does not refer to a previous experience; that is to say, to intentionality. See our book *OBBE,* pp. 140 ff.; *AEAE,* pp. 179 ff. [22 ff.]. Also see our article "God and Philosophy" in this volume.

Finally, see our lecture "Vérité du dévoilement et vérité du témoignage," in Enrico Castelli, ed., *Le Témoignage. Actes du Colloque Organisé par le Centre International d'Études Humanistes et par l'Institut d'Études Philosophiques de Rome. Rome, 5–11 January 1972* (Paris: Aubier, 1972), pp. 101–10.

The Thinking of Being and the Question of the Other

1. Does not the fact that all philosophy is theoretical—including these very reflections—signify that the forms imposed by propositions faithful to the rules of grammar and logic are encrusted in the meaning that these propositions exhibit? Does meaning not remain free in this language, disposed to unsay itself and to mean to say otherwise?

2. We note that the *theoretical,* evoked here, is not opposed to the practical, but already refers to it. Action is precisely the laying hold on the visible, where *concretely* the adequation of appearing to being only receives its signification. The connection of the *seeing* and the *grasping,* wherein the signification of the hold does not lodge solely in the skin that touches—unless the touching as such be *more* than a "sensory experience" analogous to that of all the other senses— this connection is made possible by the sovereign rest or immobility of the world, and of *esse* as rest. The original success of the laying hold, this success of the seizing, and, consequently, this first *technical success,* is not a corruption of

knowledge, nor a suspect thesis of a pragmatist epistemology, it is the first event of identification, the adequation of knowledge to being, the rise of being and of knowledge in their correlation.

3. [The French text reads, "la 'geste' d'être menée par les êtres." Literally *la geste* means an "exploit" or, in the plural, "deeds" or "doings." I translate *geste d'être* most frequently as the "gesture of being" although sometimes also as the "being's move." See "On Death in the Thought of Ernst Bloch," note 10, above.—Trans.].

4. [Although "insistence" is evidently not written with an *a* in English, I preserve the French, here, where it is so written. The example is understandable, and the suffix "-ance" is found in English words, such as "resistance," where it denotes some active or processual quality, or a capacity to do something.—Trans.]

5. [The text reads, "Il énonce une activité qui n'opère aucun changement, ni de qualité, ni de lieu, mais où s'accomplit précisément l'identification même de l'identité, la non-inquiétude de l'identité, comme l'acte de son repos" (p. 175).—Trans.]

6. [Husserl, *Formale und transzendentale Logik: Versuch einer Kritik der logischen Vernunft* (The Hague: Martinus Nijhoff, 1929). Translated by Dorion Cairns as *Formal and Transcendental Logic* (The Hague: Martinus Nijhoff, 1969).—Trans.]

7. [Although he translates the title in the present essay, Levinas cites the page (196) from the original text, *Das Ende der Philosophie und die Aufgabe des Denkens* (Tübingen: Max Niemeyer Verlag, 1968). The French translation, by Jean Beaufret and François Fédier, "La Fin de la Philosophie et la tâche de la Pensée," first appeared in 1966. English translation by David Farrell Krell in *Basic Writings: From Being and Time (1927) to The Task Of Thinking (1964)* (New York: Harper and Row, 1976).—Trans.]

8. [The text reads, "De par les signes et les mots qui les fixent ou les assemblent ou les appellent, des êtres apparaissent n'ayant de l'être que la ressemblance et la pure semblance, l'apparence étant l'envers toujours possible de leur apparoir" (p. 179).—Trans.]

9. Jacques Derrida, *La Voix et le phénomène* (Paris: Presses Universitaires de France, 1967). [Translated by David B. Allison as *Speech and Phenomena: And Other Essays on Husserl's Theory of Signs* (Evanston, Ill.: Northwestern University Press, 1973).—Trans.]

10. [On the structure of signs according to Husserl, and on the indicative reference in particular, see Derrida, *Speech and Phenomena*, pp. 23 ff.—Trans.]

11. [Cf. *Speech and Phenomena*, p. 18. "To want to say" is the literal translation of the French *vouloir dire*, which means, more succinctly, "to mean." Elsewhere, Levinas praised Derrida's translation of the German *meinen* by *vouloir dire*. See *OBBE*, p. 189n23; *AEAE*, p. 46n23 [63n2].—Trans.]

12. That which makes possible the conception of a consciousness forming a part of the world which is given to it, the famous *psychological consciousness* which Husserl opposes to the *reduced consciousness.*

13. We must put in question the Heideggerian phenomenology of affectivity, anchored in anguish, and where the fear of God should have to be reduced to the fear of sanction.

14. [In Aristotelian logic, "apophansis" refers to a statement that can be determined to be true or false.—Trans.]

15. One could not speak of the signification of the *question* for the very structure of the spiritual and of thinking without recalling the thesis of Jeanne Delhomme, *La Pensée Interrogative* (Paris: Presses Universitaires de France, 1954), and without referring to this essential book.

16. Maurice Blanchot, "Discours sur la patience," in *Le Nouveau Commerce* 30–31 (spring 1975), pp. 19–44. [Translated by Ann Smock in *The Writing of the Disaster.*—Trans.]

17. See "God and Philosophy," in this volume. Also see *OBBE.*

18. See in chapter 5 of *OBBE*, an attempt to show the birth of thematization, of discourse and of theory in ethical signification. *OBBE*, pp. 131–71; *AEAE*, pp. 167–218 [206–66].

19. On this theme, see our study "From Consciousness to Wakefulness," in this volume. Also see our study "Philosophie et éveil," in *Etudes Philosophiques* 3 (July-Sept. 1977), pp. 307–17. [For a discussion of a "pre-originary susceptiveness," see *OBBE*, pp. 122–29, *AEAE*, pp. 157–64 [195–205].—Trans.]

Transcendence and Evil

NOTE: The present text is based on a paper delivered on July 10, 1978, at the Seventh International Congress of Phenomenology, held in Paris and organized by the World Institute for Advanced Phenomenological Research and Learning. It was first published as "Transcendance et Mal" in *Le Nouveau Commerce* 41 (autumn 1978), pp. 55–78. [Translated by Alphonso Lingis in *Collected Philosophical Papers*, pp. 175–86.—Trans.]

1. J.-L. Marion, *L'Idole et la Distance* (Paris: Grasset, 1977).

2. This is an interpretation that one cannot set aside forever; through it, the thematization and discourse of science are superposed on every rupture and place transcendence in question. Without impeding the return of the lived and of the interruptive meaning. Can transcendence have a meaning which is other than ambiguous for a modern? But the same goes for the world. Cf. the lines that close the present essay.

3. Philippe Nemo, *Job et l'excès du Mal* (Paris: Grasset, 1978).

4. [John Macquarrie and Edward Robinson have translated *Zuhandenheit* as

"readiness-to-hand"; see their translation of Heidegger, *Being and Time* (New York: Harper and Row, 1962), p. 48 (p. 25 in *Sein und Zeit*). They translate *Stimmung* as "mood"; *Being and Time*, pp. 172–79 (pp. 134–40 in *Sein und Zeit*).—Trans.]

5. Cf. our attempt at a phenomenology in this direction in "Le Temps et l'autre" (*Time and the Other*).

6. ["Le Toi," which I am not translating as "The Thou" because of its resonance with the dialogical philosophy of Martin Buber.—Trans.]

7. [The French text reads, "a sens ce qui concerne l'alternative du bien et du mal extrême pour l'attente d'une âme" (p. 212).—Trans.]

8. This "audacity" is also lacking in Buber, to whom the discovery of the relation I-Thou appears immediately as a new mode of being; the You of God being only a more intense manner of being, the divinity of God losing itself thus in its mode of existence, which would be the final sense of His epiphany, as it also is of the disclosed world.

9. Nemo would not like the formula "ethics precedes ontology" for still another reason. He, like almost all the philosophical literature in our day, identifies ethics with the Law (which is the consequence of ethics), while the evil that awakes us to the You of God would be precisely contestation of the Law and of the technological spirit which, for Nemo, is tied to it. The morality of the Law would only be, for him, a technique for drawing rewards to oneself and avoiding punishments. We think that, primordially, ethics signifies obligation toward Another [*Autrui*]; we think that it leads us to the Law and to gratuitous service, which is not a principle of technique.

10. These dimensions, according to the Husserlian teachings reproduced in *Experience and Judgment* start from the position of an individual substrate, torn from the background of the world; from a substrate exposed to the "passive syntheses" of ex-plication and to the "modalization" of belief in which this position is made. These syntheses are then taken up in the *categorial activity* of the judgment properly so called. It is the dimensions of the affirmation of an impetus in its *being* and in its properties, assembled into syntheses and into a system: a coherent universe without back-worlds; a reign of the Same without any "other scene." [See Husserl, *Experience and Judgment*, §§16–21, for Husserl's discussion of passive syntheses and modalizations.—Trans.]

Dialogue

NOTE: The French version of a study entitled *Le Dialogue*, written for the encyclopedia *Christlicher Glaube in moderner Gesellschaft* (Freiburg-im-Breisgau: Herder Verlag, 1979); published in French by the Istituto di Studi Filosofici (Rome, 1980).

1. [Levinas is playing upon the etymological sense of *maintenant,* or "now," to mean "hand-holding": presence is that which we grasp figuratively or literally. The verb *maintenir,* or "to maintain, keep, or hold, or uphold," illustrates this original sense well. Hence we translate *main-tenant* as "main-tenance" even though the English term implies a carrying on or keeping up.—Trans.]

2. ["Es gehört zu den tiefsten und richtigsten Einsichten, die sich in der *Kritik der Vernunft* finden, dass die Einheit, die das Wesen des Begriffs ausmacht, also die ursprünglich-synthetische Einheit der Apperzeption, als Einheit des: Ich denke, oder des Selbstbewusstsein erkannt wird." See Hegel, *Wissenschaft der Logik. Zweiter Teil,* Georg Lasson, ed. (Leipzig: Felix Meiner, 1923), p. 211 (*Hegel's Science of Logic,* p. 584).—Trans.]

3. [Literally, "bodily there" or "corporeally present."—Trans.]

4. Husserl, *Krisis der europäischen Wissenschaften,* p. 260. [*Crisis of European Sciences and Transcendental Phenomenology,* p. 258.—Trans.]

5. [Gabriel Marcel, *Journal Métaphysique* (1914–23) (Paris: N. F. R. Gallimard, 1927), p. 207. Also see "Journal Métaphysique, III (Fragments): Le Sentiment du Profond," in *Fontaine* 51 (Apr. 1946). Also see Jean Wahl's discussion of the *Journal Métaphysique* in "Le Journal Métaphysique de Gabriel Marcel," in *Revue de Métaphysique et Morale* (Jan.–Mar. 1930). Translated into English by Bernard Wall, *Metaphysical Journal* (Chicago: H. Regnery, 1952).—Trans.]

6. [For a definition of humanity's two "primary words," see M. Buber, *I and Thou,* trans. Ronald G. Smith (New York: Collier Books, Macmillan, 2d ed., 1958 and 1987), pp. 33.—Trans.]

7. [*Selbstheit* is literally "selfhood."—Trans.]

8. [John Macquarrie and Edward Robinson have translated *Mitsein* as "Being-with"; see *Being and Time,* p. 308 (p. 264 in *Sein und Zeit).*—Trans.]

9. [The French text reads, "sur le dessein original et originel de la relation qu'on ne peut pas enfermer dans le psychisme." In French there are two adjectives for the English adjective "original." The first, *original,* implies that which is first in the sense of being novel or inventive; the second, *originel,* expresses originality as primordiality.—Trans.]

10. [Although the French infinitive *valoir* admits as a standard translation "to be worth," there is no attachment intended here between this value and human *being* or existence. This value is not situated in the first place at the level of being. Cf. *OBBE,* p. 198n28; *AEAE,* p. 158–59n28 [196 n. 1].—Trans.]

Notes on Meaning

NOTE: The ideas assembled in these notes were presented in the form of two lectures at the Facultés Universitaires Saint Louis, in Brussels, in November 1979. The present text was published for the first time in *Nouveau Commerce* 49 (spring 1981), pp. 99–127. Sections 7 and 8 were reworked, and a few material rectifications were added to the other parts of the first version thereof.

1. "Die Intentionalität wird befragt, worauf sie eigentlich hinauswill." See Husserl, *Formale und transzendentale Logik*, p. 9. [*Formal and Transcendental Logic*, p. 10.—Trans.]

2. [The French text reads, "la présence se produit main-tenant." A common word for "now," the French *maintenant* is composed of *main-*, hand, and *tenant*, from the verb *tenir*, "to hold." Levinas is here playing on the role of the hand in the production of being.—Trans.]

3. [Literally "givenness."—Trans.]

4. [See Husserl, *Logical Investigations.*—Trans.]

5. [The French text reads, "Comme si, ignorée d'autrui, que déjà dans la nudité de son visage, elle me concerne, elle 'me regardait' avant sa confrontation avec moi, avant d'être la mort qui me dévisage moi-même" (p. 245).—Trans.]

6. [See, for example, *TaI*, pp. 194–201; *TeI*, pp. 168–75; and indirectly in *OBBE*, pp. 11 ff., 86–94, 138 ff.; *AEAE*, pp. 13 ff. [25 ff.]; 108–20 [137–51]; 175 [216]—Trans.]

7. [As a salutation, "À-*Dieu*" implies "I commend you *to God*," or "Go, and God be with you." Levinas plays on the preposition and the literal sense of the construction repeatedly in this section as elsewhere.—Trans.]

8. [Cf. Chapter 5, "God and Philosophy," n. 45.—Trans.]

9. Cf. *OBBE*, p. 126; *AEAE*, p. 162 [201].

10. [The utterance is negative when it says "adieu," as a final farewell.—Trans.]

11. Abraham, father of the believers, intervened in Genesis (19:23–32) for Sodom, while recalling that it was "cinders and dust." A Talmudic apologue (Sota) reminds us that the "lustral water" that, according to Numbers 19, purifies those impurities due to contact or to the nearness/proximity of the dead, is a water in which are mixed, according to the ritual, the ashes of burnt "russet-colored cow." The rite of purification thus referred to Abraham's plea [in defense of Sodom]. The humanity of Abraham is stronger than his own death. Abraham would not have been abashed by his own mortality, which he evoked in his prayer to intervene against the death of the other man.

12. On the passage from the "for-the-other" to the equity of justice, see *OBBE*, p. 161; *AEAE*, p. 205 [250–51].

13. [Playing on the dual sense of *regarder* as "looking at" and "to concern," Levinas here writes, "Qu'il me regarde ou non, il 'me regarde.'"—Trans.]

14. Here, in the guise of a biblical fable, I will recall the books that seem to constitute the "bible" of the contemporary literary world: Kafka's works. Beyond the labyrinths and the blind alleys of the Power, the Hierarchy, and the

Administration which mislead and separate men, there rises in Kafka's work the problem of human identity, itself placed in question under the accusation, without culpability, of its right to be and that of the innocence of the very coming to pass of the adventure of being.

The Bad Conscience and the Inexorable

NOTE: First published in the review *Exercices de la Patience* 2 (Paris: Editions Obsidiane, 1981).

1. [Although the French word *conscience* can be translated as "consciousness" or as "conscience," I use the term "consciousness" in all those places where Levinas refers directly or indirectly to intentionality such as it is found in Brentano or Husserl. When speaking of intentionality, or of transcendental consciousness, Husserl uses the German term *Bewusstsein*, which English translates as "consciousness." The latter does not speak in these places of *Gewissen*, which is generally translated into English as "conscience." However, as it nevertheless makes little sense to translate "*mauvaise conscience*" as "bad consciousness," the French *conscience* is here translated as "conscience."—Trans.]

2. [John Macquarrie and Edward Robinson have translated *Geworfenheit* as "thrownness"; see *Being and Time*, 38, "Falling and Thrownness," pp. 219–24.—Trans.]

3. [The French text underscores the reflexivity of these verbs. "Structure réfléchie où l'émotion est toujours émotion *de* quelque émouvant, mais aussi émotion *pour* soi-même, où l'émotion consiste à s'émouvoir—à *s*'effrayer, à *se* réjouir, à *s*'attrister, etc." (p. 263).—Trans.]

4. [Macquarrie and Robinson translate the adjective *Zuhanden* as "ready-to-hand" and the substantive *Zuhandenheit* as readiness-to-hand; see *Being and Time*, §15, "The Being of Entities Encountered in the Environment," pp. 95–102. The term *Zuhandenes* would refer to anything that is ready-to-hand.—Trans.]

Manner of Speaking

[NOTE: First published in Jean Beaufret, Richard Kearney, and Joseph S. O'Leary, eds., *Heidegger et la question de Dieu* (Paris: B. Grasset, 1980).—Trans.]

1. Note the undated letter of Franz Rosenzweig to Martin Buber (cf. Rachel Rosenzweig, Edith Rosenzweig-Scheinmann, and Bernhard Casper, eds., *Franz Rosenzweig. Briefe und Tagebücher*, vol. 2 [The Hague: Martinus Nijhoff Publishers, in the series "Der Mensch und sein Werk," 1979], pp. 824–27), admirably commented upon and rigorously explicated by B. Casper of the Faculty

of Theology of Freiburg-in-Brisgau (see his commentary in the *Philosophisches Jahrbuch*, vol. 2, 1979 [Freiburg and Munich: Karl Alber Verlag], pp. 225–38).

In this letter the author of the *Star of Redemption*, called to give his friendly advice on the first proofs of *I and Thou*, objects to Buber over the weakness of the primary word or the *Urwort*, I-It (*Ich-Es*). Rosenzweig treats it as stunted (*Krüppel*), inadequate to the true weight of the language bearing *on* being; inadequate to the non-dialogical proposition. But the neutrality of the pronoun "It" (*Es*) designating thematized being is due, according to Rosenzweig, in the expression I-It, especially to the weakness of the *I*, which would agree, strictly speaking, with the idealist interpretation of the real, with the constitution of objects by the transcendental subjectivity of the I, but not with real reality, not with the *creature* whose absoluteness comes from God, which could not be expressed by the *I*, nor, ultimately, by the Thou. But who is He, a third person, having nothing more in common with the *he* neglected in dialogue? The true word for the being of the world would be: He-It. "He makes it live and die." The veritable importance of the proposition that is pronounced *upon* being, and of the language that uses these propositions, would be revealed, according to Rosenzweig, notably, in the very fact that the theory of the *I-Thou* which Buber's fundamental book contains, is created in this language, from one end of the book to the other. Here again we find a recourse to the model of the refutation of skepticism! But it is evident that ontological language is here claimed, not starting from the eternity and the ultimacy of being, which would be the bearer of all meaning, but from the entire theology of creation, which confers upon being its foundation or its beginning and its true weight.

M E R I D I A N

Crossing Aesthetics

Emmanuel Levinas, *Of God Who Comes to Mind*

Bernard Stiegler, *Technics and Time, 1: The Fault of Epimetheus*

Werner Hamacher, *pleroma—Reading in Hegel*

Serge Leclaire, *Psychoanalyzing*

Serge Leclaire, *A Child Is Being Killed*

Sigmund Freud, *Writings on Art and Literature*

Cornelius Castoriadis, *World in Fragments: Writings on Politics, Society, Psychoanalysis, and the Imagination*

Thomas Keenan, *Fables of Responsibility: Aberrations and Predicaments in Ethics and Politics*

Emmanuel Levinas, *Proper Names*

Alexander García Düttmann, *At Odds with AIDS: Thinking and Talking About a Virus*

Maurice Blanchot, *Friendship*

Jean-Luc Nancy, *The Muses*

Massimo Cacciari, *Posthumous People: Vienna at the Turning Point*

David E. Wellbery, *The Specular Moment: Goethe's Early Lyric and the Beginnings of Romanticism*

Edmond Jabès, *The Little Book of Unsuspected Subversion*

Hans-Jost Frey, *Studies in Poetic Discourse: Mallarmé, Baudelaire, Rimbaud, Hölderlin*

Pierre Bourdieu, *The Rules of Art: Genesis and Structure of the Literary Field*

Nicolas Abraham, *Rhythms: On the Work, Translation, and Psychoanalysis*

Jacques Derrida, *On the Name*

David Wills, *Prosthesis*

Library of Congress Cataloging-in-Publication Data

Lévinas, Emmanuel.
[De Dieu qui vient à l'idée. English]
Of God who comes to mind / Emmanuel Levinas;
translated by Bettina Bergo.
p.   cm. — (Meridian, crossing aesthetics)
ISBN 0-8047-3093-8 (cloth).
ISBN 0-8047-3094-6 (pbk.).
1. God.   2. Ontology.
I. Title.   II. Series: Meridian (Stanford, Calif.)
BD331.L45813   1998
212—dc21

97-49446
CIP

∞   This book is printed on acid-free, recycled paper.

Original printing 1998
Last figure below indicates year of this printing:
07   06   05   04   03   02   01   00